D0927881

LAST
OF THE WILD

VANISHED AND VANISHING GIANTS
OF THE ANIMAL WORLD

ROBERT M. McCLUNG

Illustrated by Bob Hines and
Robert M. McClung

Linnet Books   1997

The text of this book contains some accounts, all of them revised and updated,
from three of the author's previous books: *Lost Wild Worlds*, 1976; *Hunted
Mammals of the Sea*, 1978; and *Vanishing Wildlife of Latin America*, 1981.

Library of Congress Cataloging-in-Publication Data

McClung, Robert M.
    Last of the wild : vanished and vanishing giants of the animal
world / Robert M. McClung; illustrated by Bob Hines.
        p.   cm.
    Includes bibliographical references (p.   ) and index.
    Summary: Profiles threatened animals around the world and
discusses why they are in danger and what is being done to save
them.
    ISBN 0-208-02452-2 (alk. paper)
    1. Endangered species—History—Juvenile literature.   2. Extinct
animals—History—Juvenile literature.   3. Nature—Effect of human
beings on—History—Juvenile literature.   [1. Endangered species.]
I. Hines, Bob, ill.   II. Title.
QL83.M33   1997
591.51′9—dc20   96-35814
                                                              CIP
                                                               AC

All illustrations are by Bob Hines, except for the following by Robert M.
McClung: Kouprey, Vu Quang Ox, Chimpanzee, Birdwing Butterflies, Jaguar,
Giant Otter, Giant Peccary, Giant Anteater, Giant Armadillo, Giant Ground
Sloth, Macaws, Giant River Turtle, Giant Galápagos Tortoises, Dolphin,
Steller's Sea Lion, Dugong, Bluefin Tuna, Shark.

CONTENTS

Cow | Dugong | Manatees | Steller's Sea Lion | Elephant Seals
Walrus | Bluefin Tuna | Sharks | Other Threatened Marine
Life

MAPS

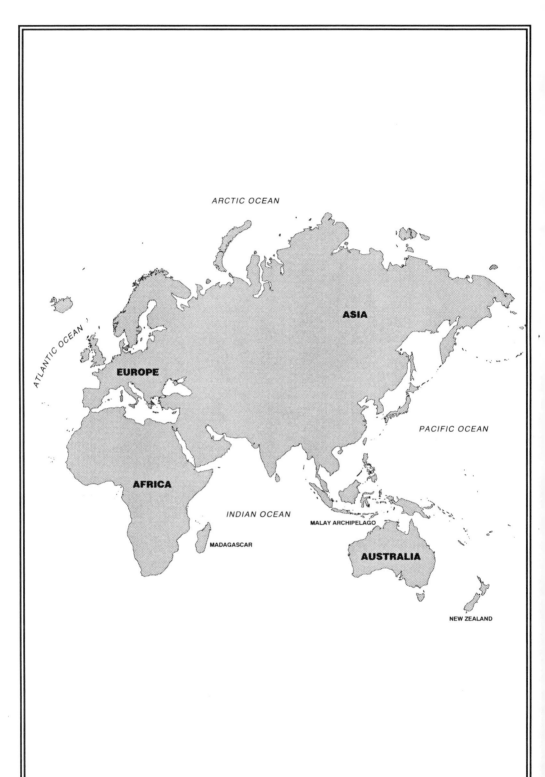

Eastern Hemisphere

*Accuse not nature! She hath done her part; Do thou
    but thine!
and be not diffident of wisdom; she deserts thee not, if
    thou
dismiss not her.*

John Milton
Paradise Lost

FOREWORD

"It really is a pity," the noted French missionary-naturalist Abbé Armand David observed in his diary more than a century ago, "the education of the human species did not develop in time to save the irremediable destruction of so many species which the Creator placed on our earth to live beside man, not merely for beauty, but to fulfill a useful role necessary for the economy of the whole."

One of the species that Père David may have been thinking of when he wrote these words was the great auk, a nineteenth-century victim of man's ruthlessness and greed. The last recorded specimen of this large flightless bird was clubbed to death on June 4, 1844, by a collector on remote Eldey Island off the coast of Iceland.

On March 6, 1971, a mounted great auk—killed in Iceland in 1821—was sold at Sotheby's auction house in London for $21,600. The successful bidder was Dr. Finnur Gudmunesson, Director of the Icelandic Museum of National History in Reykjavik.

Will mounted museum specimens such as this become the final destiny for today's endangered wildlife, too? Or will they be reduced to a few living specimens carefully preserved in zoos or managed and protected in game preserves and parks? If so, the world will be a far worse place in which to live; we ourselves will be something less than human.

Evolutionary biologist Edward O. Wilson warns, "We are in the midst of one of the greatest extinction spasms of history." Countless animal and plant species will inevitably disappear within the next few years unless effective steps are taken to save them. Mammals, birds, reptiles, fish—all living things—face this threat, as suitable habitat shrinks and the environment becomes more polluted each year.

Perched at the summit of the living pyramid, *Homo sapiens* faces the same fate, for not even humans can destroy the environment we need to support life and escape the consequences.

How has such a situation come about? The answer lies with the human population explosion, our reliance on technology, and what is happening to the earth as a result.

Wild animals are among the first victims of our dramatic ability to master and change the natural world. Many people either do not know how their activities may affect wildlife and the living earth, or they simply don't care. Many others place their own economic well-being above everything else. Motivated by greed, they ruthlessly pollute the land and seas with industrial wastes and poisons, destroy the environment, and exploit wildlife.

The account that follows tells briefly of the human rise to civilization, how we spread over the earth and explored it, and how we finally came to dominate it and alter it to our own uses. Through narrative accounts of what has happened or is happening to a number of our big and better-known wildlife species, continent by continent, this book relates how people have brought about the extinction of many of them and endangered the survival of others. It also tells how organizations and individuals of goodwill in many countries are endeavoring to reverse these destructive trends and save our fellow creatures.

The animals discussed in detail were chosen for a variety of reasons. Most of them are literally giants, as the title of this book suggests. All of them are dominant species, important to humans because of their size, habits, or economic value. Some of their histories show how destructive forces can cause a once-flourishing species to dwindle until it becomes either endangered or extinct; others illustrate how positive forces exerted by governments, conservation organizations, and individuals can work to save a threatened species. Some species have been saved through enlightened management in the wild, some by strict enforcement of protective laws. Other critically endangered forms are being preserved by safeguarding a nucleus of captive breeding stock in zoos or private game reserves. A few benefit from newly developed scientific techniques. Several major animal groups, such as the elephants, rhinoceroses, big cats, and whales, are the objects of worldwide campaigns aimed at arousing public opinion in their behalf and creating sanctuaries for them to insure their numbers.

"The campaign to save the tiger," the New York Times has observed, "does not remotely imply failure to recognize the crying social needs of that other animal—man. But the saving of tigers—and whales and wolves for that matter—is more than a cultural and esthetic compulsion. All the flora and fauna of the earth form an endlessly complex web of life, which man tears at his peril."

ACKNOWLEDGMENTS

The works of many naturalists, conservationists, historians, and geographers dating from more than two thousand years ago until today, as well as hundreds of current books, periodicals, articles, and news items, have been consulted in the preparation of this book. I gratefully acknowledge my indebtedness to the authors of all of them, many of whom are listed in the index.

Reference librarians and other staff at the Jones Library in Amherst, the Robert Frost Library at Amherst College, and the Morrill Science Library at the University of Massachusetts in Amherst, all were invariably interested and diligent in helping to track down materials. I thank them all for their valuable contributions. Any mistakes that may remain are my own, as is the responsibility for all of the statements and expressed opinions.

Finally, I deeply appreciate the care and help of my editor, Diantha C. Thorpe, who guided the book through its many stages; of the late Bob Hines, whose attractive and expert illustrations add so much to the appearance of the book; and of my wife, Gale, whose encouragement, advice, criticism, and material aid throughout the project have been of immeasurable help.

WHERE LIES TOMORROW?

One way or another, whether civilizations collapsed, were overthrown or were victims of disaster or failure, the answer always has been that the earth itself, the source of all life, was the eventual reality and the place to find certainty and ultimate truth. . . . Nature's purpose, so far as we understand purpose at all, is to perpetuate life, not to destroy it, to strengthen life, not to weaken it, to garland and fructify the earth, not blight and devastate it.

Editorial, *The New York Times*

Woe unto them that join house to house, that lay field
to field, till there be no place, that they may be placed
alone in the midst of the earth!

Isaiah 5:8

1

THE HUMAN RISE TO DOMINANCE

Be fruitful, and multiply, and replenish the earth, and subdue it: and have dominion over the fish of the sea, and over the fowl of the air, and over every living thing that moveth upon the earth.

Taken literally, this quotation from Genesis (1:28) would seem to be a clear directive for *Homo sapiens* to rule the earth and all its creatures—as we are doing today—and make of it what we want. Throughout history many people have so understood it. Most modern Bible scholars, however, would interpret the passage to indicate more human *responsibility* for the stewardship and well-being of our fellow inhabitants of the earth, rather than our dominion over them.

Read in its entirety, Genesis is a beautiful story, telling in a simple explanatory way of the creation of the earth, the emergence of life upon it, and the rise of all the various life forms. The story can be interpreted in a manner compatible with evolutionary theory, with each day of the legend representing many millions of years. Man, according to the story, was formed on the sixth day of creation. All other living things had been created before him.

3

Paleontologists, scientists who study prehistoric life, tell us that the last dinosaur on Earth died about seventy million years ago. With its passing, the Golden Age of Reptiles, which had lasted some 120 million years or more, also ended. It was then—on that symbolic sixth day—that the mammals emerged.

The first mammals, tiny insect eaters, had appeared long before, and so had the first ancient birds. Both had sprung from reptilian ancestors. When the primitive little mammals were freed from the dominance of the ruling reptiles, they began to specialize and evolve in many different directions. The Age of Mammals—the age in which we live today—had begun.

The earth gradually cooled during the millions of years that followed, while representatives of all the groups of modern mammals were evolving. This long cooling process finally culminated in the Pleistocene epoch, or Ice Age, more than a million years ago, when great sheets of glacial ice pushed outward from the poles and covered much of the earth.

The First Humans

Four times the great Arctic ice cap crunched southward, covering all of northern Europe, Asia, and North America during the coldest times, and then retreated back toward the North Pole during intervening periods of milder weather. An astounding variety of Ice Age mammals flourished during the Pleistocene: mammoths and mastodons, woolly rhinoceroses, giant bison, horses, camels, and deer, among others. It was during this period also that modern man was evolving.

Modern man's hominid ancestors—humanlike creatures that walked upright and possessed other human traits—evolved more than 4 million years ago. Fossil remains of the first true humans (genus *Homo*) were found in the 1960s and 1970s near Olduvai Gorge in Tanzania, East Africa. Scientific dating of the remains indicated that these ancient people lived about 2.6 million years ago. *Homo habilis* were hunters and meat-eaters, who used crude stone weapons and tools.

They were followed in turn by *Homo erectus*, who appeared

throughout Africa about 1.5 million years ago. These early ancestors of ours lived in family groups, wore skin clothing, made and used many kinds of tools, and used fire for warmth and food preparation. They gradually spread from Africa to Asia and southern Europe, where they appeared some two hundred thousand or more years ago. About one hundred thousand years ago, they were succeeded in Europe by Neanderthal man, archaic *Homo sapiens.*

The best known of all the prehistoric men, the Neanderthal had a brain as large as modern man's. Standing only about five feet tall, he was heavily muscled, short-legged, and beetle-browed. He lived in caves during the coldest periods and may have built primitive shelters from animal hides or branches of trees. He used fire both to warm himself and to cook his food, and he considerably advanced the art of making and using weapons of stone and flint. A skilled hunter, Neanderthal man captured small animals in snares, and with his spears and axes killed animals as big as the woolly mammoth and rhinoceros after they had fallen into natural pits or become mired in bogs. He buried his dead and had the beginnings of a crude religion.

Some thirty or forty thousand years ago, Neanderthal man disappeared quite suddenly, swallowed up by the coming of a more advanced relative: Cro-Magnon man.

Cro-Magnon Man Appears

Except for their great age, the skeletal remains of the Cro-Magnons cannot be distinguished from the remains of people living today. Cro-Magnon man's brain was just as big as our brain and equally as capable of reasoning and solving complex problems. But Cro-Magnons did not have all of the accumulated discoveries of science to back up their actions, as we have today. Already expert hunters and toolmakers, however, they were beginning to accumulate basic knowledge that would form the groundwork for all of our sophisticated science and technology. The more they learned, the more quickly their knowledge and techniques expanded. Cro-Magnon man represented a vital step in the long and fateful journey that led to modern technological man.

As the great ice sheets ebbed and flowed over the past thirty to forty thousand years, the Cro-Magnons populated much of the Old World. Sometime during that period they migrated from Asia to North America over the Bering land bridge that lay exposed between the two great land masses. This bridge was exposed when the vast ice sheets locked up such an enormous amount of water that the levels of the oceans were lowered.

These Ice Age ancestors of ours perfected the art of making weapons of stone as no other humans had done before. Working with painstaking patience and skill, they fashioned delicate but deadly blades and spearheads from flint and quartz. They made harpoon heads with sharp edges and many barbs, and created effective spear throwers from reindeer antlers. The most skillful and deadly hunters the world had yet known, they hunted mammoths and rhinoceroses, primitive horses, reindeer, and many other animals during the colder periods. In warmer weather they pursued deer and bison and wild cattle on the European steppes and in the forests. Some modern authorities believe that because of their success at hunting, they were responsible for the extinction of many of these big game animals of the late Pleistocene. The skeletal remains of some one thousand or more mammoths found at Predmost, the Czech Republic, and great bone heaps near Solutre, France, containing the remains of many thousands of horses, are awesome proof of early man's hunting abilities.

As befitted his role as hunter and predator, Cro-Magnon man worshipped the wild creatures that he depended upon for food, shelter, and life. Medicine men, or shamans, dressed in animal skins and covered their faces with animal masks during religious ceremonies and festivals. They hoped to gain favor with the spirits of the animals they represented so that the tribe would have successful hunts

By the light of flickering torches, Cro-Magnon artists painted animal shapes on cave walls. There, mixing clay of various shades with mineral oxides and charcoal, early artists fashioned pigments of red, yellow, brown, and black. They then mixed pigments with animal fat to bind the colors, and spread them on cave ceilings and walls either by hand or with some kind of crude brush or crayon.

Some archaeologists believe that the pigments were sometimes blown in powder form through hollow tubes of bone. Their vivid paintings depicted wild animals, as well as primitive hunters making their kills of bison, deer, rhinoceroses, and horses. These decorated caves were Cro-Magnon man's temples dedicated to the hunt.

In 1940 a cave in Lascaux, France, was discovered by young boys when their little dog fell into a crack in the earth. In an attempt to rescue their pet, they dug the opening wider and entered a vast cavern several hundred feet long. Awestruck, they gazed at hundreds of paintings on the walls depicting animals of the Ice Age.

The Advance of Civilization

Bit by bit, Cro-Magnon man began to change his nomadic life as he learned different methods of utilizing the land and animals around him. Some groups stayed by the shores of lakes and became fishermen, fashioning nets and traps and building crude canoes and boats. Others learned how to grow crops and began to live in one place instead of wandering from one area to another. They also began to domesticate wild sheep, cattle, and horses, and many tribes were supported by the meat, milk, and wool that their stock produced.

These prehistoric humans eventually learned how to use metals such as bronze and iron instead of stone for their weapons and tools. The use of metal was the beginning of a new era. People living by the sea built larger boats in which they could take long voyages. Trade and commerce with neighboring peoples began to flourish. So did arts and religion.

A host of early Old World civilizations rose and fell. In the lands bordering the Mediterranean Sea, they culminated in the glories of ancient Egypt and Greece, and ultimately in the power of Rome; in Asia they led to highly developed civilizations in Persia, India, and China. All of these expanding cultures began to exert powerful pressures and changes on the environment.

The swift rise of humans from those early beginnings to their dominance in today's world is well documented in recorded history.

In the continuous struggle for power, many wars were fought as man increased his knowledge and applied skills. In the eighteenth century, Western man made the great scientific breakthrough known as the Industrial Revolution. This revolution was the result of thousands of years of accumulated knowledge that led to a rapid series of inventions. Humans learned how to harness steam as a source of power and to manufacture many kinds of products more efficiently and cheaply. And along with the escalating technology, advances in agricultural knowledge and medicine allowed more people in the Western world to live longer.

The human population of the earth, which was almost stationary or rose very slowly during the preceding million years, suddenly began to increase in startling fashion. From 500 million people in 1650, the world population of *Homo sapiens* doubled to one billion in 1850, just 200 years later. Only eighty years were needed for the next population doubling to some two billion in 1930. In 1995 the world population was about 5.5 billion, with the possibility of doubling again in the next fifty years. And the more people there are, the more pressures are exerted upon our planet Earth, thereby increasing the dangers to all living things—including human beings.

Technological Man

As humans increase in numbers, we change the earth more and more. The last great wilderness areas of the world—the Amazon jungles, the Alaskan and Siberian tundra, the forests of New Guinea—all are being attacked by eager exploiters. Newly emerging African and Asian nations are working feverishly to clear lands for more crops and development. As a result, the wildlife of every continent is losing more and more of the natural habitat that it needs for survival.

The rich nations of the West express their alarm at the rising populations of many of the poorer nations, and the widespread famines, malnutrition, and deadly epidemics that flourish among them. The less-developed countries, for their part, blame the advanced Western nations for selfish and conspicuous waste of food and natural resources—much of it at the expense of the poor nations—in order to maintain their accustomed high standards of living. These poor nations understandably want their fair share of the world's riches; they want a higher living standard for their peoples too, and are fiercely determined to achieve it.

The simple truth is that the earth cannot begin to produce all of the food and other resources necessary to support the peoples of the world in anything like the luxurious standard of living now enjoyed by the majority of Americans and Western Europeans.

Most of the world is at least aware of the problems brought about by rising populations and dwindling resources. What to do about them is the crucial question humans now face. In answering that dilemma we must recognize that the animal and vegetable life of the earth—their complex relationships and their preservation—are closely bound up with our own ultimate well-being.

No man is an island, entire of itself; Every man is a piece of the continent, a part of the main. . . . Any man's death diminishes me, because I am involved in mankind; And therefore never send to know for whom the bell tolls; it tolls for thee.

John Donne
Devotions upon Emergent Occasions, No. 17 (1642)

2

EUROPE
Cradle of Western Civilization

After the last great retreat of the glaciers, some ten thousand years ago, most of temperate Europe was still a forest wilderness, the home of many barbarian tribes. To the southeast, it merged with the steppes, endless plains stretching from the Caspian and Black seas eastward into central Asia. All of this vast area of temperate Europe was unaffected by man's influence until approximately two thousand years ago, when civilization in the form of Roman legions arrived.

Civilization had come much earlier to parts of southern Europe, and the shores of the Mediterranean were among the first lands to be scarred by man. Until the rise of the Phoenicians and Greeks, however, those marks were still minimal.

The Phoenicians and Greeks

The Phoenicians, well established at the eastern end of the Mediterranean, had already explored the shores of that great landlocked sea, and by 1400 B.C. they had colonized many coastal areas. In the eighth century B.C. they established Carthage as a powerful outpost on the rim of North Africa. During this same period the power and greatness of the Greeks were emerging, and with them came an expansion of man's knowledge of his world.

About 320 B.C. Pytheas, an adventuresome Greek scientist and navigator who was a citizen of Massilia (Marseilles), sailed his ship through the Pillars of Hercules—the Rock of Gibraltar in Europe and the promontory of Jebel Musa in Africa—and out into the open Atlantic. Heading northward along the coast of the Iberian Peninsula, he is said to have sailed his ship all the way around Britain, bringing back to his wondering countrymen tales of the barbarians who inhabited that strange land to the north. A few years later, Philip of Macedonia was extending Western knowledge of Asia, leading his armies eastward to the headwaters of the Indus River. In the process, he battled oriental princes who opposed him with battalions of elephants. Greek power was at its zenith at this time, with the influence of Greek civilization being felt throughout the Western world and into Egypt and Asia as well.

Roman Civilization

Greek power began to fade several centuries afterward, and gradually many of the Grecian colonies were taken over and absorbed by the Romans, who were starting to establish one of the great empires of history. Especially good at organization and engineering, the Romans borrowed whatever they needed of science and the arts from Greece and other civilizations. They then adapted the knowledge for their own needs. By 290 B.C. the Romans had finally defeated their rivals, the Carthaginians, and thereafter were the undisputed rulers of the Mediterranean regions. Africa and Asia lay open to their armies and so did the unknown interior of barbarian Europe.

In 58 B.C. the Roman general Gaius Julius Caesar marched into Gaul—now France and the Low Countries—and quickly conquered it. He followed this victory by invading Britain in 55 B.C. and inaugurating a long period of Roman rule there. The next two hundred years saw the extension of Roman power and rule over a

great empire, extending from Scotland in the north to the Mediterranean rim of Africa in the south, and from Spain through all of western Europe to Egypt and the Near East. Throughout this vast territory the Romans bestowed order and stability through the *Pax Romana* and organized the wild tribes and their lands to serve Rome.

The emperor Trajan, who reigned from A.D. 99 to 117, built 47,000 miles of Roman roads that linked the farthest points of the empire and opened up Europe's interior to exploration and conquest. These roads provided the Romans with efficient land travel that was not equaled again in Europe until the nineteenth century. They were so well engineered that some are still used today.

The first notable observer of nature in the Western world was Aristotle, the Greek philosopher and naturalist who lived more than three centuries before Christ. But the Romans observed the new worlds they conquered with lively curiosity, too. In the first century A.D. Pliny the Elder of Rome compiled his *Naturalis Historia,* a thirty-seven volume encyclopedia of natural history. A few of the subjects covered were the sun, moon, stars, and other heavenly bodies, earthly phenomena, animals, birds, insects, plants, and minerals. A great deal of the material was inaccurate, but a number of scientifically sound accounts, most of them taken from Aristotle, were included.

The Roman citizens, however, were able to observe the wild beasts of the empire and the world beyond it in quite a direct fashion. In the third century B.C., the consul Metellus exhibited 142 elephants captured at Carthage. Later rulers celebrated their military victories by entertaining the populace with contests setting beast against beast, and beasts against men, in exhausting life-and-death struggles, along with chariot racing staged in large arenas. The Circus Maximus, a mammoth structure 2,000 feet long and 600 feet wide, which seated more than 150,000 people, was the largest of these arenas.

In the autumn of 55 B.C. the Roman general Pompey the Great celebrated one of his many triumphs with the killing of twenty elephants in the Circus Maximus, where he also exhibited 600 lions and 400 other big cats. Not to be outdone, Julius Caesar celebrated his triumph over Pompey in 46 B.C. in similar fashion, and was escorted to and from the capitol by forty elephants. The emperor Augustus, during his reign from 27 B.C. to A.D. 14, is said to have imported about 3,500 animals for the twenty-six celebrations, or *venationes,* he staged during his rule. As though trying to top all of his predecessors, the emperor Titus brought 9,000 animals in the year A.D. 80 to be killed in a hundred-day show at the opening of the Coliseum. Mercifully, the emperor Constantine issued an edict against such spectacles in the year A.D. 326, and they gradually faded away. By this time the Roman Empire was fading as well, and soon the period known as the Dark Ages settled over Europe.

The Dark Ages

After the disintegration of the Roman Empire, Europe sank into an unenlightened period that lasted almost one thousand years, during which time there were few significant advances in science, the arts, or knowledge of any kind. Secure in their cloistered monasteries, monks became the keepers of all wisdom of past ages. Most of the people lived in walled and fortified towns, in small city-states, or under the protection of feudal lords who were always on guard against possible attacks by neighboring rulers. The trade and commerce that had flourished in ancient times with Asia and Africa was greatly curtailed.

Little changed during this period. Northern Scandinavia remained as wild as ever, with its frozen steppes and treeless plains inhabited only by hardy, wandering nomads who hunted reindeer. The vast forests of northern and eastern Europe were the home of the moose, bison, and the aurochs, or wild ox. Shaggy brown bears also roamed the forests, and the howls of wolves could be heard from one end of the continent to the other.

There were no animal shows and circuses as there had been in Roman times, but a few medieval towns had bear pits where the people could see a European brown bear or two. Once in a while a traveling showman came to town with a tame dancing bear. Except for these few contacts, most people thought of wild animals as fierce meat-eating beasts—such as wolves and bears—or as harmless and tasty game species to be hunted at the risk of punishment from an irate feudal lord who considered them his quarry.

The Renaissance

After almost a thousand years of comparative darkness, science and the arts began to flourish once again with the coming of the Renaissance. Backward city-states became consolidated, and exploration and commerce expanded in many directions.

In the year 1317 the powerful city-state of Venice, already carrying on a flourishing business with Asia and Africa, opened a ship service with regular trading routes between the Adriatic Sea and northern Europe. "By means of those galleys," observes the historian A. P. Newton in his book *The Great Age of Discovery*, "the ginger of Malabar and the cloves of Ternate, the cinnamon of Ceylon and the nutmegs of Malacca, the camphor of Borneo and the aloes of Socotra, not to mention the chinaware from China found their way into English homes."

European man had not yet conquered the known world, but as a result of the Renaissance he was beginning to make his presence known throughout the Old World. How his expanding trade and civilization affected some of Europe's wildlife is reflected in the following accounts.

WOOLLY MAMMOTH
Elephas primigenius

Some fifteen thousand years ago a little band of Ice Age hunters gazed happily at the huge beast that stood trapped and helpless before them. Here was a source of abundant food for the entire band. A hairy elephant had stumbled into a natural pit lined with huge boulders and scoured out by glaciers—a deadly hazard for lumbering beasts such as this one. There were many such traps in this area that we now know as France.

Trumpeting with rage, the giant animal struggled to free itself, but succeeded only in wedging its vast bulk more firmly into the crevasse. Nine feet high at the shoulder hump, the mammoth was covered with long shaggy hair. Thick yellowish tusks, each measur-

ing nearly eight feet along its crescent sweep, jutted out on either side of its grasping trunk.

The band of hunters attacked the helpless giant with clubs and spears tipped with sharp stone points. The victim's bellows echoed and reechoed across the valley as the attack continued. Soon blood streamed down from the beast's wounds. Even so, many hours passed before it finally died. Then the primitive hunters hacked it to pieces with their stone knives and axes. Afterward they feasted in celebration; the mammoth's meat would feed the band for many days.

The years went by, and a river of ice buried the bony remains of the mammoth under many feet of glacial debris. The giant's bones remained buried for thousands of years while the vast ice sheet ebbed and finally receded.

During excavation for a cathedral in southern France during the late Middle Ages, workmen uncovered the huge bones. These remains were a source of much wonder. Could giant men have lived there before the great flood described in the Bible? Could the great curving tusks be the horns of legendary unicorns? Some men, more learned than others, pointed out that the bones and tusks were very much like those of elephants—those giant beasts that the ancients were said to have used in war. Could these be the remains of an elephant brought over from Africa by the renowned Carthaginian general Hannibal, when he marched on Rome in 218 B.C.? The possibilities were many, but no one knew for certain.

In years to come mammoth bones and tusks were found in other European countries. In 1611 an enterprising Englishman named Josias Logan exhibited in London a mammoth tusk that he had brought from Russia. In 1692, a Dutch diplomat, Evert Ysbrants Ides, traveled to China on a mission to the Chinese emperor K'ang-Hsi, on behalf of Russia's ruler, Peter the Great. Upon returning, he reported on the many mammoth remains he found in northern areas he had visited. "But the old Siberian Russians affirm that the *Mammuth* is very like the *Elephant*," he declared. Other Siberian travelers related that both the Siberians and Chinese had for many hundreds of years conducted a flourishing ivory trade with the tusks.

In 1799 the eminent zoologist Johann Friedrich Blumenbach stated that, based on the evidence of remains that he had been studying for years in Germany, an elephant had indeed once lived in Europe. It had tusks that curved in a great arc, much more of a curve than the tusks of the living Indian elephant. Blumenbach named this beast *Elephas primigenius*. His conclusions were reinforced by the discovery in 1864 of an Ice Age carving of a mammoth on a piece of ivory at La Madeleine in northern France, as well as later discoveries of mammoth paintings in caves of the Dordogne region of southern France.

There certainly were no mammoths still living in Europe in the nineteenth century, and scientists speculated that the species had evidently shifted its range to northern Asia when Europe's climate warmed up after the last glacial retreat. An incredible number of mammoth remains, some in remarkable stages of preservation, were found in Siberia. In the nineteenth century the semi-autonomous republic of Yakutsk in east central Siberia was the world center for a flourishing trade in mammoth tusks. As much as twenty-five tons of ivory were put on the market every year. Even today the trade continues.

In 1901 an almost perfectly preserved mammoth was found in a melting glacier along the banks of the Berezovka River, a tribu-

tary of the Kolyma, in Siberia. The remains were taken to the zoological museum in St. Petersburg, where they were studied in
detail. The Berezovka mammoth had a thick coat of reddish wool,
with long, black guard hairs. Its stomach contents showed that it
ate grasses and other tundra vegetation. Blood samples showed that
as a species it was closely related to the Indian elephant of today.

No one knows when the last mammoth died, or why. Some
believe that the changing climate after the last ice sheet may have
caused its extinction. Others believe that primitive man may have
hastened its disappearance by overhunting. And a very few die-
hards say that the species may still survive today in Siberia's far
northern wilderness.

In 1920 an old Russian hunter told a strange story to the
French chargé d'affaires in Vladivostock that seemed to support
this possibility. As related by Bernard Heuvelmans in his book *On
the Track of Unknown Animals*, the old hunter told how he had
followed huge circular tracks in the snow while traveling in northern Siberia: "All of a sudden I saw one of the animals quite clearly,
and must admit I really was afraid. It had stopped by some young
saplings. It was a huge elephant with big white tusks, very curved;
it was a dark chestnut color as far as I could see. It had fairly long
hair on the hindquarters, but it seemed shorter on the front. . . ."

A tall tale? Practically every student of the mammoth or of
zoology would probably agree that it was.

TARPAN, OR EUROPEAN WILD HORSE
Equus caballus

Our modern horse is a descendant of the dawn-horse, or *Eohippus*,
a small browsing animal that appeared in North America, Europe,
and probably Asia as well, during the Eocene epoch, forty million
years ago. About the size of a fox, *Eohippus* had four toes on each
front foot and three on each hind foot.

This distant ancestor of the modern horse eventually died out
in the Old World, but in North America it flourished and evolved.
Through millions of years of natural selection it gradually increased
in size and changed in shape, while the number of functional toes
on each foot was reduced to one encased in a protective hoof.

Tarpan, or European Wild Horse

During the Upper Pliocene epoch, more than a million years ago, the genus *Equus* evolved in North America. This is the group to which our modern horse as well as the zebras and wild asses belong. Some of these relatively recent horses migrated to Asia over the Bering land bridge at the beginning of the Ice Age. Others spread into South America. Before the beginning of recent times, however, horses had died out in the Americas, and did not reappear there until early Spanish explorers reintroduced them in the fifteenth century. But in the Old World *Equus* spread far and wide, reaching Europe and penetrating southeastward to the shores of the Mediterranean and into Africa and Asia.

Wild horses were abundant throughout much of Europe during the time of prehistoric man, who hunted them for food. Cro-Magnon painters depicted wild horses on the walls of many European caves. At some point before recorded history, man also captured and tamed wild horses—probably foals only a few days old. Ever since, man has used horses as faithful mounts and beasts of burden. The domestication of the horse may well have taken place on several different continents at roughly the same time.

Egypt and other early civilizations had domestic horses. By the beginning of the Christian era the Romans had refined the horse by selective breeding and were using it extensively as a riding and work animal. At the same time, nomadic tribes of central Asia were domesticating the shaggy wild ponies around them. Eventually the Huns would ride their hardy little mounts westward, to invade and conquer much of Europe during the Dark Ages.

The tarpan was the historic wild horse of Europe. It is still debated whether it stemmed from wild stock that had naturally wandered westward from Asia during prehistoric times or descended from horses that had been domesticated by man during prehistoric times and then had returned to the wild. Whatever its origin, the tarpan survived well into the nineteenth century.

A small stocky horse with a tan coat and short black mane, the tarpan once ranged in bands throughout the forests and steppes of eastern Europe. In 1768, the German naturalist and explorer Samuel Gmelin collected four specimens in the Russian Ukraine north of the Crimea. Forty years later another German zoologist, Peter Simon Pallas, reported that the tarpan still ranged over parts of the Russian steppes and beyond into central Asia. One of the tarpan's last refuges was a royal game park near Bilgoraj, Poland. The band was protected there but its numbers declined during the years 1810 to 1820, and one particularly harsh winter all but decimated the herd. The remaining few were reportedly killed to feed hungry peasants.

By this time the species was on the decline nearly everywhere. Hunted and killed for food by modern as it had been by prehistoric man, the tarpan quickly disappeared in Europe. The last recorded specimen, an aged female, died in 1876, in Askaniya Nova, an area of the Ukraine.

Many zoologists claim that the tarpan and the still-surviving Asiatic, or Przewalski's, horse of central Asia may be the same animal or, at most, different races of the same species. Others say that the tarpan was a distinct species.

AUROCHS, OR EUROPEAN WILD OX
Bos primigenius

In 58 B.C. Julius Caesar marched north from Rome and into the forests of Gaul to conquer those backward lands and add them to the Roman Empire. Writing of his adventures in his *Commentaries*,

Aurochs, or European Wild Ox

he later described a species of wild cattle that he called urus, which lived in the forests of Germany:

> [This is] . . . an animal somewhat smaller than the elephant, with the appearance, color, and shape of a bull. They are very strong and agile, and attack every man and beast they catch sight of. The natives take great pains to trap them in pits, and then kill them. . . . It is impossible to domesticate or tame the urus, even if it is caught young. The horns are much larger than those of our oxen, and of quite different shape and appearance.

In Caesar's day the European wild ox was a widespread species that roamed throughout the forested areas of the continent. Standing about six feet high at the shoulder, the bull was blackish brown and had long, sharp horns that swept out and forward in a broad curve, then flared upward and in. Cows were a lighter brown than the bulls, and calves were a reddish color, evidently somewhat like the young of the American bison. Living in small herds, these wild oxen ventured out of the sheltering woods into open areas during the summer. In the fall they browsed on forest vegetation and munched on acorns and other nuts.

Emperor Charlemagne is reported to have hunted the aurochs near Aix-la-Chapelle, France, in the ninth century, and the Crusaders saw them as they passed through parts of Germany in the eleventh century. By 1400, however, the species had disappeared nearly everywhere except in Poland, a casualty of hunting and the clearing of forests for settlement and agriculture. And in Poland, their last refuge, the number of aurochs dwindled, generation after generation. By 1599 there remained a small herd of only twenty-four aurochs living in a royal preserve in the Jaktorovka Forest, some 35 miles southwest of Warsaw.

In 1602, just three years later, the herd had dwindled to four individuals. And in 1620—the same year the Pilgrims landed at Plymouth Rock—there was but a single survivor, which lingered on until 1627. Afterward the aurochs was gone forever.

Present-day cattle in all likelihood were domesticated from the aurochs. The Greeks and peoples of the Middle East had herds of domestic cattle four thousand years ago. And even today there are wild, or feral, cattle that resemble the aurochs in the Camargue region of southern France, and in wilderness areas of Corsica and Spain.

WISENT, OR EUROPEAN BISON
Bison bonasus

Most of us tend to think of the bison as an exclusively American animal, but Europe has a closely related, though distinct, species of bison. Paralleling the misfortunes of the American bison, the European species almost became extinct during the nineteenth century, but was saved through the efforts of a few dedicated conservationists.

Quite similar in appearance to the American bison, the wisent is less stocky and has longer legs and a longer tail. Its shoulder hump is less pronounced, and its woolly mane is thinner. More of a browsing (leaf-eating) than a grazing (grass-eating) animal, it travels in small bands and inhabits woodlands.

Wisent, or European Bison

In ancient times the wisent ranged over most of the forested areas of temperate Europe, eastward to the Caucasus of southeastern Russia. The Romans, busy subduing the stubborn Franks, saw wisent in the wilderness forests of Germany and at various times exhibited them in amphitheaters. By the time of the Middle Ages, however, a thousand years of hunting, clearing, and settling the land had caused the wisent to disappear over much of Europe.

By 1800 as few as a thousand individuals of the southern, or Caucasian, race still roamed the steppes north of the Black Sea, and only several hundred of the northern wisent survived in protected forested areas of the Polish-Russian frontier.

One of these areas was the 300,000-acre Bialowieza Forest, a royal hunting preserve—first for the Polish kings, then for the Russian czars. During the Napoleonic Wars, the wisents of Bialowieza dwindled to about three hundred animals. By 1857, however, the herd, carefully managed and protected, had increased to nearly two thousand in this forest refuge. A few years later, in 1865, Czar Alexander II had a bull and three cows from the Bialowieza herd sent to a reserve breeding center in the Pszczyna forest in Upper Silesia. This group had increased to seventy animals by the start of World War I in 1914; at the same time the herd in Bialowieza had decreased to 737 animals.

During the war many German and Russian troops fought in and around Bialowieza, and many of the bison were slaughtered. Following Russia's armistice with the Germans, most of the remaining individuals were killed by marauding peasants and revolutionaries. By 1921 the last wild bison in the preserve had disappeared. The same fate befell the band of wisent in Upper Silesia, with only three individuals preserved in captivity. The last wild survivor of the Caucasian wisent was reportedly killed by a poacher in 1919. A few of them, however, may have survived until 1925. At that time the only remaining wisent in the world were about fifty-five specimens in zoos and in several small private preserves.

Alarmed that the species was about to suffer the same fate as the tarpan and aurochs, zoo officials and conservationists met in 1923 at the Berlin Zoo and founded the International Association for the Preservation of the European Bison. They then took immediate steps to protect the remaining stock and kept records so that the pure-blooded individuals (those without any American bison or domestic cattle blood) would be known. Among these were a few members of a small herd that the Duke of Bedford, an ardent English naturalist and conservationist, had carefully nurtured on his Woburn Abbey estate in England.

In 1929 two survivors of the old Silesian herd were joined with two cows sent by Sweden's Skansen Zoo and a bull from Germany. These five were sent to Bialowieza in a brave attempt to reestablish the wisent in its native habitat. The bison were kept in a fenced enclosure and by 1939, on the eve of World War II, had increased to thirty head. In spite of the hazards of war, this band survived; six years later, in 1945, they numbered forty-four animals. Twelve additional specimens survived in German zoos and in several other animal collections throughout the world. The European Bison Society, for its part, had kept careful pedigree records, and the bloodlines of these individuals were well-documented.

Today, thanks to such careful preservation efforts, there are more than three thousand European bison worldwide, and the number continues to grow larger. Several hundred of them are in Poland's Bialowieza preserve and the Russian preserve beside it.

With such a pool of both captive and free individuals, the future of the species seems secure.

Pure-blooded animals of the Caucasian wisent are now officially extinct, but a herd of about five hundred with a very small amount of American bison blood now roams the Caucasus National Park in Russia.

The Status of Other European Animals

Most of Europe's wildlife populations have fared better through the centuries than one might expect. Ironically, as a result of hunting— for centuries a favorite pastime of the European aristocracy—many animal species have been saved from extinction. Because the ruling classes valued a plentiful supply of game to kill, their hunting lands were usually off limits to everyone except royalty. Many game parks and preserves were established on these restricted lands where wildlife was managed and protected from large-scale killing. Consequently, most animals that existed in Europe in Greek and Roman times survive to some extent even today.

The predatory animals have, of course, suffered the most. Men have always feared and hated them and viewed them as competitors in the hunt. Two thousand years ago lions still roamed southeastern Europe, but the ancient Greeks and their contemporaries exterminated them. The European brown bear was killed off in England in the eleventh century; it disappeared from Germany during the nineteenth century and from the Swiss Alps by the early twentieth century. A few of these brown bears, perhaps forty or fifty, still maintain a precarious existence in the Cantabrian Mountains of northwestern Spain, and another twenty-five may survive in the Pyrenees. Small remnant populations still roam in remote areas of the Far North, the Balkans, and Greece, but Russia is the only European country that still has a sizable population of brown bears.

Wolves have fared somewhat better. Spain, Romania, and Poland each have substantial populations of 1,000 or more, and smaller populations survive in the mountains and forests of most of the other countries of western Europe. But only in Russia, the Ukraine, and other former Soviet Republics in Asia, can wolves be found in substantial numbers. All in all, 50,000 to 100,000 of them roam the forests and plains of the former Soviet empire.

A few European wildcats survive in remote wild areas, but the rarest predator of them all is probably the Spanish lynx, a subspecies of the European lynx. It is found solely in the mountains and delta region of Spain, where there may be only a very few pairs left.

Europe's deer, managed and protected as game animals for many centuries, have survived in good numbers. The red deer and the roe deer are managed and hunted much as the American white-tail deer. In far northern Europe, the nomadic Lapps tend their herds of reindeer. The European moose had all but disappeared from the forests of Sweden and other Scandinavian countries by the early 1800s. It has recovered well under protection, however, and Sweden now harvests the animals in annual hunting seasons without affecting the stability of the population. Russia's northern borders also support a healthy moose population.

Stretching from the shore of the icy Arctic Ocean to the warm waters of the Indian Ocean, from the Mediterranean to the Pacific, the earth's largest landmass . . . possesses the highest mountains, the vastest deserts, the wildest stretches of forests and steppes, the most desolate tundras, the deepest lakes, and several of the longest rivers in the world.

Pierre Pfeffer
Asia: A Natural History

3

ASIA
The Immense Land

Largest of all the continents, Asia encompasses nearly 30 percent of our planet's land and more than half of its human population. Asia stands apart, not only for its vastness, but also because of its endless variety of life forms. Situated at the world's crossroads, Asia is closely linked with all the other continents except South America. Throughout the ages Asia has been a source of plants, animals, and culture to the other continents.

The two most populous nations in the world—China and India—are in Asia. Each of these great countries boasts a civilization and heritage thousands of years old. Since World War II they have been struggling to emerge from centuries of subjugation and exploitation at the hands not only of Western colonial nations but also of invading neighbors and their own rulers and warlords. Today these two countries have more than two billion people between them, and the numbers increase every year. Much of Asia suffers from overcrowding of the human species, especially in the southeast. But other areas of the continent are empty—too inhospitable for people to inhabit.

In Asia's far north lie thousands of miles of frozen tundra, and endless stretches of subarctic taiga: forests of larch, fir, and spruce, intermixed with birch and aspen. Below lie the steppes: great plains and grasslands stretching from China to the Balkan lands of Europe. In prehistoric times the steppes were a gateway to and from Europe for many forms of wildlife; and within the past two thousand years they have served as a highway for the Huns and other invading tribes. To the south of the steppes, and around them, are the vast deserts of central and southwestern Asia—burning hot in summer and freezing cold in winter—and below range the awesome, snow-covered peaks of the Himalayas. To the south and west of these mountains lie the temperate forest lands and the rice bowls of China, as well as the steaming, tropical rain forests of India, Indochina, and Malaya.

With hundreds of soaring snow-covered peaks, higher than any other mountains in the world, the Himalayas forge a craggy barrier, an almost insurmountable dividing line between the zoogeographic region know as the Palaearctic realm of the north, and the mostly tropical Oriental realm of southeastern Asia. All in all, the continent forms a vast treasure-house of human history and of countless living things as well.

Early Asiatic Civilizations

Western civilization rose along the shores of the Mediterranean and reached its highest accomplishments in Europe. But while this smaller continent was still largely wilderness, with a few tribes just beginning to emerge from barbarism, Asia was already the homeland of many complex and highly sophisticated civilizations.

In Bible lands of the Near East—especially in that fertile spot between the Tigris and Euphrates rivers that used to be called Mesopotamia and is now in the modern state of Iraq—a bewildering succession of dynasties and kingdoms had already come and gone. For good reason this area has been called the Cradle of Civilization. Among the first advanced peoples in this area were the Sumerians,

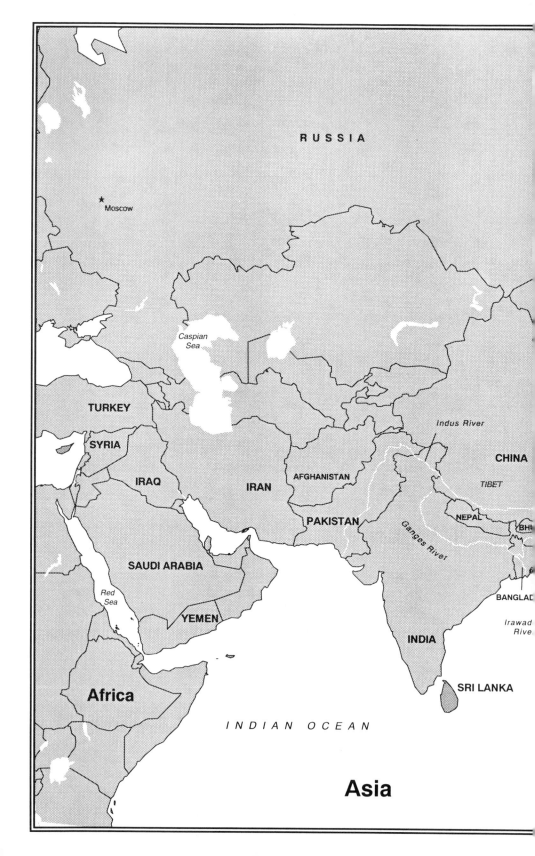

who developed a sophisticated civilization as early as 3500 B.C. Building on the Sumerian foundation, the Babylonians advanced the practice of agriculture, irrigation, and animal husbandry, and they further developed arts and architecture. Many other groups rose to temporary prominence in this region and vied with one another for power. Among them were the Hittites, Assyrians, Chaldeans, and Persians.

Persia (today's Iran) reached its summit of power under King Cyrus and his immediate followers about 500 B.C. Under their vigorous military leadership, Persia conquered Egypt and most of the Near East and ruled an empire that stretched from Egypt to India. Less than two hundred years later, however, the Greeks challenged Persian dominance and marched toward India under Alexander the Great.

India was the meeting ground where many different peoples— Aryans, Mongols, Huns, and countless primitive tribes—met and mixed over thousands of years of invasion, migration, and assimilation. By the time of Alexander, the great southern peninsula boasted a number of highly developed civilizations. All of the world's principal religions—Judaism, Hinduism, Buddhism, Christianity, and Islam (each of them Asiatic in origin)—finally met in India, a meeting place of travelers and merchants from all points of the compass. The influence of these religions spread both east and west. In the same way, the civilizations and peoples of India influenced all the other Asiatic countries around them, especially those of southeastern Asia and the islands of the Malay Archipelago.

China, that vast land to the north and east of India, has had an equally ancient and advanced civilization. When the philosopher Confucius wrote his maxims for life's conduct, about 500 B.C., China (known to its inhabitants as the Middle Kingdom) already had a long, respected history as a civilization of cultivated arts and sciences.

Ancient Trade Routes between Europe and Asia

Trade and commerce had flourished between the Mediterranean and the lands of southern Asia long before written history. Ancient caravan routes wound their way through high mountain passes and across the steppes and deserts, bringing silks and spices and other produce of the East to the civilizations of the Mideast and southern Europe, in exchange for their timber, ivory and gold from Africa, and the purple dye and fabrics for which the Phoenicians were famous. Sea routes were also used for commerce, for the Arabs had from earliest times sailed under the monsoon winds from the Red Sea to India. From these ancient mariners, the Phoenicians and others also learned the favored sea routes to southern Asia.

When the Romans became dominant in the Mediterranean, Europe's commerce with Asia further increased. Silk from distant China was highly prized by the luxury-loving Romans, and they spared no efforts in obtaining it. The Chinese kept the source and production of this beautiful fabric a well-guarded secret until the sixth century A.D. In the year 536, however, two monks serving as missionaries in China smuggled silkworm eggs back to Europe in hollow bamboo staffs. With this introduction, the production of silk finally began in Europe.

The intermingling of Eastern and Western cultures increased with the rise of Islam—the fervent and expansionist religious movement of the Moslems in the seventh century A.D. Mohammed the Prophet was born in 570 in Mecca, an Arab city near the shores of the Red Sea. He died in A.D. 632, but his followers swiftly spread his religion and influence far and wide—westward to Morocco and eventually Spain, and eastward to China and the exotic Spice Islands of the far Pacific. During this time Rome collapsed; the Western world broke up into many splintered parts as Europe descended into the time known as the Dark Ages.

Led by Genghis Khan, the Mongols of northern Asia invaded Europe in 1236, sweeping across Russia with their fierce cavalry, devastating Poland and Hungary, and dominating these eastern European lands for some two hundred years. The Mongol horsemen swept over the Mideast as well, capturing Baghdad in 1258. Two years later Kublai Khan, the grandson of Genghis Khan, was elected the Great Khan of the Chinese empire.

At this time Marco Polo, Venetian merchant, traveled with his father to the Great Khan's court and there entered his service for over twenty years—from 1271 until his return to Venice in 1295.

The Travels of Marco Polo

Polo was "the first traveler to trace a route across the whole longitude of Asia," one of his biographers, Sir Henry Yule, says, "naming and describing kingdom after kingdom which he had seen with his own eyes . . . the first Traveller to reveal China and all its wealth and vastness . . . to tell us of the nations on its borders with all their eccentricities of manners and worship."

The Book of Marco Polo, which he wrote after his return to Venice, forever linked the knowledge of East and West. His detailed descriptions were colorful and generally accurate. He gave many vivid word pictures of the life of the people and their relationship to the animals around them. "The emperor has numbers of leopards trained to the chase," he wrote, "and has also a great many lynxes taught in like manner to catch game, and which afford excellent sport. He also has several great lions, bigger than those of Babylonia, beasts whose skins are colored in the most beautiful way, being striped all along the sides with black, red, and white."

When the emperor went on a hunting expedition, Marco Polo noted, "He takes with him full ten thousand falconers, and some five hundred gerfalcons besides peregrines, sakers, and other hawks in great numbers; and goshawks also to fly at the waterfowl." He further described what must have been one of the earliest kinds of game management and protection. "Throughout all the emperor's territories, nobody however audacious dares to hunt any of these four animals, to wit, hare, stag, buck, and roe, from the month of March to the month of October. . . . And thus the game multiplies at such a rate that the whole country swarms with it. . . . Beyond the term I have mentioned, however, to wit, that from March to October, everybody may take these animals as he list."

Marco Polo pointed the way, but another two centuries were to pass before the modern era of Western exploration and exploitation of Asia and the fabled Spice Islands would really begin. Only then did the complex variety of the land and wildlife of Asia gradually begin to be more completely known.

ASIATIC ELEPHANT
Elephas maximus

Native to India and southeastern Asia, the Asiatic elephant in appearance looks like a throwback to the mammoths of the Ice Age. Indeed, it and its African relative are the only two surviving members of a huge and diverse group that once included many species that wandered over most of the world, except Australia. Both the Asiatic and African elephants have been domesticated by man, but the Asiatic species has been used to a far greater extent.

Weighing up to six tons, and with a shoulder height of nine feet or more, the Asiatic elephant has incredible strength and endurance. Possessing a high level of intelligence, it has been a servant and companion to people for thousands of years and is useful in many different roles: as an efficient beast of burden, as a hunting platform, as a bulldozer in road building or a carrier of logs in forestry operations, as a performer in religious ceremonies and circuses, and as a tank or battering ram during wartime.

The use of elephants in battle goes back thousands of years. When Alexander the Great campaigned in Asia, Darius of Persia opposed him in 331 B.C. with fifteen elephants supporting his armies of men. The Persian forces were routed, however, and the elephants captured. Later described by Aristotle, they became part of recorded history. Just five years later, at the Battle of Jhelum, the Indian King Dorus opposed Alexander's advance with "200 elephants like walking ramparts in the center of his army, with archers in the wings."

Elephants were well known in Rome and its provinces during the flowering of the Roman Empire, for they were featured in many spectacles and circuses at the arenas and the Circus Maximus. Ever since those days, elephants have been popular animals in zoos and circuses all over the world.

There were several traditional ways of capturing wild elephants for domestication. One method was to construct a pit, cushioned at the bottom with branches and leaves and camouflaged with leafy branches across the top. After falling in, the elephant was trapped. A sloping ramp was then dug down into the pit and the shackled victim led out, usually escorted by a tame elephant. Another method of capture was the use of a noose that snared the beast by the leg.

The most famous method, however, was the capture of an entire herd of elephants at one time in a huge and stoutly built stockade known as a *khedda*. The *khedda* had a comparatively narrow opening, from which long extensions of the wall flared wider and wider outward, forming a funnel. Trained men called beaters would surround a group of wild elephants and herd them toward the *khedda* by beating drums and making loud noises. Hurrying through the arms of the stockade, the frightened animals were funneled through the narrow opening. The heavy gates were then closed, and the elephants trapped. Reliable tame elephants were used to separate and calm the wild captives. Before 1945 the *khedda* was the prevalent method used for capturing elephants in British colonial India. During the twentieth century, however, the use of domestic elephants began a steady decline. This decrease began after World War I, when cars and trucks were introduced into India and Burma. The trend away from elephants was even more marked after World War II, when India gained independence from Britain and much wild country began to be opened up for agriculture and forestry activities. Many of the forests, which had for centuries provided food and sanctuary for elephants, were cleared for crops and destroyed in extensive lumbering operations. Once the pride of India, the elephant has now been relegated to the status of unwanted animal in many areas, especially regions where wide-ranging bands of elephants ravage and destroy crops. Every year, many elephants are killed illegally by ivory poachers, too.

Throughout their entire natural range, the numbers of Asiatic elephants continue to shrink annually. From an estimated hundreds of thousands a century ago, the wild population has dwindled today to less than fifty thousand in all of Asia. Some authorities believe that no more than half that number survives. There are probably an additional ten to fifteen thousand in captivity.

The wild elephants roam in isolated bands in scattered pockets of their old range, which once extended from the Tigris-Euphrates valleys to China's Yunnan Province, Borneo and Sumatra. There may be 20,000 surviving in India; 5,000 in Burma; 1,500 in Thailand; less than 1,000 in peninsular Malaysia; 500 to 2,000 in Borneo; 2,000 to 4,000 in Sumatra; and perhaps 2,500 in Sri Lanka—once the island kingdom of Ceylon. There are no estimates for Indochina.

The problems elephants face in Sri Lanka illustrate the problems they are facing everywhere. As early as 1831, the island instituted a bounty system to reduce its elephant herds, for already there were too many beasts for the size of the country and its expanding human population. Close to ten thousand elephants were shot on the island of Ceylon during the nineteenth century. By 1953 fewer than five thousand remained. A few years later, a study and survey of the island's elephants indicated a population of just fifteen hundred. The Wildlife Department of Sri Lanka disagreed, saying that at least five thousand elephants remained. Whatever their numbers, most of the survivors were concentrated in national reserves. Today these wild elephants—except for dangerous rogues—are legally protected. But their jungle habitat is fast disappearing.

The Asiatic elephant's future everywhere depends on the establishment of a number of large reserves that can provide the herds with all the sanctuary and food they need, plus added protection against ivory poachers.

PÈRE DAVID'S DEER
Elaphurus davidianus

Abbé Armand David, the noted French naturalist and missionary, was born in 1826 in the little French town of Espelette on the River Nive. From earliest boyhood he was an enthusiastic observer of nature and possessed a keen eye, a lively curiosity, and a sense of wonder. As a young man he took the vows of priesthood and in 1861 went to China as a missionary and naturalist. There Père David set up and directed a school for boys in Peking (Beijing), but he also spent a great deal of his time exploring the Chinese countryside, taking detailed notes on the plants and animals that he observed and gathering specimens to send back to Europe. Birds were his main interest, but he also studied and collected insects, plants, reptiles, fish, and mammals. In 1865 he made a notable discovery—a new species of deer—as he described in a letter written on September 21 to his friend, Henri Milne-Edwards, a well-known zoologist, who was then director of the Museum of Natural History in Paris:

A mile from Peking lies the vast Imperial Park, which may be a dozen miles around. . . . No European can go into the Park, but this last spring, climbing on the wall, I was lucky enough to see, although rather far away, a herd of over 100 of these animals which looked to me like moose. Unfortunately they had no antlers at that time. What characterizes the animals I saw was the length of the tail which was proportionately as long as a donkey's. . . . The Chinese gave this animal the name of Mi-lou, and more often that of Ssu-pu-hsiang, which means "The four characters which do not fit together," because they find that this reindeer belongs to the stag by his antlers, to the cow by its feet, the camel by its neck, and the mule by its tail.

In his journal, Père David later noted that, although there was reported to be a death penalty for anyone who killed one of these animals in the Imperial Park, the soldiers who supposedly guarded the animals sometimes secretly killed them for food. In 1866, however, the resourceful Père David managed to obtain two skins of the deer—perhaps by bribing the guards—and sent them to his friend, Milne-Edwards. The French zoologist thereupon described the animal and gave it the scientific name, *Elaphurus davidianus*, in honor of the priest-naturalist who had sent the specimens to him.

Two living Père David's deer reached the London Zoo in 1869, through the efforts of Père David and the British minister in Peking. During the next few years others were sent to zoos in Paris, Berlin, and, once again, London. Père David, the discoverer of the species, considered that it had long since been killed off in the wild and had been preserved only by being protected in captivity, perhaps for hundreds of years, in the royal preserve. As later determined by the discovery of fossil remains, the original range of Père David's deer evidently included considerable portions of East Asia—mostly low flatlands along the Yellow River and other waterways from Peking to Shanghai.

The most notable feature of this deer is its unusual set of antlers, quite different from those of any other species. These antlers divide into two main branches, and the forward branch then forks again. Along the nape of the neck there is a skimpy mane of black hair. In winter the animal's coat is dull brown; in spring and summer, it is a warm reddish color. During the mating season, large glands below the eyes of the stag are very noticeable. The rutting stag often becomes quite ill-tempered, digging in the mud with his antlers and bellowing with a loud, hoarse grunt. At this time he may on occasion charge any man or animal nearby.

After having survived in the protected enclosure of the Imperial Park near Peking for so long, Père David's deer suffered a major setback at the close of the nineteenth century. Floodwaters of the Hun Ho River breached the walls of the park, and many of the deer drowned or escaped only to be killed for food by hungry peasants. As few as thirty survived. Most of them were subsequently killed in 1900 during the Boxer Rebellion, when European soldiers broke into the park and slaughtered the deer for venison. Only two surviving animals could be counted at Peking in 1911. Ten years later there were none.

Fortunately, there were still some surviving specimens in Europe, descendants of those sent from China years before. Those in zoos had usually been kept by pairs or as individual specimens in small enclosures, and most of them had failed to breed. But the Duke of Bedford, the enthusiastic and determined English naturalist, purchased zoo specimens of Père David's deer wherever and whenever he could. By the turn of the century he had assembled a small herd, which he kept on his 4,000-acre ancestral estate at Woburn Abbey.

Conditions there were very much as they had been at the Imperial Park in China, and the deer prospered. By 1914 the duke's herd had increased to about ninety specimens. After the hard years of World War I, however, these animals had dwindled to about fifty. In 1921 they were the only Père David's deer left in the world, for all of the specimens in China and in European zoos had died.

Happily, the Duke of Bedford's herd flourished during the 1920s and 1930s. After World War II, the duke decided that all the specimens should not be kept in one place, in case disease or other disaster should strike. He sent some to Whipsnade, the large animal park operated by the Zoological Society of London. In December, 1946, two bucks and two does were also sent to the New York Zoological Society's Bronx Zoo—the first Père David's deer ever seen in the New World. These quickly adapted to their new home and were soon breeding there.

A number of other zoos have since received breeding stock as well, and, in 1956, four specimens were sent from England to China—the land from which they had come in the first place. By 1974 the population of Père David's deer had increased to about seven hundred deer, held in some seventy zoos and game parks throughout the world. By 1996 there were about fifteen hundred of them, six hundred at Woburn.

In 1985 twenty-two more specimens from the Woburn herd were introduced into Nan Haizi Milu Park, the former Imperial Park south of Beijing, where Père David had first seen them in 1865. The next year another eighteen specimens were introduced. By the early 1990s the Chinese herd had increased to about 130 animals, and plans were underway to release some of them in another reserve on the Yangtze River in Hubei Province.

The future of Père David's deer in captivity now seems assured. The species is an outstanding example of an animal that was exterminated in the wild but successfully preserved for many hundreds of years in captivity. It is hoped that some of this captive stock may eventually be released in other carefully chosen wild preserves in the animal's natural habitat in China. There Père David's deer can once again be counted as a wild species that has survived—both in spite of man and *because* of man.

GIANT PANDA
Ailuropoda melanoleuca

Traveling through western Sichuan Province in 1869, Père David wrote in his journal for March 23:

> My Christian hunters return today after a ten-day absence. They bring me a young white bear, which they took alive, but unfortunately killed so it could be carried more easily. The young white bear, which they sell to me

Giant Panda

very dearly, is all white except for the legs, ears, and around the eyes, which are deep black. . . . This must be a new species of *Ursus*, very remarkable not only because of its color, but also for its paws, which are hairy underneath, and for other characters.

Within the next two weeks, the hunters brought him other specimens. They knew the giant panda as *hua-hsiung*, "spectacled bear," or sometimes as *pei-hsiung*, "white bear."

Today the rare and beautiful giant panda is used as the symbol of the World Wildlife Fund, an international organization devoted to helping endangered wildlife. Judging from fossil remains, ancestors of the giant panda ranged widely over southern China during the Ice Age. Today, however, the main population is apparently confined to an area less than 200 miles from north to south in the remote mountain country of central and northern Sichuan Province.

Usually living at altitudes of 6,000 to 10,000 feet on rugged mountain slopes covered with mixed forests and thick stands of bamboo, the giant panda apparently feeds almost entirely on the leaves and shoots of the latter. Each of its front paws is equipped with an unusual small pad, which assists the panda in grasping stalks of bamboo and pulling them down to its powerful grinding teeth. When it is feeding, the panda may wander in a zigzag pattern over a mountain slope, stopping at one bamboo thicket after another. Sometimes it even climbs trees. It sleeps in nests under ledges or at the base of trees.

Ever since Père David brought the species to the attention of the Western world, scientists have disagreed about whether it is more closely related to the bear or the raccoon family, or whether it is perhaps in a family of its own. The giant panda certainly *looks* more like a bear than anything else; but its little cousin, the reddish-colored lesser panda, is decidedly raccoonlike.

Although the panda skins collected by Père David were sent to Europe, the first recorded specimen shot by Westerners was taken in 1929 by Theodore and Kermit Roosevelt, the adventuresome sons of President Theodore Roosevelt. This specimen was placed in the Chicago Field Museum of Natural History, where it still may be seen.

Mrs. Ruth Harkness, however, was the one who brought the first living panda to the Western world. In 1935 the New York Zoological Society had talked with her husband, W. H. Harkness, about capturing a live panda for the Bronx Zoo collections. Shortly after beginning his quest for a specimen, Harkness died in Shanghai in February, 1936, before he could reach panda country. Mrs. Harkness, who had accompanied her husband, carried out the search in his place. Aided by Quentin Young, an experienced animal collector, she finally succeeded on the ninth of November, as she later recorded: "From the old dead trunk of the tree came a baby's whimper. Quentin reached into the hollow trunk of the tree. Then he turned and walked toward me. In his arms was a baby panda." Weighing two and a half pounds, eyes still closed, and probably no more than two weeks old, the baby thrived under Mrs. Harkness's care. Thought to be a female (later found to be a male), the cub was named Su-Lin and ended up in Chicago's Brookfield Zoo—the first giant panda ever seen in captivity.

In quick succession during the next five years, eleven other pandas were brought out of China and delivered to Western zoos. The last two that came out before World War II were Pan-dah and

Pan-dee, acquired by the New York Zoological Society in December, 1941. The war and the upheaval in China stopped all panda exports for some years—and probably just as well.

At war's end in 1945 the trade began again. Many of the prized black and white animals were sent to western zoos in subsequent years. In 1957 China elevated the species to the status of goodwill ambassador, and during the next twenty-five years gave twenty-four pandas to nine different countries as expressions of friendship and respect. In this manner a pair of pandas, Ling-Ling and Hsing-Hsing, came to the National Zoo in Washington in 1972.

China kept many pandas in its own zoos, and in 1963 the Beijing Zoo proudly exhibited the first panda cub bred and born in captivity. During the next twenty years nearly fifty litters were born to captive Chinese pandas—several of them the result of artificial insemination. Other panda births occurred at the Chapultepec Zoo in Mexico City, Tokyo's Ueno Zoo, the Madrid Zoo, and the National Zoo in Washington, D.C. None of the infants born in Washington survived.

In the wild, meanwhile, giant panda numbers were declining at an alarming rate, as more and more forest habitat was destroyed by farmers and loggers, and as poachers hunted them down for illegal profits. In Hong Kong, Taiwan, and Japan panda pelts sold for as much as $10,000 or more on the black market.

In 1980, acknowledging the seriousness of the threats to panda survival, a team of Chinese scientists and George Schaller, noted American field naturalist and conservationist, went into the mountains of Sichuan Province and launched a five-year study of the panda. They needed to learn more about its habits and requirements in the wild. Pandas were captured and fitted with radio collars, then released, so that their travels could be followed. As part of the program, a panda conservation, research, and breeding center was completed in 1984 at the Wolong Reserve—some 8,000 square miles of panda habitat situated about 80 miles northwest of Chengdu, Sichuan Province.

A widespread bamboo die-off in panda habitat occurred in 1983, and the Chinese used it as an excuse for a massive panda trapping program. Over a hundred animals were captured—

"rescued" according to the Chinese—during the next four years. Of these, about a third died in captivity, a third were relocated to other wild habitat, and the remainder were kept in captivity.

Soon the Chinese government began to rent out some of these captive pandas to zoos around the world, in return for hefty payments to the government. By 1988 some thirty North American zoos were vying with one another to secure import permits for these prized exhibits. George Schaller was highly critical of this rent-a-panda program. "The politics and greed, coupled with the shameful indifference to the panda's welfare that has characterized much of the rental business, will not vanish," he noted in his 1993 book, *The Last Panda*. "But I fervently hope that it will be contained. . . . The panda has not evolved to amuse humankind."

The Fish & Wildlife Service suspended all U.S. panda import permits in 1993. That same year the Chinese government and the World Wildlife Fund began to implement a $100 million, ten-year program to expand the thirteen existing panda preserves and create fourteen new ones. Plans were made to establish and preserve undeveloped corridors of land to link isolated panda habitats, and to relocate farmers who were clearing forest areas needed by the animals.

Today perhaps a thousand pandas still survive in the wild, scattered in about twenty-four small and isolated populations. China keeps about a hundred pandas in captivity, some thirty of them taken as cubs from the wild. Loved by children and adults throughout the world, the unique black and white bear clings to survival by the slenderest of margins.

SAIGA ANTELOPE
Saiga tatarica

A stocky, short-legged antelope, the saiga is distinguished by its curiously swollen nasal chambers and downward curving nostrils. These adaptations may prove useful in moistening and warming the dusty, dry air breathed by the saiga in the areas in which it lives. Besides the inflated nose, the male saiga antelope is equipped with foot-long, slightly curving horns.

Traveling in herds, the saiga historically ranged across the

Saiga Antelope

steppes of Europe and central Asia. It was hunted enthusiastically by the Tartars, Mongols, and other Asiatic tribes, and for hundreds of years the exported horns formed the basis of a flourishing trade with China. The Chinese ground up the horn, which was then used in oriental medicines for its curative properties.

The slaughter of the saiga for its horns, and for its meat and hides as well, reached its peak in the middle of the nineteenth century—about the same time as the mass slaughter of the American bison. Sometimes entire herds of saiga antelopes numbering hundreds or thousands were driven into fenced corrals, then killed en masse. By the early years of the twentieth century only scattered remnants of the once huge bands were left, possibly no more than a thousand antelope in all.

After the overthrow of the czarist government in Russia, the revolutionaries passed a decree in 1919 forbidding the hunting of the endangered saiga. During the next twenty years field biologists conducted detailed observations of the species in the wild, learning its habits and requirements. The animal, they noted, was responding dramatically to protection.

By 1960 the saiga population in Kazakhstan, Russian Asia, had ballooned to an estimated one-and-a-quarter million animals. An additional half-million roamed the steppes west of the Volga River. The increase illustrated graphically how an endangered species could make a dramatic comeback under protective management. By 1975 the total population was estimated at more than two million animals, permitting a controlled hunting season and a sizeable harvest of animals yearly without causing a decline in the overall population.

In recent years, however, the cycle of human greed and illegal overkill has victimized the saiga antelope once again. The species has been exterminated in China because of the belief that its horns have curative properties. Now China imports horn from Russia—some eighty tons in 1990. Many of the victims are killed by poachers. As a result, saiga populations are plummeting. Entire herds have been wiped out, and according to some reports the overall population has declined by 90 percent. In 1994 the Convention on International Trade in Endangered Species (CITES) listed the saiga antelope as a threatened species requiring strict export controls.

PRZEWALSKI'S WILD HORSE
Equus przewalski

Exploring central Asia during the 1870s, a Russian naturalist, Nikolai Mikhailovitch Przewalski, collected many animal specimens for scientific study as well as a great deal of information about the wildlife of the region. He was especially intrigued by a unique wild horse—an animal quite different from the mounts of the nomadic Mongol tribesmen. These wild horses were small and stocky, with an erect black mane but no forelock. With big heads and short legs, they were generally yellowish brown in color, with a light belly and a dark streak down the back. They looked very much like the cave drawings of Europe's Ice Age horse, the long-extinct tarpan.

When he returned to Europe, Przewalski brought back with him a skin and skull of this wild horse he had found. In 1881 I. S. Poliakov, a Russian zoologist, wrote the first scientific description of the animal, naming it after its discoverer.

A few foals were subsequently captured, and in 1900 three living specimens were kept on a Russian estate. At this time the Duke of Bedford, the English animal enthusiast, commissioned Carl Hagenback of Hamburg, Germany, to capture six specimens of Przewalski's horse for his collections at Woburn Abbey. The most noted animal collector of his time, Hagenback had a worldwide network of agents and collectors. He promptly sent agent William Grieger to the Gobi Desert to organize the capture. There, with the aid of nearly two thousand Kirghiz horsemen to run down foals and pregnant mares, Grieger succeeded in capturing fifty-two Przewalski's horses. Of them, twenty-eight survived to be transported to Europe in the fall of 1901. From this nucleus have come practically all of the captive stock of Przewalski's horses alive today.

The species once ranged over much of southwest Mongolia and parts of the Gobi Desert. Traveling in bands, the little wild horses summered on the high, dry plains and wintered on the southern slopes of the mountains or in protected valleys. They competed for food and water with the domestic stock of nomadic tribesmen, and at times there may have been hybridization with Mongol ponies. The wild population decreased steadily. By the 1940s it had almost disappeared, and by the 1950s Przewalski's horse was considered extinct in the wild.

There have been a few subsequent sightings, however, and possibly a handful may still roam free. Although nominally protected, the only hope for their survival is the establishment of a native preserve from which all domestic horses are excluded.

The survival of the species so far has been assured by the descendants of the animals collected by William Grieger at the turn of the century. Today there are hundreds of Przewalski's horses in zoos and other animal collections around the world. A stud book containing a careful record of all these captive specimens is kept at the Prague Zoo in the Czech Republic.

Captive animals such as these are no substitute for wild populations. They may serve, however, as seed stock that will eventually make possible the return of Przewalski's horses to the wild.

The first step in such a return has already taken place. Sixteen zoo-bred Przewalski's horses, raised in San Diego, Berlin, and Munich, have been sent to China, where they live in a 1,000-acre enclosure in the desert of the Junggar Basin of northern Xinjiang Province. If the group thrives in this area and breeds successfully, some of them may eventually be liberated. Another captive group is being kept in Gansu Province, with the same goal.

In November 1995, a scientific expedition in northeastern Tibet reported finding another Stone Age horse in a high icy valley closed off from the surrounding country by passes about 16,000 feet high. The Riwoche horse, as it is called after the region where it was found, is a rugged pony about four feet high, with a beige coat and bristly mane, a black stripe down its back, and black lines on its lower legs. Michel Perissel, the leader of the expedition, declared that the little horses "looked completely archaic, like the horses in prehistoric cave paintings." The expedition caught several of them, took blood samples, then filmed and released them. "It will be interesting to compare the genetic markers to those of other wild horses" (such as Przewalski's wild horse), Steve Harrison, a geneticist with the expedition, remarked. It could turn out that the Riwoche horse and Przewalski's are one and the same.

GREAT INDIAN RHINOCEROS
Rhinoceros unicornis

A relic of prehistoric days, the great Indian rhinoceros almost seems a creature from another world. Its thick hide hangs over a bulky frame in folds that suggest armor plate. Rough warts, or protuberances, on the skin remind one of rivets. With a shoulder height sometimes well over five feet, and a weight of two tons, the overall impression is of a living tank. Indeed, Indian rulers in ancient days are said to have used the rhinoceros in warfare, fastening an iron trident over the animal's horn. If kept under control, the terrifying beast undoubtedly could move everything in its path.

Great Indian Rhinoceros

The horn of the rhinoceros has long been prized as an aphrodisiac, and this belief has contributed significantly to the animal's endangered status. The horn has no bony core. It is composed of compressed fibrous material attached at the base to a rough supporting area of skin. Growing continuously, horns have measured up to two feet in length and may weigh as much as three pounds.

In times past the species had other supposed attributes that made it a handsome prize for poachers. Rhinoceros blood was believed to speed departing souls on their way to life after death, the urine was said to be an excellent disinfectant, and drinking vessels made from the horn allegedly rendered poisons harmless.

In much of Asia, rhino horn is considered more precious than gold. Even though the animal is legally protected nearly everywhere at the present time, it is still killed illegally for the horn, which is sold on the black market at fabulous prices. George Schaller reports that China uses about 1,400 pounds of horn every year, and the illicit traffic in the product is widespread in that country, as well as in Taiwan, Thailand, and South Korea. Wholesale prices are around $1,000 per pound for African rhino horn, ten times that much for Asian horn.

The Convention on International Trade in Endangered Species (CITES) banned all trade in rhino products in 1987. Under increasing international pressure, China's State Council prohibited the manufacture of rhino horn medicines and forbid all domestic trade in such products in 1993, but the underground market continues to thrive.

The range of the great Indian rhinoceros once covered parts of northern India and Nepal. Today, however, the species has disappeared from much of its former range because of poaching and the clearing of large areas of its habitat for timber and agricultural use. Most of the wild population, estimated to be two thousand or slightly more, lives in protected sanctuaries.

India has set aside a number of such refuges, the principal one being the Kaziranga National Park, 166 square miles of habitat located on the south bank of the Brahmaputra River in the state of Assam, northeastern India. In 1912 there were less than one hundred rhinos in the area, but now there are about 1,500, thanks to an effective anti-poaching program in recent years. For the same reason, Nepal's Chitwan National Park now has about 465 rhinos, up from about a hundred in 1973.

Besides the wild population, there are about one hundred Indian rhinos in zoos around the world. Two-thirds of these were born in captivity.

ASIATIC LION
Panthera leo persica

The lion has long been considered the king of beasts, a living symbol of power and majesty. A large male lion, with his imposing mane and tawny coat, certainly commands respect, and even fear, especially if the beast is angry. Then his eyes seem to glow with fierce light, his tail twitches menacingly, and his lips draw back in a snarl. He may roar, showing his enormous teeth. Noisiest of all cats, the lion vents its feelings with what the explorer Samuel Baker has described as "awe-inspiring notes, like the rumble of distant thunder."

In ancient times the lion ranged widely over much of the Old World, including some parts of eastern Europe. When Xerxes, the

Asiatic Lion

Persian conqueror, marched through Macedonia in 480 B.C., some of his baggage camels were killed by lions, as recorded by Herodotus, the Greek historian. Many lions, he noted, could be found in Thrace (southeastern Europe) at that time. By A.D. 100 the big cats had disappeared from Europe, killed off by humans. Lions, however, were a familiar sight to the Romans. They imported them from North Africa and the Mideast by the hundreds, and featured them in their numerous circus spectaculars.

The lion was still common in the Near East during Biblical times, but it disappeared from Palestine by the thirteenth century, at about the same time that Marco Polo was heading for China. In Iraq, the last lion was seen in the early 1800s, and in Pakistan the last reported killing of a lion was in 1842. A few persisted in Persia (modern-day Iran) until this century, with several sightings recorded as late as 1942.

Once widely spread throughout India, the Asiatic lion, like the tiger, furnished royal sport to Indian princes and colonial nabobs alike. Colonel George Acland Smith boasted that he had shot 300 Indian lions during the mid-1800s. With such attrition, the lion had disappeared from the entire Indian Peninsula by the 1880s except for a few survivors in the Gir Forest, in the state of Gujarat in southwest India. There they seemed to be making their last stand, and in the 1890s the British naturalist Richard Lydekker stated: "A few years will probably witness the extinction of the lion throughout the peninsula."

The Nawab of Junagarh held jurisdiction over the Gir Forest, and in 1900 he extended complete protection to the lions there. The estimated population of the big cats at that time was fewer than one hundred—some said perhaps only twenty-five animals. Under protection, the population slowly increased to about three hundred by 1950.

During the next twenty-five years the number of lions began another decline, mainly due to habitat destruction. A century ago the Gir Forest had covered three-quarters of a million acres, but by 1975 it had shrunk to less than half that amount. Once there had been many teak and other hardwood trees in the forest, but most of them had long since been cut down for lumber. Groups of seminomadic people invaded the sanctuary with large herds of domestic animals, and much of the remaining forest deteriorated to overgrazed scrub, with encroaching areas of semidesert around its borders. Such land supported very little food or cover for the lions and their natural wild prey: sambar and chital deer and wild pigs.

Vigorous programs were instituted to reduce habitat damage and restrict access to the sanctuary by domestic livestock. The lion population—down to 180 in 1975—began to increase once again. By 1990 there were nearly three hundred lions in the Gir Sanctuary—perhaps more than the remaining suitable habitat could comfortably support. Lions often roamed twenty or thirty miles outside the refuge boundaries, killing livestock and attacking humans with increasing frequency. From 1978 to 1991 there were an average of fifteen lion attacks on humans and two resulting deaths every year. In the years since, there has been a sharp increase in the frequency of the attacks—most of them occurring on land outside the sanctuary. Villagers, understandably, have become increasingly hostile to the lions.

To alleviate the problem, plans are underway to compensate villagers for livestock losses, prohibit lion baiting as a tourist attraction, and reduce the lion population either by culling or by relocating some of the animals to two other sanctuaries—Palpur

Kuno in the state of Madya Pradesh and Sitamata in the state of Rajasthan.

The Asiatic lion is the only race that is seriously threatened at the moment. But two African races—the Barbary lion of North Africa and the Cape lion of South Africa—have both been exterminated at the hand of man. Populations of the big cat are dwindling in many other parts of Africa as well. The lion will eventually disappear everywhere in the wild unless we humans reassess our attitude toward this magnificent creature.

SNOW LEOPARD
Panthera uncia

Considered by many as the most beautiful of all the cats, the snow leopard has a coat of pale smoky gray that shades to white on the undersides, with numerous black splashes and rosettes on the body. The tail is long and thick and fluffy, and the eyes, as described by zoologist George Schaller, are "pale, with a frosty glitter softened only by a twinge of amber . . . the eyes of a creature used to immense solitudes and snowy wastes."

The habitat of the snow leopard includes the high steppes and slopes of the mountains of central Asia, from Afghanistan, Pakistan, and Kashmir to Mongolia, Tibet, and western China. A solitary and nocturnal animal, it preys on musk deer, wild sheep and goats, hares, and other small game. Driven by hunger during the harsh winters, it sometimes leaves the high slopes and descends into the valleys, where it may feed on domestic stock.

Nominally protected in much of its range, it is hunted as a destructive predator in some areas. Possessing one of the most luxurious coats in the world, the species is also killed for its fur. No one knows how many snow leopards survive, but its numbers are declining everywhere, and it is presently classified as a species in imminent danger of extinction. The zoos of the world have more than one hundred of them in their collections, most of them captive bred.

TIGER
Panthera tigris

In his *Book,* Marco Polo reported that there were beautiful "striped lions" in the Sichuan and Yunnan areas of China, and that the great Kublai Khan sometimes used them in the hunt. Marco Polo had evidently never seen a tiger before, but the Romans of some fifteen hundred years earlier were well acquainted with the beasts. They imported tigers for their spectacles and pitted them against other beasts or gladiators.

In the centuries since, visions of the great striped cats have fired the imaginations of men, women, and children everywhere. The tiger has long been a symbol of power and courage, a beautiful predator to be admired and feared.

Two centuries ago, the poet William Blake wrote:

> Tyger! tyger! burning bright
> In the forests of the night,
> What immortal hand or eye
> Could frame thy fearful symmetry?

Today the "tyger" whose fortunes burned so brightly in William Blake's time is in dire distress. As the late naturalist Gerald Durrell observed, "The great beast has faded to a twinkle in the overgrazed forests of the night." Within a very few years, the species may be snuffed out completely in the wild.

Tiger

In Blake's time, the tiger (*Panthera tigris*) ranged across suitable habitat from Turkey and the Caspian region westward to southeastern Siberia and Korea, and southward through China, India, and Southeast Asia to the islands of Sumatra, Java, and Bali. At the beginning of the twentieth century perhaps 100,000 of them still roamed this vast territory. Today, an estimated five to six thousand remain.

Over the years, scientists have recognized eight subspecies of the big orange-and-black cats, based on subtle differences in size, color, markings, and other minor characteristics. These are the Bengal, Siberian, South China, Indo-Chinese, Sumatran, Bali, Caspian, and Javan tigers. The last three are now considered extinct.

The last Bali tiger (*P.t. balica*), a victim of uncontrolled hunting, was killed in 1937. The Caspian tiger (*P.t. virgata*), which once ranged from eastern Turkey and the southern Caucasus into northern Iran and Afghanistan, was last recorded in Iran in 1959, and in Turkey in 1973. The Javan tiger (*P.t. sondaica*) had been reduced to a handful of survivors in eastern and southern Java by

1970. Six years later, these had dwindled to an estimated three to five lonely survivors, and the last reliable sighting occurred in 1983.

The Sumatran tiger (*P.t. sumatrae*) was abundant in the late nineteenth century. Today, only a remnant population—perhaps four to five hundred individuals—survives in remote jungle areas. Nominally protected, they are still heavily hunted by poachers.

The South China tiger (*P.t. amoyensis*) once roamed through much of the Yangtze Valley and the Sichuan border region, southward through central and southern China. During the 1950s and 1960s, it was actively hunted and killed in government programs to eliminate pests. As many as 3,000 tigers were reported to have been destroyed in these official campaigns. In 1956 alone, the People's Liberation Army of China's communist government is said to have killed more than 530 tigers and leopards. By the 1980s, only an estimated one hundred South China tigers were left, and today fewer than thirty may remain.

The Siberian, or Amur, tiger (*P.t. altaica*) was one of the world's rarest animals half a century ago, with no more than an estimated two or three dozen remaining in the Soviet Far East. Once ranging over large forested areas of southeastern Siberia, Manchuria, northern China, and Korea, this race had long been a prime target for hunters. Largest of all the tigers, it has longer fur and is generally paler in color than its southern relatives. Big males sometimes measure twelve feet in length and weigh more than 700 pounds.

In the 1950s, when the Siberian tiger had almost reached the vanishing point, the Soviet Union belatedly instituted strict laws protecting it. The population slowly increased, and a 1969 census counted an estimated 150 tigers in Soviet territory. A few others survived in northeastern China and in neighboring Korea. By 1983 the population had climbed to perhaps four hundred. Then, with the demise of the Soviet Union in the early 1990s, near-anarchy came to much of the Russian Far East. Desperate for foreign exchange, the territorial government sold logging rights in vast areas to international companies, and the great northern forests—prime habitat for tigers and other wildlife—began falling before the ax and saw.

While timber companies invaded the forests, poachers had a field day killing tigers and selling their skins and other parts to countries to the south. In the winter of 1993–94, an estimated eighty to ninety Siberian tigers were taken illegally. As few as four hundred may now survive in the wild.

In 1989 a meeting between Dr. Maurice Hornocker, the director of the Idaho-based Hornocker Wildlife Research Institute, and Russian wildlife biologists from the Soviet Academy of Sciences led to the formation of the cooperative Russian-American Siberian Tiger Project to observe, study, and protect the great cat. The field studies of the Russian-American team have been conducted in the Sikhote-Alin Nature Reserve, part of a wilderness area north of Vladivostok known as Ussuriland. Backed by grants from the National Geographic Society, the National Fish and Wildlife Foundation, Exxon (whose symbol is the tiger), and the National Wildlife Federation, Americans have brought new equipment and techniques to the project.

The Indo-Chinese tiger (*P.t. corbetti*) ranges from Burma south through Thailand and the Malay Peninsula to Cambodia, Laos, Vietnam, and extreme southern China. Portions of this range, especially the dense and nearly impenetrable jungles on the borders of northern Vietnam and Laos, are still largely unexplored by scientists, and any estimate of tiger numbers in the region is mostly guesswork. Perhaps a thousand to fifteen hundred Indo-Chinese tigers still roam its wild reaches. *P.t. corbetti* gets its scientific subspecific name from Jim Corbett, a legendary British hunter, conservationist, and author of the 1946 best seller, *Man-Eaters of Kumaon*. Corbett spent years tracking and killing man-eating tigers in the United Provinces of northwestern India.

The Bengal tiger (*P.t. tigris*), which once ranged across the Indian subcontinent from northwestern India and southern Nepal to the Irrawaddy Valley of Burma, is the most numerous surviving race. Both India and Bangladesh claim it as their national emblem. During the heyday of the British Empire, the Bengal tiger was the most prized quarry of Indian princes, British colonials, and trophy hunters from all over the world. In the 1993 book *Tiger-Wallahs: Encounters with the Men Who Tried to Save the Greatest of the Great Cats*, Geoffrey and Diane Ward note that more than 100 thousand tigers, most of them Bengals, may have been shot during the nineteenth century. By 1900 some forty thousand Bengals may still have remained, still plenty to sate the lust of wealthy sportsmen. In 1939 the king of Nepal killed forty-one tigers during one hunt on his private reserve. And as recently as 1965 another maharajah wrote to naturalist George B. Schaller, confessing that "my bag of tigers is only 1,150." Besides being shot as trophies, Bengals were hunted from the earliest times because of their threat to humans and livestock. Since 1948 tigers have killed more than eight hundred people in the Bangladesh Sundarbans, the mangrove jungles at the delta of the Ganges River. A few villagers there and in India continue to fall prey to man-eaters.

Bengal tigers were still plentiful a half-century ago, but since then their numbers have dwindled steadily. Alarmed by a 1972 census that counted only 1,827 left in India, the World Wildlife Fund spearheaded Operation Tiger, an effort to save the embattled species. As part of its own Project Tiger, the Indian government passed legislation and set up reserves to protect Bengals. In 1993 Indian officials celebrated the twentieth anniversary of Project Tiger by announcing that their country's tiger population had increased to 4,300, but impartial experts regarded this number as padded for the benefit of corrupt bureaucrats. They pegged a more realistic total at three thousand.

A chief culprit was the loss of habitat, for India's burgeoning population had placed under siege its much-heralded system of national parks and reserves. (India's population is 900 million and still climbing, despite state birth-control programs. Indians account for 16 percent of the world's population but are squeezed onto just 2 percent of the world's land.)

Expanding human numbers threaten all Asian wildlife, but tigers face the added threat of poaching. A tiger's skin may sell for more than $3,000, and virtually every other part of the animal is prized in traditional oriental medicines and pharmaceuticals. According to the Wards:

The catalogue of physical ills which tiger bones and the elixers brewed from them are supposed to cure includes rheumatism, convulsions, scabies, boils, dysentery, ulcers, typhoid, malaria, even prolapse of the anus. Tiger remedies are also said to alleviate fright, nervousness, and possession by devils. Ground tiger bone scattered on the roof is believed to bar demons and end nightmares for those who sleep beneath it.

Pulverized tiger bone, which sells for as much as $100 a pound on the illegal market, is used for making "tiger wine" and other cure-alls. And in Taiwan, a bowl of tiger-penis soup can fetch $320.

Because of its numbers, the Bengal tiger is the chief victim of this illegal trade. Both the People's Republic of China and Taiwan pay lip service to attempts to stop or control the illegal trade, but tiger products are sold more or less openly in their markets. In April 1994 President Clinton imposed limited sanctions against Taiwan for its lack of progress in curbing the trade, but he sidestepped imposing any penalties against mainland China.

Tigers will survive in captivity, of course. Today there are at least a thousand or more Siberian tigers, the most numerous zoo race, living and breeding in captivity on every continent—more than twice as many as there are in the wild—and the total number of tigers of all races in zoos may total more than fifteen hundred.

The future of tigers in the wild, however, remains bleak. The world's human population is constantly increasing, and the relentless pressure on the tiger's living space continues. Unless the trend is reversed, the tiger and countless other species will soon have nowhere to go except oblivion. Cat specialist Peter Jackson, of the International Union for the Conservation of Nature and Natural Resources (IUCN), believes the tiger may become extinct in the wild by the year 2002.

Yet hope remains, and conservationists continue to do what they can. In October 1994 Congress authorized the spending of $50 million in behalf of the tiger and the rhinoceros, two animals particularly hard-hit by the trade in endangered-species parts. A month later, delegates from the 122 countries that have ratified the

CITES convention gathered in Fort Lauderdale, Florida, to debate measures to protect key wildlife species. At that meeting, nine Asian nations pledged their support for tiger rescue and conservation programs. But the results of Congress's current budget-cutting mania do not augur well for endangered species.

Meanwhile, our own species continues to wage its deadly war of destruction against wildlife and the environment on every continent. The future of the tiger lies in the balance.

KOUPREY
Bos sauveli

The kouprey or forest ox was unknown to Western scientists until 1937, when a young male was received at the Vincennes Zoo in Paris, together with a shipment of young gaur—another species of wild ox—from Saigon, Indochina. It was described that year by Achilles Urbain, the zoo director. Three years later, Harold J. Coolidge, Jr., a noted field naturalist and conservationist, compiled all available information about the kouprey in the wild, and wrote a detailed description of the species and what little was known about its habits.

The adult bull kouprey is an imposing animal, weighing about 2,000 pounds and measuring six feet in height at the shoulder hump. Its color is black or dark brown, with white stockings. It has an impressive dewlap—a fold of loose skin hanging from the neck—that nearly reaches the ground, and widespread horns that may measure thirty inches around the outside curve. One distinctive feature of the horns is that they are often frayed at the tip. The light gray female is much smaller than the male, and has lyre-shaped horns.

Almost nothing was known of the kouprey's behavior and requirements in the wild until 1952, when biologist Charles Wharton conducted a field study of the species in Cambodia, during which he located, observed, and photographed half a dozen separate groups. The total population at that time was perhaps five hundred animals. By 1970, due to hunting and habitat destruction, the number had shrunk to about one hundred.

For most of the past half-century, the kouprey's living space has been the scene of savage warfare and revolution. The rare forest ox was one of war's victims, relentlessly hunted and killed by marauding soldiers and hungry peasants. As a result, only a few dozen may survive today. A biologist sighted a bull in Vietnam's Du Lap Province in 1990—the first sighting by a scientist in nearly twenty years. Since then, none.

Today the kouprey is probably the most endangered large land mammal in the world.

SAO LA OR VU QUANG OX
Pseudoryx nghetinhensis

In 1992, British field biologist John MacKinnon led an expedition into the Vu Quang Nature Reserve, an almost unknown and unexplored "lost world" of rugged slopes and tropical rain forest in the Annamite Mountains of northern Vietnam, near the Laos border. Recently opened by the government to Western scientists, the Vu Quang reserve promised many prizes to MacKinnon and his staff as they started a preliminary survey of its animals and plants.

In the homes of several villagers MacKinnon saw the skulls and straight, foot-long horns of a large hoofed animal—the remains of a species that he realized was unknown to science. The villagers, however, knew the animal. They hunted it for food and called it *sao*

la, or spindle horn. From their descriptions, the adult sao la evidently stood about thirty-five inches high at the shoulder and weighed perhaps 200 pounds. The scientists were able to obtain several of the skulls and horns, as well as some pieces of skin and hair. Subsequent DNA analyses indicated that this new species was a survivor of a primitive bovid (cud-chewing, even-hoofed) ancestor that eventually split to evolve into two different types of hoofed animal—modern cattle and buffalo, and spiral-horned antelopes. The sao la was the first hitherto unknown large mammal to be discovered to science since 1937, when the kouprey appeared.

In 1994 two young sao la were captured and exhibited briefly in Hanoi, where they died. Vietnam is proud of the sao la and other biological treasures of the Vu Quang reserve, however, and wants to preserve and protect them. The government recently enlarged the reserve from 60,000 to 150,000 acres and imposed bans on hunting and logging.

Another new species of hoofed animal—a giant barking deer or muntjak—was discovered in the area in 1994. About one and a half times the size of the largest previously known muntjak, it has massive canine teeth and eight-inch antlers which are bowed, with long brow tines.

Other Asian Animals

Today Asia is a vast continent in turmoil as its human populations strive to build better lives for themselves under difficult circumstances. The booming birth rate adds many more millions of hungry mouths each year to those that already must be fed. By the year 2000 an estimated 3.8 billion people will struggle for existence in Asia.

Since World War II there has been a large-scale introduction of Western technology and agricultural practices into the continent to help the Asian nations cope with the problems of too many people, too little food, and antiquated methods of agriculture, sanitation, and health care. Vast areas of the continent—particularly Indochina and Southeast Asia—have been wracked by long wars that have destroyed a great deal of forest and cropland. Many clearing and drainage projects have been instituted, and huge areas have been sprayed with DDT and other pesticides for disease and pest control. As one inevitable result of all these activities, there has been a grave reduction of natural habitat throughout the continent. The effects of this loss on native wildlife have been dramatic.

The large-hoofed mammals show the trends most graphically. Mainland Asia is the homeland of at least five different species of wild cattle, all of which are now in serious danger. The water buffalo has been domesticated for thousands of years, but today's wild herds are mere remnant populations threatened with imminent extermination. The yak, another species long domesticated by tribes of the central highlands and used for meat, milk, and as a beast of burden, has also been almost exterminated in the wild. The gaur, or seladang, of Southeast Asia, largest of all the world's cattle, survives only in scattered bands, as does the banteng of Burma and Indonesia.

Many Asiatic deer are in imminent danger of disappearing. The beautiful barasingha of India has declined drastically in recent years due to hunting and loss of habitat to crops and domestic stock. So has the brow-antlered, or Eld's, deer. This species is notable for its unusual antlers, in which the long brow tine and the beam form an unbroken sweeping curve, somewhat like the rocker on a rocking chair. Its numbers have been dangerously reduced by overhunting, clearing of the forests, and the use of defoliants and other environmentally damaging operations during the long Vietnam War. At least four Asiatic races of the red deer, a close relative of our American elk, or wapiti, are either extinct today or imminently threatened with that fate, principally because of overhunting. So are various races of the little spotted sika deer of East Asia's mainland and islands.

A number of Asiatic antelope are threatened because of excessive hunting, poaching, and loss of suitable habitat. The once-abundant blackbuck of India has practically disappeared. So have the Arabian and Dorcas gazelles, dainty little antelopes of the Arabian Peninsula and neighboring areas.

Asia is the ancestral homeland of many magnificent wild sheep and goats, and it still supports populations of various races of the ibex, the markhor, the bharal, the argali, and the takin (one of the goat antelopes) in remote and mountainous areas. All of these animals have long been pursued for their meat or as hunting trophies, and their populations are either decreasing or barely holding their own. The same can be said for the various races of the Asiatic wild ass, several of which may soon disappear.

Bactrian camels survive in the wild only as tiny remnant populations: perhaps five hundred in the forbidding climate of the Taklimakin Desert in western China, and about three hundred in the Great Gobi Desert National Park in southern Mongolia. Although they are legally protected in the park, their numbers have dwindled in recent years because of drought and predation by wolves, which lie in wait for young camels at waterholes. In 1988 park authorities captured about a dozen young to start a captive breeding herd. If the program proves successful, some of the young bred and born in captivity may eventually be released to run with the wild bands.

Besides the tiger and snow leopard, a number of other meat-eating animals are threatened with extermination because of habitat loss and hunting. Among them are several races of leopard. The Amur leopard, a beautiful northern subspecies that once ranged widely through eastern Siberia, the Koreas, and northern China, is the most critically endangered. It is now considered extinct or very nearly so throughout most of its range. On the other side of the continent, only one or two hundred Arabian leopards remain. Another endangered meat-eater is the clouded leopard of India, Nepal, and Southeast Asia. It has already disappeared in many parts of its former range, and is hard-pressed in regions where it still survives.

Asian bears are being pursued and killed nearly everywhere, victims of the trade in oriental medicines. Bear gall bladders are used in the treatment of burns, fevers, ulcers, and other ailments. Bear bile fluid, according to George Schaller, is many times more valuable per ounce than gold. In one single year, 1989, the Japanese imported 1,500 pounds of bear bile from China. Bear paws are a much prized luxury food in Tokyo, where a banquet of them may cost hundreds of dollars. In Russia's Kamchatka Peninsula, more than 5,000 bears have been illegally killed since 1991—about half the estimated population—according to a scientist at the Kronotsky Nature Reserve.

Asia's crocodiles—the marsh crocodile of Southeast Asia, the Siamese crocodile, the Indian gavial, and the Chinese alligator—are all presently endangered by heavy hunting and poaching for their hides. Many snakes, the spectacular big pythons in particular, are also being killed for their beautiful skins.

The endangered species listed here are but a few of those that may disappear within the next few years. As a result of human pollution, destruction of natural habitat, widespread hunting and poaching, and the drenching of vast areas with insecticides, increasing numbers of wildlife species will be exterminated unless more sanctuaries and protective measures are instituted.

Where the south declines toward the setting sun lies Ethiopia. There gold is obtained in great plenty, huge elephants abound . . . and the men are taller and longer-lived than anywhere else.

Herodotus

4

AFRICA
Land of the Last Great Herds

The ancient Mediterranean civilizations knew Africa only as a vast, undefined land of mystery to the south. Phoenicians and other seafarers skirted its coasts; sometimes they landed and traded with native tribes. The ancient Egyptians knew the fertile borders of their mighty Nile River as far as the third or fourth cataract (rapids), several hundred miles inland, but little more. The sources of that mighty river were not learned until the nineteenth century. These early civilizations were curious to discover Africa's secrets, and bit by bit they began to uncover them.

The Phoenicians, chief sailors of the ancients, founded Carthage on Africa's north rim about 900 B.C. and sailed their ships both east and west on voyages of exploration. The ancient Egyptians also sought to learn more about the lands outside their sphere. About the year 600 B.C., Necho, King of Egypt, repaired an already ancient canal that linked the Nile to the Red Sea and sent forth an expedition manned by Phoenicians to explore the African coastline.

Heading southward on the prevailing winds, the expedition lasted for two years, as recorded by Herodotus. Sailing clockwise around Africa, the expedition finally returned to Egypt through the Straits of Gibraltar and the Mediterranean Sea. Even though he recorded this remarkable voyage, Herodotus found it hard to believe. A similar voyage around Africa in the opposite direction did not take place until more than twenty centuries later.

Exploring Unknown Coasts

About 500 B.C., the Phoenician Hanno sailed from Carthage through the Straits of Gibraltar and southward along the west coast of Africa. Passing the delta of the River Niger, he ventured as far as Cameroon Mountain, just above the equator in present-day Cameroon. Hanno recorded seeing live volcanoes and visiting an island with strange, hairy savages on it, which the interpreter for the expedition called "gorillae." Three of these animals were killed, and their skins brought back to Carthage. Whether they were actually gorilla skins or those of some lesser ape, no one will ever know.

The Romans finally defeated their Carthaginian rivals in 146 B.C., at the end of the Third Punic War. After conquering Egypt as well, they ruled the Mediterranean world for several hundreds of years thereafter. Hanno's voyage to Cameroon, however, was not duplicated, as far as we know, until the fifteenth century when the Portuguese began to probe farther and farther southward along Africa's west coast.

In 1487, Bartolomeo Diaz sailed as far as the Cape of Good Hope, near Africa's southern tip, before turning back. Ten years later Vasco da Gama sailed past the Cape and on to Zanzibar, proving once and for all that Africa was a great continent with open ocean to the south of it.

The island of Zanzibar had long been a flourishing trading center. Strategically located on the shores of the Indian Ocean below the horn of eastern Africa, it served as an outlet for slaves, ivory, and other goods from Africa's interior, as well as a depot for products from both the Mediterranean and the Far East. Arab navigators were probably the first to sail the monsoons (periodic

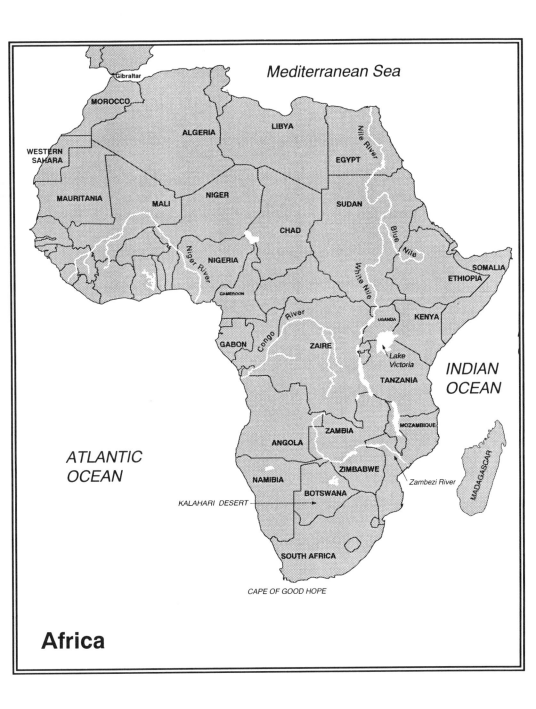

Mediterranean Sea

Gibraltar

MOROCCO

ALGERIA

LIBYA

Nile River

EGYPT

WESTERN
SAHARA

MAURITANIA

MALI

NIGER

SUDAN

CHAD

Blue Nile

Niger River

NIGERIA

CAMEROON

White Nile

SOMALIA

ETHIOPIA

GABON

Congo River

ZAIRE

UGANDA

KENYA

Lake
Victoria

INDIAN
OCEAN

TANZANIA

ATLANTIC
OCEAN

ANGOLA

ZAMBIA

MOZAMBIQUE

NAMIBIA

ZIMBABWE

Zambezi River

MADAGASCAR

KALAHARI DESERT

BOTSWANA

SOUTH AFRICA

CAPE OF GOOD HOPE

Africa

winds) across the Indian Ocean to India and the Orient, but in time the Phoenicians, Greeks, and Romans learned the secret, too.

Below Africa's narrow green strip of Mediterranean coastland lies the vast Sahara Desert, which acted as a highly effective barrier to inland exploration by the Phoenicians, Greeks, and Romans. Toward the end of the Ice Age, this area had been pleasant and productive grassland, the home of many tribes and wild animals. But, four to six thousand years ago, the grasslands began to dry up, possibly because of the changing climate or owing to man's habit of overtilling the soil and overgrazing the vegetation. Gradually the desert spread, replacing the fertile land. Here and there were palm-shaded oases, separated by hundreds of miles of barren dunes. Hardy desert tribes and their dromedaries traveled the caravan routes that connected the oases, but few others ventured into the wastes of burning sands. Timbuktu, the fabled city at the crossroads of these caravan trails, was only a vague reference to fifteenth-century Europeans.

The Source of the Nile

The valley of the Nile, however, was another matter. As early as 700 B.C., the Egyptians had explored the Nile valley as far as the fourth cataract, where the Blue Nile comes out of the mountains of Ethiopia and joins the White Nile. Today the Sudanese city of Khartoum lies in the fork. The Egyptians had also explored parts of Ethiopia. Herodotus, who visited much of the known world of his day, ascended the Nile as far as Aswan—the first cataract—in 470 B.C., and speculated about the river's source. Several hundred years later Ptolemy of Egypt claimed that the sources of the river were twin lakes fed by the legendary "Mountains of the Moon."

Emperor Nero attempted to solve the riddle about A.D. 60, when he sent Roman centurions on a voyage of exploration. The Roman writer Seneca, in his *Questiones Naturales*, reported that they came "to immense swamps, the area of which is unknown even to the natives and which no one can tell. For the water plants there are so closely intertwined that no one can measure this water, either on foot or in a boat. . . . There we espied two rocks, between which the Nile gushed forth in mighty fulness."

The enterprising centurions, however, were evidently not the first Europeans to pass this way. Nearly a century before, as recorded at the time by the Syrian geographer Matinus of Tyre, a Greek merchant, Diogenes, is said to have left a place called Rhapta—an East African coastal settlement, perhaps not far from Zanzibar—and "travelled inland for a 25-days' journey and arrived in the vicinity of two great lakes, and the snowy range of mountains whence the Nile draws its twin sources."

The ancients came close to learning the sources of the Nile, but not until the nineteenth century did explorers settle the matter to the satisfaction of Victorian geographers.

Modern Exploration of Africa

The industrious Portuguese were the first to build a way station and fort at the Cape of Good Hope, the southernmost tip of Africa. They were displaced in 1652, however, by the Dutch, who promptly began the settlement of South Africa. During the next two centuries almost all of the continent was brought under the colonial yoke as many European countries vied for territory and commercial benefits. In the process, the continent was opened up and its secrets explored.

Determined to solve the puzzle of the Nile's source, the English explorers Richard Burton and John Speke struck inland from Zanzibar in 1857 and the following year reached Lake Tanganyika, where Burton fell ill. Speke pushed on by himself to find Lake Victoria, which he proclaimed as the true source of the Nile. Four years later Speke made his way into Uganda, where he reached the left bank of the Nile at the mighty Ripon Falls.

Less than ten years later another Victorian explorer, Samuel Baker, discovered Lake Albert and the Murchison Falls, where "the river drops in one leap 120 feet into a deep basin, the edge of which literally swarms with crocodiles."

Meanwhile, the noted missionary-explorer David Livingstone was blazing new trails for Europeans through the southern half of the continent. Sent to Bechuanaland (Botswana) in 1840, "determined to open up the country," he crossed the Kalahari Desert and explored the Zambesi River during the next fifteen years, and in 1854 mounted an expedition into the Congo basin, eventually opening up a trade route across Africa from the Atlantic to the Indian Ocean.

During the same period, an American explorer, Henry Stanley, was surveying Lakes Victoria and Tanganyika and discovering Lake Edward. Stanley followed the Congo down its course and rediscovered Ptolemy's "Mountains of the Moon," the Ruwenzori range. He also made much of the fact that he had "found" the missing David Livingstone, who had not really been lost in the first place.

The Land and People

Today the land and people of Africa are well known, and so are its animals, although there are those who say that some of its zoological marvels are still undiscovered. Since World War II, the many nations of the continent have to a great extent broken their colonial ties, and most of them are endeavoring to build better lives for their peoples.

Africa harbors a great diversity of people with widely divergent physical attributes, languages, and cultures. They are as varied as the Egyptians and other Arab peoples of North Africa; the nomadic Masai of the East African plains, who measure their wealth in cattle; the warlike Kikuyu of Kenya; and the primitive Pygmies who live in the equatorial rain forests. South Africa harbors equally primitive Bushmen, who hunt and forage in the hostile barren areas of the Kalahari Desert. In South Africa are also the proud Zulus, who early in the nineteenth century united with other Bantu tribes under the dynamic leader Shaka and carved out a powerful empire before the coming of the European colonizers.

Today these diverse Africans face a bewildering number of problems—problems complicated by rising populations, the colonial past, and above all by the facts of geography. In the north is the vast Sahara Desert, and in the southwest the Kalahari Desert. Both of these merge into wooded steppes and extensive grasslands and plains on either side of the vast rain forests of the Congo. The southern end of the continent is a varied country, with coastal swamps and grasslands backed up by mountains and semidesert areas, as well as productive croplands in the interior. All of these habitats affect both the wild animals and the people that live in them. Today Africa still has the greatest herds of wildlife left in the world—elephants and buffalo, gnus, wildebeest, and antelopes of many kinds—but they are fast dwindling under relentless human pressures.

AFRICAN ELEPHANT
Loxodonta africana

A huge African elephant bulldozes its way through thick brush, heading for a water hole. Pausing, it lifts its trunk and trumpets loudly. Then it crashes onward, and the earth trembles. Like no other animal, the African elephant is a beast that inspires awe.

It is even bigger than the Asiatic elephant and has larger fan-shaped ears. Instead of a back elevated in the middle, like that of the Asiatic species, the African elephant has a shoulder and a rump elevation, with a dip between the two. A big bull may weigh six or seven tons, stand eleven feet high at the shoulder, and carry tusks as long as nine or ten feet; the largest tusks on record were about eleven feet long and weighed 293 pounds.

These awesome beasts once ranged over much of Africa, from the southern rim of the Sahara to the Cape of Good Hope. In ancient times they were tamed and trained for use in battle, especially during the period of the Punic Wars between Rome and Carthage. The great Carthaginian leader Hannibal led his armies and elephants across the Alps in 218 B.C. and defeated the Romans at the battle of Cannae. And a year later African elephants played an important role in a battle waged in the Sinai Desert between Seleucus Antiochus III of Syria and Ptolemy IV of Egypt. The Egyptians finally won the day, even though their African elephants were reportedly terrified by the better-trained Indian elephants.

Such ancient wartime use of African elephants declined, and the art of capturing and training the beasts was evidently discontinued many centuries ago. Reinstituting it was a dream of King Leopold II of Belgium, however, and in 1900, with his blessing, an enterprising Belgian colonial officer named Jules LaPlume established an Elephant Domestication Station at Vira Vunga in the northeastern Belgian Congo (now Zaire). The station was later relocated to Gangala-na-Bodio, just south of a vast wilderness area of long-grass savannah and forest—prime elephant country. In 1938 this area was established as Garamba National Park. Wild elephants were captured in Garamba, then trained and domesticated at the station. The project was so successful that by 1948 more than one hundred elephant graduates were earning their keep by working on Congo plantations.

Belgian Congo gained its independence in 1960. During the resultant years of turmoil and disorder, the trainers and their domesticated elephants took refuge in the bush. When order was finally restored, they returned to Garamba and found the park in very poor shape after years of neglect, with poaching rampant. A long period of restoration began, helped immeasurably when Garamba was named a World Heritage Site by the United Nations Education, Science, and Cultural Organization (UNESCO) in the 1980s.

Today three of the domesticated elephants that had retreated to the forest with their trainers during the years of unrest still live and work around the park headquarters, and carry tourists on sightseeing trips through Garamba. Far to the south, Botswana has followed the lead of Zaire by establishing another elephant training station.

Some modern elephant experts believe that Africa once supported as many as fifteen million elephants. Others put the top figure at three million. Whatever the numbers, elephants were abundant and dominant animals over much of Africa in the late nineteenth century.

Killing the beasts for their tusks was a common activity all over the continent. At least two million elephants, according to one estimate, were shot from 1880 to 1910. As early as 1861 explorer Paul Du Chaillu observed: "Ivory comes down the river from the interior by inland journey in great quantities. Upward of 80,000 pounds are taken from the Gaboon River yearly . . . elephants must finally disappear."

Describing the scene in 1934, another hunter related that in the Sudan: "I heard of a Greek who must have been responsible for shooting over four thousand elephants in his lifetime. . . . My informant told me that he could remember the days when elephants used to pass the borders of the Belgian Congo, the Sudan, and Uganda, in herds of thousands. . . . There is no doubt that the last thirty years have seen the elephant of Africa vastly reduced by the frantic hunt for food and ivory."

Wasteful and cruel, the killing of elephants has continued unabated until the present time. In 1930 Africa's elephant population was perhaps five million—some say twice that number. By 1979 the total had plummeted to about one-and-a-half million. At the same time the price of ivory had soared to almost $100 a pound— twenty-five times its value in the 1960s. Little wonder that the elephant slaughter reached a peak in the 1980s, when poachers killed seventy thousand or more every year. The illegal kill was especially devastating in the middle African nations of Kenya, Tanzania, and Uganda.

Because of the slaughter, the Convention on International Trade in Endangered Species (CITES) in 1989 declared the African elephant endangered, and placed a moratorium on all international trade in elephant ivory. By the end of the next year, 105 member nations had ratified the moratorium, with only five opposing it.

Kenya immediately stepped up its war against poachers, and during the next two years its agents shot and killed more than a hundred poachers caught in the act. As a symbolic gesture, Kenya also burned more than twelve tons of confiscated ivory.

Because of the CITES ban, the value of ivory, now illegal for trading purposes, plummeted, and the elephant kill by poachers was drastically reduced nearly everywhere.

In spite of this, five nations in the southern part of the continent—South Africa, Zimbabwe, Botswana, Malawi, and Zambia—opposed the ban. All of them had healthy and stable or increasing elephant populations as a result of careful management and conservation practices. South Africa's 8,000-square-mile Kruger National Park, for instance, supported a population of over seven thousand elephants—the maximum number the area could support without changing the character of the habitat and diminishing its value for other wildlife species. When there are too many elephants in a restricted area, their travels and feeding habits cause marked changes in the environment. "Elephants, with their path-making and tree-splitting propensities, will alter the character of the very densest brush in a very short order," the American writer and naturalist Peter Matthiessen has noted in *The Tree Where Man Was Born*. "Probably they rank with man and fire as the greatest force for habitat change in Africa."

To prevent such changes in Kruger Park, from 1967 on South Africa has kept the elephant population balanced in two ways: capturing and relocating family groups (a very expensive proposition); and culling the herds, killing several thousand elephants yearly. The meat of the culled animals is used for human food, the hides tanned and sold, and the ivory stored under guard.

Both Zimbabwe and Botswana have increasing elephant populations. Both have established strict conservation programs to sustain their elephants as a valuable natural resource, and have encouraged their people to view them in this light. Zimbabwe's management plan gives villagers a vested authority over the wildlife on their lands, and the people have come to appreciate elephants and other wild game as valuable resources for food, safaris, and tourist attractions, and to view the actions of poachers as stealing from the people.

In contrast to the conservation programs of these southern African countries, Kenya's wildlife managers have long promoted a "laissez-faire" or "let nature take its course" attitude. The government appreciates the tourist value of elephants and other wildlife— worth about $50 million a year—but deplores any culling of elephant herds when they get too big. As a result, elephant herds have destroyed much natural habitat in certain areas. The same thing has happened in neighboring Tanzania's Serengeti National Park. Kenya's elephants have begun to increase in numbers since the ivory ban and the war on poaching, and human-elephant encounters have also increased. Between 1990 and 1992, the number of people killed by elephants quadrupled.

In spite of conflicting views and programs, there is no doubt about the success of the CITES ban on ivory. Prices of ivory have collapsed, and poaching incidents have dropped dramatically. In the long run, however, Kenya and other African nations will probably have to adopt some of the elephant management practices of the nations further south. In order to meet the demands of the continent's burgeoning human population in future years, more and more living space and agricultural lands will be needed. Because of this land-and-people squeeze, Africa's elephants will have to be managed, and their numbers controlled. In 1996 their total population was estimated to be about 540,000.

BLACK RHINOCEROS
Diceros bicornis

The black rhinoceros, like the elephant, looks prehistoric, a relic of ages past. And indeed it is. Rhinoceroses were dominant and widespread animals in the Ice Age, and those that survive today are the last representatives of ancient lines. Unless we guard them better than we have in recent years, however, these survivors will have disappeared in the wild by the dawn of the twenty-first century and will be known to future generations only in a few protected game reserves and through zoo and museum specimens.

Standing five to five-and-a-half feet tall at the shoulder, the

Black Rhinoceros

black rhino is not quite as big as its cousin, the white rhinoceros, but it is a formidable beast, weighing up to 4,000 pounds. Its skin is relatively smooth and hairless, without any sign of the folds of the Indian rhinoceros. It has two horns, of which the forward is the longer. The record length is slightly more than fifty-three inches. Its sight is very poor, but it has keen hearing and sense of smell to compensate. Perched on the rhino's back, oxpeckers, or tick birds, eat ticks that infest the rhino's skin, and also help warn their host of danger.

Many cases in which rhinos charge human beings are the result of the beast coming closer to investigate a possible threat. On occasion, the black rhinoceros even charges automobiles and trains.

A browser, with a pointed prehensile upper lip designed for grasping leaves and twigs, the black rhinoceros once ranged the open plains of Africa in great numbers, from the Cape to the southern fringe of the Sahara Desert. But during the nineteenth century, rhinos were slaughtered by the thousands for their meat and hides, as game trophies, and especially for their horns, which Asians have prized for centuries as a cure-all for many human ailments.

All five species of rhinoceroses have suffered because of this belief; and, as the numbers of Asian rhinos have dwindled in recent years almost to extinction, poachers have shifted most of their activity to Africa. The stakes are high, for rhino horn may sell for as much as $5,000 or more a pound in Asia. Little wonder that poachers take many risks to search out and kill their quarry. Under such pressure, black rhino numbers have plummeted dramatically.

In 1970 the population of black rhinoceroses throughout Africa was about sixty-five thousand, but ten years later the total had shrunk to just thirteen thousand as a result of the illegal kill. In 1988 only forty-five hundred were left—small remnant populations in scattered areas. Zimbabwe had probably the last viable breeding population, about five hundred black rhinos living in the valley of the Zambesi. To protect them, the government instituted a "shoot on sight" war against poachers.

In 1997 perhaps thirty-four hundred black rhinos still survived in pockets of their former range, most of them in protected sanctuaries. Kenya, which had about twenty thousand of them in the early 1970s, now has a little more than four hundred living in well-guarded reserves. It is one of the few African countries, however, that has a stable—or even slightly growing—black rhino population today. With the help of the World Wildlife Fund, Kenya is now working on a plan to transport rhinos from small fragmented populations to a number of new, well-guarded sanctuaries. Most of Africa's other black rhinos live in Namibia, South Africa, and Zimbabwe. All three of these nations have experimented with programs of tranquilizing rhinos with darts and sawing off their horns in order to render the animals valueless to poachers. The programs have proved of limited value, however, for the horn may grow back at the rate of one-and-a-half to three inches annually. In just one year the horns of one dehorned animal could grow enough to be worth several thousand dollars on the illegal market.

All of the African nations that still have black rhinoceroses within their borders recognize their endangered status and are doing all they can to protect them. Other nations have joined the battle as well. In October 1994 the U.S. Congress authorized the spending of $50 million during a five-year program, to start in 1996, to help save endangered tigers and rhinos.

WHITE, OR SQUARE-LIPPED, RHINOCEROS
Ceratotherium simum

Somewhat larger than its black relative, the white rhinoceros stands six to six-and-a-half feet at the shoulder, measures thirteen feet or more from snout to tail, and weighs three to four tons. A grazing animal instead of a browsing one like the black rhino, it has a square muzzle, which it uses to crop grasses. Although a slightly lighter hue than its relative, the white rhinoceros is no more "white" than its cousin is "black." Both species enjoy wallowing in mud, and their skin takes on the shade of the dried mud in the area in which they live.

Formerly ranging widely throughout southern Africa as well as in a restricted area of central Africa, the white rhino was not recognized as a distinct species or described scientifically until much later than the black. William Burchell, a noted nineteenth-century naturalist and African explorer, bagged his first white rhinoceros in 1812, near Kuruman, south of the Kalahari Desert in South Africa. Several years later he described the animal in a scientific journal and gave it its specific name, *simum*.

Throughout the nineteenth century, the white rhinoceros suffered heavily at the hands of poachers, Africans, and white hunters. Observing the hunting scene during the closing years of the nineteenth century, one famous hunter, Frederick Selous, remarked, "Thousands upon thousands of these huge creatures were killed by white hunters, and natives armed with the white man's weapons, and the species had become practically extinct." Selous was referring to the South African population of the white rhinoceros, the only one that was known when he started his hunting career. Almost all of this population had disappeared by the 1890s, and by 1902 only twenty to fifty of them survived in Zululand, South Africa. Experts considered the species doomed.

Another population, however, was discovered in a small area of central Africa, including the southern Sudan and adjacent parts of the Belgian Congo and Uganda. Described as a separate race (*C.s. cottoni*), this northern population was promptly pursued by hunters and poachers in the same way that the southern race had been.

Today the northern white rhino is an endangered animal, with an estimated total population of only several hundred animals. In 1963 there were about a thousand of them in just one preserve—the Garamba National Park in the Belgian Congo (now Zaire). Early in 1963, however, rebels from the southern Sudan invaded the park and, among other atrocities, killed off most of the white rhinos. By the end of that year the rhino population in Garamba had plummeted to under one hundred animals. The killing continued, and in 1971, eight years later, there were only twenty or thirty survivors in the park. When political order was restored in the area, the rhinos received increased protection and most of the poaching ceased. Today more than thirty white rhinos live in Garamba, and there had been no confirmed poaching of them for twelve years until the spring of 1996, when two were killed.

Uganda had about ninety white rhinos in its Ajai Reserve in 1971. During the early 1960s twelve animals from this reserve were captured and transplanted to Murchison Falls National Park, where they thrived and multiplied.

Meanwhile, the handful of twenty or so southern white rhinos that survived in Zululand in the early years of the twentieth century were given rigid protection. Saved in the nick of time, their numbers slowly increased. By the early 1960s there were more than two thousand of them in Umfolozi Game Reserve in northeastern Natal.

This increasing population became such a heavy burden for the available habitat that the Natal Parks Board began "Operation Rhino," in which surplus rhinos were captured and transported to other South African parks and sanctuaries, as well as to refuges in Kenya, and other African nations. Today, the total population of white rhinos is more than eight thousand, and nearly four thousand have been relocated in the continuing "Operation Rhino" program. Every year the Natal Parks Board earns about $1.5 million selling white rhinos to private game reserves, where they serve as tourist attractions and, in a few cases, as the quarry of trophy hunters. Many have been sent to zoos in other nations as well. There are more than six hundred white rhinos in captivity worldwide, and they are breeding well under captive conditions.

CHEETAH
Acinonyx jubatus

Crouching on its belly, the lithe spotted cat peers through the tall grass. Ahead, a band of Thomson's gazelles are feeding. Stalking slowly and silently forward on long, lean legs, the cheetah approaches to within a hundred yards of its unsuspecting prey. Then suddenly it bounds forward with great speed. Surprised and confused, the gazelles scatter.

Light as thistledown, the big cat overtakes one of the antelope, brings it down, and quickly kills it. Often considered the world's fastest mammal, the cheetah can move at speeds of 60 miles an hour, more for short distances, enabling it to overtake gazelles and other swift antelopes. Living in an open grassland environment— only 5 percent of Africa below the Sahara Desert is suitable—it hunts by sight and is most active during daylight hours. Slender and slight of build, it weighs only 120 to 130 pounds, and it has claws that are only partially retractable. It seldom defends its kill if challenged by other predators such as hyenas or Cape hunting dogs.

The cheetah once ranged westward from India across southern Asia and North Africa and southward through the African plains and savannahs to South Africa. Today it has disappeared from much of its African territory and has been exterminated practically everywhere in Asia in spite of its former abundance there.

The name cheetah comes from the Hindi word *chita*, which means "spotted," and Indian rulers once delighted in using their tame captive cheetahs to bring down blackbuck and deer, much as falconers use birds of prey to capture smaller animals. The sixteenth-century Mogul emperor, Akbar the Great, reportedly kept a thousand trained cheetahs for the hunt.

The cheetah has long been considered extinct in India; the last one was reported killed in 1951. In 1990, however, a field director for the Simlipal Project Tiger reported that he had seen one in the Bulunda forest block. A very few may still survive in northwestern Afghanistan and eastern Iran. Elsewhere in Asia the cheetah has been wiped out.

In Africa, the cheetah has fared somewhat better, but it will eventually disappear there also, unless the trend changes. Today there may be ten to twenty thousand African cheetahs left. Many of them survive in East Africa where they are protected in parks such as Serengeti National Park in Tanzania and Kenya's Tsavo National Park.

Through the years, however, the African cheetah has been hunted relentlessly, not only for its beautiful spotted fur but because it is a predator that sometimes preys on domestic stock. Thus, it has been virtually exterminated from ranch country in Kenya, Zimbabwe, and South Africa. Even where it is protected, poachers kill it for its handsome spotted hide. In 1968 and 1969 a total of 3,168 cheetah skins were imported into the United States. Five years later, renowned field biologist Norman Myers declared in *International Wildlife* magazine, "in 1969 there were probably twice as many cheetahs as there are now." He believed that the species had already almost lost the survival battle because of relentless hunting and loss of suitable habitat.

Geneticists have long known that the cheetah is a very difficult species to breed successfully in captivity. Extensive research has shown that cheetahs are all practically uniform genetically. Scientists theorize that the species suffered a population crash for some unknown reason about ten thousand years ago and almost became extinct as a result. The few survivors, they say, experienced a genetic bottleneck because of inbreeding, producing male cheetahs with low sperm counts and making both sexes much more susceptible to disease. In spite of all of Akbar the Great's efforts to breed his one thousand or more cheetahs, he had to be content with a lone litter. In modern times, the first success in breeding cheetahs in captivity went to the Philadelphia Zoo in 1956. There has been more success in recent years, however. The 1993 International Zoo Yearbook records 699 cheetahs in 120 zoos throughout the world, 555 of them bred in captivity.

The Center for the Reproduction of Endangered Species (CRES), operated by the San Diego Zoological Society, has done extensive research on cheetah breeding and reproduction, including artificial insemination. Other zoological institutions are studying the problems as well. In 1995 the Cincinnati Zoo's Angel Fund—named for its "cat ambassador," a captive cheetah named Angel—was instrumental in the purchase of a 19,000-acre farm in

Namibia to be used as a base for the Cheetah Conservation Fund, dedicated to research on conservation of the species.

LEOPARD
Panthera pardus

One of the most beautiful of all the big cats, the leopard has tawny yellow fur decorated with dark spots clustered together in rosette shapes. With a wide range, it roams suitable habitat in Asia from the Caucasus to eastern Siberia and southward through India and all of Southeast Asia to Java. It is also present over much of Africa. Many races of this powerful cat have been described.

Although neither as fast nor as lithe as the cheetah, the leopard is a far stronger animal. A forest dweller, it is an excellent climber and usually hunts at night, often waiting on a tree branch and springing down upon its unsuspecting victim.

At least five different races of leopard have virtually or completely disappeared: the Sinai leopard, thought to be extinct; the Arabian leopard, which may be extinct as well, killed off by shepherds to protect their flocks; the Barbary leopard of Morocco, Algeria, and Tunisia, with an estimated population of only a few hundred animals; the Anatolian leopard of western Asia and Trans-caucasia, now very rare; and the Amur leopard of eastern Siberia, which is also in imminent danger of extinction, with an estimated population of fifty to one hundred.

Although its overall population has declined sharply in recent years, the leopard still roams many parts of southern Asia, where a melanistic form—the black leopard—lives. The big cat is fairly common in much of Africa south of the Sahara as well. Legally protected as a game animal in some countries, it is hunted down as vermin—a danger to people and domestic stock—in others. In all areas its habitat is shrinking and its prey species are being de-pleted as forests are cleared for agricultural crops and other human projects. And everywhere it is stalked by poachers who take its handsome spotted hide for the fur trade. During the 1960s, a single poaching center in Ethiopia exported about eight thousand leopard skins annually. Very few big game species can stand attrition like that for long.

Fortunately, several things happened in the 1970s that helped to reduce the pressure on leopards. Wildlife conservationists every-where were campaigning vigorously to stop the use of wild furs of any kind for coats and other luxury items. In 1971, bowing to in-creasing pressures, the International Fur Trade Federation sug-gested a three-year ban on use of leopard skins until the results of a worldwide survey of the species could be evaluated. This sugges-tion was merely a recommendation, however, and in 1973 some twenty thousand leopard skins for the fur trade were shipped out of Africa, most of them going to Europe.

That same year, the Convention on International Trade in En-dangered Species (CITES) was ratified, and all trade in leopard products (and many other species of endangered wildlife as well) was either banned or subject to severe restrictions between nations that signed the convention. This effectively stopped the importation of leopard skins for commercial purposes into the United States.

The leopard is still under siege in many countries in Africa and Asia. Of all the big cats, however, it is still the most widespread and has the largest total population.

GORILLA
Gorilla gorilla

> Nearly six feet high (he proved two inches shorter), with immense body, huge chest, and great muscular arms, with fiercely glaring large deep gray eyes, and a hellish expression of face, which seemed like some nightmare vision: thus stood before us, this king of the African forests.
>
> He was not afraid of us. He stood there, and beat his breast with his huge fists till it resounded like an immense bass drum, which is their mode of offering defiance; meantime giving vent to roar after roar . . . we fired and killed him.

Thus did explorer Paul Du Chaillu describe one of his encounters with a gorilla in the Congo forest more than a century ago, when the gorilla was a virtually unknown beast. Du Chaillu was able to observe the gorilla better than any other European of his time, but he did little to dispel the evil reputation that our near relative has had since primitive times.

Compare Du Chaillu's attitude with that of George Schaller, the well-known ethnologist (student of animal behavior) who in 1959 and 1960 made the first detailed study of the mountain gorilla in the wild. "I was little prepared for the beauty of the beasts before me," he relates in his book, *The Year of the Gorilla.* "Their hair was not merely black, but a shining blue-black, and their black faces shone as if polished. . . . The large male . . . was the most magnificent animal I had ever seen. His brow ridges overhung his eyes, and the crest on his crown resembled a hairy miter. . . . He gave an impression of dignity and restrained power, of absolute certainty in his majestic appearance."

As demonstrated by the experiences of Schaller and other trained observers such as Dian Fossey, the gorilla is in truth a shy and reticent animal, one that lives at peace with other animals of its habitat, and with man as well, unless attacked or approached too closely. Then the gorilla may bluster and bluff, trying to scare the intruder away with short charges and breast-beatings, but only after great provocation. The two observers mentioned above lived in close contact with gorillas for months or years at a time and were never harmed. Indeed, they were finally accepted.

Dian Fossey, under a grant from the National Geographic Society, lived near mountain gorillas on the slopes of the Virunga Volcanoes from 1967 to 1971 and spent thousands of hours observing them. She gained their confidence by imitating their daily activities: sampling the foods they ate, scratching herself when they scratched, and imitating their various cries. Slowly they became used to her.

Gorillas usually live together in small bands of three to twenty individuals, with a mature male, or silverback, as the leader. Vegetarians, the gorillas wander from place to place feeding on leaves, fruits, and pithy stalks. At night they sleep in makeshift beds constructed of leafy boughs and other vegetation. Females and young often build their nests in the trees, but the bigger and heavier males make theirs on the ground at the base of the tree trunk. There they can act quickly as sentinels on guard.

A large male gorilla in the wild may measure five-and-a-half feet in height and weigh 450 pounds. Adult females seldom weigh more than 250 pounds. Devoted mothers, they keep the young with them for three years or so. During a lifetime that might reach thirty years, a female may bear four or five young.

The western lowland gorilla (*G.g. gorilla*), the only gorilla known before this century, ranges through the tropical rain forests of West Africa, from southern Nigeria to Gabon, and inland about 500 miles almost to the Ubangi River, a tributary of the Congo. About 85 percent of the estimated population—thirty thousand to fifty thousand in all—is in Gabon. Suitable habitat for this form dwindles steadily, year after year, because of logging, mining, clearing of land for agricultural use, and other human activities. Throughout its range, it is hunted for meat, and infants are sometimes taken for the pet trade. In Brazzaville, Congo, a gorilla orphanage has been established to rehabilitate foundling gorillas rescued from pet sellers and eventually reintroduce them into protected reserves.

Separated from the western lowland gorilla population by more than 700 miles of tropical forest, gorillas are found once again in the lowland forests of eastern Zaire, the Virunga Mountains at the borders of Zaire, Uganda, and Rwanda, and the Bwindi Forest of southwestern Uganda. Until 1970 all of these eastern gorillas were considered to belong to the race known as the mountain gorilla (*G.g. berengei*). In 1970, however, mammalogist C. P. Groves divided the eastern population into two forms, designating those living in the lowland forests of eastern Zaire as a new subspecies (*G.g. graueri*). This eastern lowland gorilla has an estimated population of about six thousand, most of them living in the Kahuzi-Biega National Park in eastern Zaire.

The true mountain gorilla has an estimated population of only about six hundred individuals, half of them living on the slopes of the Virunga Volcanoes, the rest in the Bwindi Forest of southwestern Uganda. Mountain gorillas in general can be distinguished from the two lowland forms by their thicker and darker fur, narrower face, and the more pronounced crest on the head of the adult males.

The early twentieth century was an active time for collecting gorillas for museums. From 1902 to 1925 more than fifty gorillas were taken from the Virunga Volcanoes alone. In 1921 the eminent sculptor and collector, Carl Akeley, shot five specimens in this area for the American Museum of Natural History in New York City. Mounted in lifelike poses in the museum's African Hall—the huge male standing and thumping his chest in full glory—the group has been observed by many millions of museum visitors.

After collecting the animals he needed for his habitat groups, Akeley persuaded the Belgian government to set aside a gorilla sanctuary in the eastern Congo. The Albert National Park was created in 1925 and enlarged in 1929 to include the entire chain of Virunga Volcanoes that lay within the territory of the Belgian Congo.

Despite all the activity of collecting gorillas for museum exhibits and of making detailed anatomical studies, little had been discovered about the real nature of the beast—how it lived, what it ate, all the habits of its natural existence. This ignorance contributed greatly to the poor luck that plagued attempts to keep the gorilla in captivity. Only within the last half century has this species been maintained successfully and eventually bred and raised in captivity.

The honor of recording the world's first birth of a gorilla in captivity went to the Columbus Zoological Gardens in Ohio when a baby lowland gorilla was born there on December 22, 1956. Within a few years many other zoos were reporting similar successes. In 1993, as recorded in the *International Zoo Yearbook*, there were 633 gorillas in zoological collections worldwide, and 362 of these, more than half, were bred in captivity. In 1995 the first test-tube gorilla baby was born at the Cincinnati Zoo, the fruit of eggs collected from Rosie, a western lowland gorilla there. The eggs were fertilized in vitro, with sperm collected from a male at the Henry Doorly Zoo in Omaha, and three embryos were then transferred back to Rosie, who successfully carried one to full term and birth.

Everyone, responsible zoo administrators included, would shudder to recall the former practice of killing adult gorillas to capture their young. George Schaller reported that sixty gorillas were killed in 1948 near Anguma, Zaire, in order to obtain eleven infants for sale. Of these young, only one survived. Most such atrocities—insofar as they relate to capturing gorillas for exhibition or scientific research—are happily in the past.

George Schaller, Dian Fossey, and others who have studied the gorilla in its native habitat have expressed deep concern about the constant reduction in size and deterioration of the gorilla's natural habitat through human encroachment. Since the mid-1940s the areas occupied by the mountain gorilla have undergone drastic changes. Much of its habitat has been destroyed by the effects of war and an expanding human population. The same can be said for the two lowland forms. Everywhere the steady erosion of the gorilla's natural living space continues as people and cattle and timbering interests destroy the forest land they need to survive. The irony will be bitter if *Homo sapiens* eliminates his close animal relative in the wild. But that eventuality may very well happen unless determined efforts are made to protect and save this magnificent species.

CHIMPANZEES
Pan troglodytes and *Pan paniscus*

The chimpanzee (*Pan troglodytes*) and the bonobo or pygmy chimpanzee (*Pan paniscus*) are our closest living relatives. Their genetic similarity to humans means that they share many of our characteristics and behavior. Living in bands or small communities, they can by turns be loving and tender, cruel and calculating, deceitful and scheming. Under certain circumstances they are show-offs, exhibitionists, or clowns. They often exhibit a lively sense of humor as well as an ability to plan ahead and solve problems. They sometimes wage war to the death with others of their kind, just as humans do.

These close relatives of ours have a wide but discontinuous range in the forests of Equatorial Africa. Perhaps 175,000 to 200,000 of them survive today, but their population is steadily dwindling because of many pressures throughout their range. Chimpanzees are widely hunted by humans for meat, or captured for export to other countries for use in medical research. In the United States alone, about seventeen hundred captive chimpanzees are kept for research on AIDS, hepatitis, respiratory diseases, and other ailments. Young chimpanzees are captured for the pet trade— and for every infant taken, several other chimpanzees are usually killed. Their best habitat is being destroyed as forests are cleared in lumbering, mining, and agricultural operations. Today chimpanzees have disappeared completely from five nations where they once lived.

Three geographic races or subspecies of the chimpanzee are recognized. The western race (*P.t. verus*), which ranges from southern Senegal to central Nigeria, is the most seriously endangered, with a surviving population of perhaps fifteen to seventeen thousand, most of them in Guiana. More than 90 percent of the chimpanzees captured for the overseas export trade—much of it illegal—are members of this race.

The central chimpanzee (*P.t. troglodytes*) is found from Nigeria east of the Niger River southward to the Congo River, Congo, and Gabon. Most of the estimated eighty thousand of these chimps live in Gabon. The eastern chimpanzee (*P.t. schweinfurthi*) ranges north and east of the Congo River, eastward to the Great Rift Valley on the western border of Tanzania. Perhaps fifty to eighty thousand of them still live in this area.

The bonobo or pygmy chimpanzee (*P. paniscus*) was not described as a separate species until 1933. Almost as big as the other chimpanzees, it has a smaller head, a black face, and pink lips. About fifteen thousand pygmy chimpanzees range through the forests of central Zaire.

Jane Goodall, the leading authority on chimpanzees, began her studies of them in 1960, under the sponsorship of paleontologist Louis Leakey, who for years had been probing the origins and relationships of ancient man. Goodall did most of her field studies and observations in Tanzania's Gombe National Park, near Lake Tanganyika. Time and infinite patience on her part revealed many hitherto unknown things about chimpanzees, their social and community relationships, their behavior and intelligence. She came to know all the individual members of a number of chimpanzee bands. She gained their trust and friendship, and observed their interactions.

Over the years she and her followers gained many surprising insights about the species. Although their primary food is fruit, chimpanzees, unlike the other great apes, are also meat-eaters. They kill and devour small animals—at times, even infants of their own kind. They shape and use tools, trimming twigs or grass blades to probe termite nests, selecting stones as hammers to crack the shells of nuts. They sometimes wage prolonged wars against others of their kind, the males of one community attacking and killing the males of another group until one band or the other is destroyed. They have been observed searching out and swallowing the leaves of certain plants of known therapeutic value, evidently to relieve stomach pains or other ailments. Perhaps most interesting of all, each chimpanzee band or population may demonstrate unique behavior and customs. Like human tribes, each particular group may have habits that differ from those of other groups. In other words, many chimpanzee communities have specific cultures.

In recent years, Goodall has spent most of her time traveling and speaking to audiences all over the world, promoting the conservation of chimpanzees and the preservation of their habitat. She campaigns against the illegal trade in infant chimpanzees, and urges more humane treatment and better living conditions for the captive chimpanzees used in medical research. Backed by financing from Conoco, Inc., she established a 65-acre sanctuary at Point-Noire, Congo, for orphan chimpanzees confiscated by the government from illegal traders, and also helped to set up several halfway houses in other African countries for orphaned chimpanzees. She started a "Roots and Shoots" program to raise environmental awareness among Tanzanian children. This idea has spread, and there are now more than 250 Roots and Shoots groups in the United States, Canada, Germany, Japan, and more than twenty other countries.

Jane Goodall is tireless and dedicated. If her way prevails, the future is hopeful for Africa's chimpanzees and other endangered wildlife.

QUAGGA
Equus quagga

Portuguese mariners were the first modern Europeans to round the Cape of Good Hope and open the ocean route to the Far East. The Dutch, however, were the ones who first settled at the Cape in 1652. It was a convenient place for ships to lay over for repairs or to stock up on food and fresh water before sailing on. Permanent settlers soon began to spread out over the land and stake out homesteads on the grasslands, or *veldt*, as the Boer (Dutch colonial) farmers called it.

The veldt teemed with great herds of various kinds of antelope, to each of which the Dutch gave a name: springbok, blesbok, bontebok, hartebeest, and wildebeest. They also encountered great numbers of little wild horses, which the native Hottentot people called *quahkah*, accenting the last syllable in imitation of the shrill barking neighs that these animals frequently emitted. The Dutch adapted the name to *quagga*.

The quagga had black stripes on its head, neck, and shoulders, but the rest of its body was a light brown color with a dark brown stripe running down the middle of its back. The tail and all four legs were white. Quagga were very abundant and customarily moved about in small herds, often in association with wildebeests and ostriches. Because they competed for grass with the cattle of the settlers, the Dutch hunted them down and killed them by the thousands. The meat was used to feed slaves and farm workers, and the hides could be used for many different items.

English naturalist William Burchell witnessed a quagga hunt and roundup in 1811. Describing the sound and the fury of great herds of quagga galloping past, he wrote: "I could compare it to nothing but to the din of a tremendous charge of cavalry, or to the rushing of a mighty tempest. I could not estimate the accumulated number at less than fifteen thousand, a great extent of the country being actually chequered black and white with their congregated masses."

Not surprisingly, the quagga had disappeared from the Cape Colony by 1840, although it was still plentiful in relatively unsettled areas to the north and east. But not for long. In 1814, the Dutch had been forced to cede Cape Province to the English, and their determined desire for independence led them in 1836 to start a great trek northeastward to found the Orange Free State and the Transvaal in the northeastern section of present-day South Africa. Once again farming and the quagga came into conflict, with the same inevitable result; by 1870 the little half-zebras were gone everywhere in the wild. A few had been sent to zoos from time to time, but they were never given the right conditions for breeding in captivity. The world's last living quagga, an old female, died in the Amsterdam Zoo in 1883.

The Boers also found another species of wild horse in abundance in the Orange Free State and Transvaal—a true zebra with stripes over most of the body but with white legs. They named it bontequagga, or painted quagga, but the English called it Burchell's zebra (*Equus burchelli burchelli*) after the naturalist who described it. Hunted in the same way as the quagga, Burchell's zebra was very rare by 1859, and by the end of the nineteenth century it had disappeared completely in the wild. Three other races of the same species survive today, although all of them are hard pressed for living space. They include Chapman's zebra (*E.b. antiquorum*), which ranges from the Transvaal to Angola; Grant's zebra (*E.b. bohmi*), which is found from Zambia to Ethiopia; and Selous's zebra (*E.b. selousi*) of Mozambique, Zimbabwe, and Malawi.

Cape Mountain Zebra

GREVY'S ZEBRA AND CAPE MOUNTAIN ZEBRA
Equus grevyi and *Equus zebra zebra*

Writing nearly two thousand years ago, Roman historian Dio Cassius described zebras picturesquely and splendidly as "horses of the sun which resemble tigers." He was probably speaking of the species we know as Grevy's zebra, which once ranged from Ethio-

pia and the southern Sudan through northern Kenya and Somalia—a region that the Romans knew a little about because of their
exploratory trips up the Nile. Grevy's, with its many narrow stripes,
is the largest of the zebras and one of the handsomest. Today it is
also one of the most endangered for it has disappeared completely
from much of its original range and its numbers elsewhere continue
to shrink.

The third full species of the handsome horses of the sun is the
mountain zebra of southern Africa. One race of this species, the
Cape Mountain zebra, ranged over the southern parts of Cape Colony when the Dutch first settled there.

Smallest of the zebras, the Cape Mountain zebra is only forty-
eight inches high at the shoulder and has very wide black stripes.
Like the quagga, it was hunted relentlessly by the settlers. By 1656
it had become so scarce that it was awarded special protection by
Jan van Riebeeck, one of the Dutch governors of Cape Province.
Linnaeus, a Swedish botanist and systematist, described the species in 1758. When the British took over the Cape, they relaxed
hunting laws, and the Cape Mountain zebra, along with the quagga,
quickly dwindled.

By the early years of the twentieth century only several hundred were left, due to hunting pressure, competition from domestic
stock, and loss of habitat. Several conservation-minded Boer fami-
lies saved the Cape Mountain zebra, however, protecting a few
small bands of them on their farms.

From this seed stock, six individuals, including one mare,
were sent in 1937 to the Cape Mountain Zebra Park, newly established by the government of South Africa. There were fewer than
fifty surviving animals at this time.

With only one mare, this original group of six did not thrive at
the park. They had died out by 1950, when eleven new animals
with a more equal sex ratio were brought in. Results were encourag-
ing this time. By 1964 the park had trebled in size with an additional 12,700 acres, and thirty new animals were added to the herd.
By 1980 the total population of the Cape Mountain zebra had increased to more than two hundred, with nearly three-fourths of
them at Cape Mountain Zebra National Park.

A lightly-colored form of the species, Hartman's Mountain zebra (*Equus z. hartmannae*), has a considerably larger population. Ranging widely in southwestern Africa and Angola, this subspecies has a total population of several thousand.

GIANT SABLE ANTELOPE
Hippotragus niger variani

In 1909 the Trans-African Benguela Railroad was being constructed between the Angolan port of Lobito and the copper mines of Rhodesia, some thirteen hundred miles to the east. One of the supervisors of this project was H. F. Varian, an English engineer. A wildlife enthusiast, Varian was especially taken with the magnificent giant sable antelopes that he observed in small herds along the railroad right-of-way. He had never seen sable antelopes like them anywhere.

Standing close to fifty-five inches high at the shoulder and weighing about 600 pounds, the male giant sable flaunts great crescent-shaped horns that grow up to sixty-five inches in length. The animal's coat is glistening black, with contrasting white facial markings, belly, and buttocks. The somewhat smaller females are a rich golden-chestnut color.

Varian procured the type specimen—the original specimen from which a description of a new species is made—of the giant sable antelope in 1913, and the zoologist Oldfield Thomas described it in 1916. It was the last of the large African animals to be officially discovered and scientifically described.

Long before, however, the giant sable had been known as one of the world's most outstanding big-game hunting trophies. Boer immigrants had killed many of these magnificent creatures in the 1870s for their meat, hides, and horns. The hunting was still going on when Varian discovered them, and he was alarmed at its extent. He persuaded officials of Portuguese West Africa (now Angola) to declare the sable antelope "royal game" so that over much of its range it could be taken only under special permit.

Despite such measures, trophy hunting and poaching of the giant sable continued. In 1933 one African traveler declared that he had "heard several Portuguese brag of killing ten sable a month. At that rate, this magnificent animal will soon be extinct."

Besides the pressure of such illicit hunting, the pressures of an increasing human population were also beginning to encroach upon the giant sables' habitat, which is restricted to an isolated area in central Angola. The wooded savannahs frequented by the species were invaded by pastoral tribes with herds of cattle, and much of the woodland was cut, cleared, and burned. The big antelopes were forced out, and their population began to decline. By the late 1950s only an estimated five hundred or so were left. But the imposition of a stiff $3,500 fine helped to control the poaching.

In 1957 the Angolan government created the 4,000-square-mile Luanda Natural Integral Reserve to protect the giant sable. Some years later, a second protected area—Cangandala National Park—was created. In 1970 the estimated total population of giant sable antelopes in and around these two areas was from one to two thousand animals.

In 1961 guerilla warfare erupted in Angola, and continued until 1975, when Portugal granted independence. The three rival rebel groups continued to struggle, however, fighting one another for control of the country. The warfare continued until the 1990s, from time to time sweeping across Malange Province, where most of the surviving giant sables live. No reliable estimate of the present population is available, but the sable's numbers are certainly reduced because of the fighting and habitat destruction.

OKAPI
Okapia johnstoni

In 1899 the High Commissioner for Uganda, Sir Harry Johnston, rescued a group of Pygmies—people of the Belgian Congo's Ituri Forest—from the greedy clutches of a wandering German entrepreneur who planned to exhibit them at the forthcoming 1900 Paris Exposition. The Pygmies lived with Sir Harry for several months before he was able to return them to their forest home, and they became friends. Among other things, they told him about a strange animal that lived in the Ituri Forest, a creature they called *okapi*. From their description, the animal was evidently rather like a mule in shape and was dark colored with contrasting light zebra stripes.

Sir Harry knew of no such animal, but he recalled that Henry Stanley, in his book *In Darkest Africa*, published in 1890, had mentioned a beast that might fit that description. Stanley had written: "The Wambutti knew a donkey and called it 'Atti.' They say that they sometimes catch them in pits."

His curiosity whetted, Sir Harry determined to do his best to track down this unknown beast when he returned the Pygmies to their homeland. Arriving at Fort Mbeni in the Congo Free State, he questioned the Belgian officers there and learned that although they had never seen the animal alive, they knew it through the local hunters who killed it for its delicious meat. The Belgians promised to get him a complete skin of the animal. Sir Harry wrote to Dr. Sclater of the London Zoological Society on August 21, 1900, telling him what he had learned and stating that he would send samples of skin and other parts as soon as he got them. Two strips of skin, bartered from local hunters, duly arrived, and on the basis of them, Dr. Sclater named the unknown animal *Equus* (?) *johnstoni*, in honor of Sir Harry Johnston. His question mark indicated that he was not certain that this newly described species belonged to the horse family.

Not long thereafter a Swedish officer in the Belgian service, Karl Ericksson, sent Sir Harry a whole skin plus two skulls of the animal. They were sent off to London in June 1901, and on examining them, Professor Ray Lankester rechristened the animal, giving it the generic name *Okapia*.

The okapi's closest living relative is the giraffe, and the species itself must closely resemble the long-extinct *Samotherium*, which roamed Europe and Asia some fifteen million or more years ago. Male okapis have short, skin-covered horns, and in the case of both sexes the velvety coat is dark chocolate in color, with many contrasting white stripes on the flanks and legs. The animal's head is long and pointed, and the prehensile tongue can be extended to considerable distances to reach out and pull foliage into the mouth.

That an animal as large and distinctive as the okapi was not discovered by scientists until the twentieth century seems remarkable. But the region in which it is found, a 700-by-140-mile strip of tropical rain forest in the northeastern Congo, was at that time one of the world's least explored areas—and for good reason. The dense jungle growth made it almost impenetrable.

The immensity of wilderness is appalling; over eighteen hundred miles without a break, it stretches more than half way across the continent, from the coast of Guinea to the Ruwenzori. In spite of tropical luxuriance, it is one of the most dismal spots on the face of the globe, for the torrid sun burns above miles of leafy expanse, and the unflagging heat of about one hundred degrees, day and night, renders the moist atmosphere unbearable. Over the whole area storms of tropical violence thunder and rage almost daily. Here natives have become cannibals, and the graves of thousands of white men are merely a remembrance of where youthful energy and adventure came to a sudden end.

The writer of this passage was Herbert Lang, a zoologist and wild animal collector, who in 1909 was commissioned by Dr. Henry Fairfield Osborn, then the president of both the American Museum of Natural History and the New York Zoological Society, to head up an expedition to the Congo to collect museum specimens and live animals for both of these institutions. Departing from New York in the spring of 1909, Lang remained in the Congo until 1915. Okapis were the expedition's most-desired specimens: first, for a habitat group at the museum; and second, if possible, a live animal for the zoo.

Lang was successful in achieving the first objective, for he soon learned that the Pygmies often hunted it for its meat and hide, and the Bantu tribes trapped the okapi in snares and pitfalls. Local hunters assured Lang that a Mangbetu chief named Zebandra had some years before taken eleven okapis within a week's time by using some eight hundred native beaters to flush the animals out of the forest and drive them into snares, pitfalls, and nets. But Lang's expedition failed to bring back a live okapi, after being within sight of success. A week-old calf was actually captured, and it lived until it had exhausted the stock of canned milk. No substitute food was available, and the little animal soon died. The expedition had to return to New York in 1915 without a live okapi.

In 1937 the Bronx Zoo finally got a male okapi. The first of its species ever seen in America, it lived at the zoo for many years. Today there are about eighty okapi in the world's zoos, most of them captive bred.

Although evidently not uncommon within its rain forest habitat, the okapi has a very restricted range, and its total population during historic times must always have been quite small. Until recent years it has been protected by the remoteness and inaccessibility of its habitat. Unfortunately, such protection diminishes year by year. Roads built by the Belgians now penetrate into the heart of the okapi's home forest, and much of this wild habitat is being lost because of logging, the expanding charcoal industry, and clearing of the forest for coffee plantations. Although nominally protected by national law since 1933, the species is increasingly hard pressed by human activities such as these. Conservationists, however, hope to have a core region of the Ituri Forest designated a protected national park and nature reserve. Only by actions such as this can the okapi's future be assured.

AFRICAN, OR NILE, CROCODILE
Crocodylus niloticus

The mighty Nile sweeps more than 4,000 miles from its sources in the heart of Africa to the Mediterranean, bringing life—and sometimes death—to the people who live along it. On its banks lie great reptiles basking in the sun, armored dragons surviving from the age of dinosaurs, hundreds of millions of years ago. Their amber cat eyes gleam with the reflected gold of the sun; their gaping jaws reveal jagged rows of long, sharp teeth. A rugged armor of bronze green covers the squat body and the long saw-toothed tail, all except for the belly, which has yellow leathery plates.

Silently one eighteen-foot monster slides into the water and floats like a submerged log, with only eyes, nostrils, and ears above water. An unwary waterbird drifts toward the log, which moves imperceptibly forward to meet it. One snap, a startled squawk, and the bird disappears. Satisfied for the moment, the crocodile sinks beneath the surface.

Little-changed from the animal that coexisted with the dinosaurs, the Nile crocodile is a fearsome-looking beast. Once abundant on the Nile and most of Africa's other rivers, it has long been feared and persecuted. In ancient times, however, it was held sacred in some areas. Legend has it that Mona, the first king of Egypt, was saved from wild dogs by jumping onto the back of a crocodile at Lake Moeris, after which the obliging beast carried him to the safety of the opposite bank. To some Egyptians the crocodile was the symbol of Sebek, the water god, who caused the Nile to rise and spread out over the land, fertilizing and irrigating it.

But in Africa today the crocodile is feared as a destroyer of game animals and livestock and occasionally of unwary human beings as well. In many areas it is killed as vermin; in others it is hunted for its handsome hide, which has long been in great demand for use in leather products.

David Livingstone observed a lot of crocodile hunting in his travels more than a century ago, as recorded in his 1865 book, *The Zambezi and Its Tributaries:*

> Crocodiles in the Rovuma [a river which forms the present boundary between Tanzania and Mozambique] have a sorry time of it. Never before were reptiles so persecuted and snubbed. They are hunted with spears, and spring traps are set for them. If one enters an inviting pool after fish, he soon finds a fence thrown around it, and a spring trap set in the only path out of the enclosure. Their flesh is eaten and relished. The banks, on which the female lays her eggs at night, are carefully

searched by day, and all the eggs are dug out and de-
voured. The fish-hawk makes havoc among the few that
escape their other enemies.

Crocodiles were abundant throughout Africa's waterways during Livingstone's time, and in many regions they remained common
until a few years ago. But now, after years of relentless killing,
the species is disappearing in many areas. It has been completely
exterminated in Egypt and along the lower Nile in recent years,
and it is in difficulty in East Africa. Traditional crocodile breeding
grounds in countless areas are being destroyed by the pressures of
human settlement: the clearing and altering of stream banks, drainage projects, sewage, and pollution.

Poaching has also been a principal cause of the crocodile's
downfall. Philip Crowe, in his 1971 book, *World Wildlife, the Last
Stand*, tells of one poacher, Bobbie Wilmot, who worked the Kalahari region and the Chobe River area between southern Zaire and
Bechuanaland. "Wilmot's main business is still hunting crocodiles," he relates. "Since he started crocodile hunting in 1954, he
has killed about 42,000 of them and of late years has averaged
2,000 skins a year. These are worth about twenty-five dollars for a
prime skin. In the future, however, he is going to run a crocodile
farm where he will raise his own stock."

Today such farming is a thriving industry in several African
countries. *Oryx*, the journal of the British Fauna and Flora Preservation Society, reported in its July 1994 issue that Zimbabwe has a
very successful crocodile ranching program, using tens of thousands of eggs that are gathered from wild nests every year. The
young are hatched and reared on the farms until they are about two
years old, when they are killed and their skins exported under
CITES permits. Enough eggs are left undisturbed in the wild, however, so that the wild population remains unharmed.

At egg-laying time the wild female crocodile digs a hole in a
sandy shore and lays a clutch of as many as fifty eggs. Covering the
nest, she remains close by for three months, guarding the eggs until
they hatch. As they hatch out of the eggs, the young grunt, a signal
to the mother to uncover them, which she does. Leading or carrying

her offspring in her jaws to shallow water, she continues to watch over them for six weeks or more until they have a reasonable chance of survival on their own.

If a boat comes too close, the female crocodile may abandon her nest area or her young. With the mother absent, predators often move in to devour the eggs or young. Some common predators are the big Goliath heron and the marabou stork, both of which probe for the eggs with their long beaks and also gulp down the young whole. Fish eagles, kites, and monitor lizards prey on them too, as do such mammalian predators as baboons, hyenas, and honey badgers. More than half of the nests and eggs in the Kabalega (Murchison) Falls area in Uganda have been reported destroyed by such enemies when the mother crocodile is driven away.

The issues of crocodile hunting, poaching, and ranching are still being debated. Should legal and controlled hunting be permitted, and should crocodilians be farmed as a valuable source of fine leather? Or should a worldwide ban be established on all traffic and use of crocodilian skins? The future of the Nile crocodile, and all other crocodilians, hinges on how these questions are answered.

The Future of Africa's Wildlife

In the post-colonial period, most countries in Africa have endured long periods of violence and political instability. Many governments have risen and fallen because of coups, revolution, civil war, genocide, and famine. The resulting turmoil has had a deadly effect, not only on humans, but also upon any and all attempts to protect and conserve the continent's wildlife.

What lies in store for the wildlife of Africa depends very much upon which of various conflicting attitudes and policies will eventually prevail. They are still in flux, and time grows very short. Africa's wildlife becomes hemmed in more and more every year by an ever-increasing human population. The animals continue to be pursued relentlessly by hunters, killed off by poachers, and harassed by hordes of tourists from all over the world. At best, Africa's wildlife faces a very clouded future on a continent that is becoming crowded with hungry human beings.

Human population in Africa has been increasing at a rate of 3 to 4 percent yearly, a doubling of the total population every twenty-four years. The rising tide of humanity needs more land for crops, more land for grazing animals, more land for industry and development. All over the continent forests are being cut, grasslands fenced and plowed or overgrazed, and wildlife destroyed when it competes with cattle for food. And poaching continues to take an appalling toll of the continent's wildlife.

Africa was still a paradise for hunters in 1900, in spite of centuries of slaughter. First to be exploited was the wildlife of North Africa, which started its decline some two thousand years ago in Roman times. In South Africa the killing began in the seventeenth century, and whole wildlife populations were slaughtered there in the same ruthless manner that the bison was later exterminated in most of North America.

Africa's heartland, the tropical rainforests and the rugged country of the middle of the continent, remained relatively unexploited until the twentieth century, because of the difficulties in penetrating the vast stretches of forest and also because of the dangers posed by the tsetse fly and other disease-carrying pests. During the past fifty years, however, these difficulties have been conquered to some extent, and now the exploitation of both land and wildlife is well under way there too.

On the northern rim of the continent the Sahara advances steadily, creeping relentlessly into neighboring savannah and bush country. The desert-making process is hastened by overgrazing by domestic animals, and the attempts of pastoral tribes to raise crops on land not suited for tilling. Such practices, heightened by extended periods of drought, have brought famine and death to untold thousands of people and their domestic animals during the past few years alone. Under such conditions, what hope does the future hold for either wildlife or people in Africa?

In spite of all the difficulties, a number of African nations have taken positive steps aimed at safeguarding their wildlife heritage. Many game preserves and national parks have been established, and active antipoaching programs have been instituted. A number of African leaders promote parks and wildlife preserves enthusiastically, for they realize that Africa's spectacular wildlife is one of the continent's most valuable natural resources, a prime attraction for tourists and their dollars. These same leaders are beginning to realize that wildlife could be an important source of food for their hungry people if it could be managed and harvested as needed. Many Africans, however, view the matter quite differently. They say that the parks were established *by* Europeans *for* Europeans and that they are an intrusion on traditional hunting grounds, established for the benefit of foreign tourism with which the local people have very little contact. Furthermore, farmers and herdsmen understandably do not want elephants or rhinos invading their croplands, or herds of wild hoofed stock competing with their domestic animals for grass and water.

The East African plains have long been a center of conflicting interests between stock raisers and wildlife conservationists. This whole rich region—especially Tanzania's Serengeti Plain—is blessed with the most spectacular wild animal herds left on earth. Thousands of wildebeest, zebra, hartebeest, and gazelles, as well as plentiful populations of rhinos, giraffes, lions, leopards, and hyenas roam the grassy plains. The region is also the homeland of the cattle-raising Masai and other pastoral tribes. Much of the area has been taken for the raising of domestic stock at the expense of wildlife.

Ideas about the best way to preserve African wildlife are still being vigorously debated. Wildlife reporter Bill Keller declared in 1992 that "the most contentious debate in Africa is whether, and when, 'using' wild animals may be the best way to save them." Animals, plants, and landscapes, he noted, "are best protected if they are worth something to the humans living around them."

Wildlife professionals in some African countries believe that the only way to safeguard the continent's wildlife and eliminate poaching is to legalize and strictly control the taking of wildlife for meat, hides, and other products. Such a policy, they maintain, would eliminate the huge profits that poachers presently enjoy, and would make the rewards of illegal hunting not worth the risks. They argue that Africa's wildlife should be strictly managed, with surplus stock being harvested yearly to feed hungry people. Under management, they say, Africa's game animals could provide a continuous supply of protein and other products at a cheaper cost than domestic livestock, which are not as well adapted to marginal lands nor as disease-resistant as native wild animals. If wildlife is not made a paying proposition, they declare, it will eventually be exterminated and the land put to other uses.

The ultimate fate of Africa's wildlife is still undecided. Its future will be determined by the extent to which various management and protection programs are implemented, and their degree of success. In many African nations the will to implement any such programs is very much in doubt.

*Madagascar . . . that vast, fantastic land with a fauna
so extraordinary that it has evoked for itself the name
Promised Land of the Naturalist.*

Archie Carr
The Land and Wildlife of Africa

5

MADAGASCAR AND
ISLANDS OF THE INDIAN OCEAN

Almost a thousand miles long and from 200 to 300 miles wide,
Madagascar is—after Greenland, New Guinea, and Borneo—
the world's fourth largest island. Separated from Africa by the 250
mile-wide Mozambique Channel, it began to drift away from its
huge continental neighbor about 145 million years ago. Because of
this long isolation without competition from more advanced forms,
its evolving plants and animals have developed forms unlike those
found anywhere else in the world. As a result, Madagascar has
sometimes been called a Noah's ark of ecological riches.

Human beings did not find this lost world and settle on it until
the third or fourth century A.D., fifteen hundred years ago. The first
settlers were not Africans, as one might expect, but people of Ma-
laysian stock who left their home islands somewhere in the East
Indies in search of new living space. Their graceful outrigger canoes sailed across the Indian Ocean before the prevailing trade-
winds, perhaps hopping from island to island in the same way that

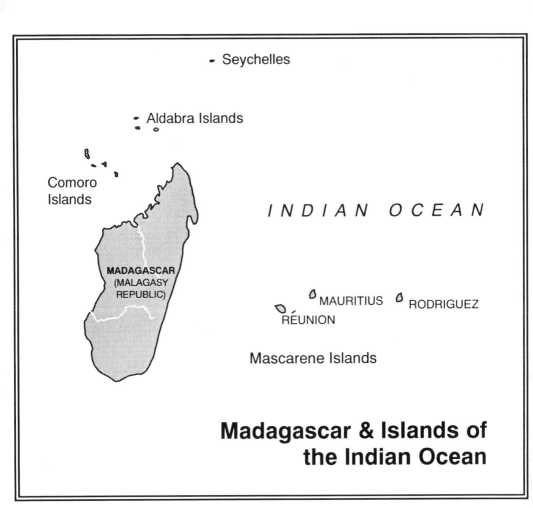

Madagascar & Islands of the Indian Ocean

the Polynesians fanned east and south through the Pacific to colonize the South Sea Islands. Eventually the pioneering adventurers from the East Indies came to the great island of Madagascar.

Man Changes the Face of the Land

When these early settlers first arrived, Madagascar's eastern highlands, blessed with abundant rainfall, were clad with lush evergreen forests, while the western coastal areas facing Africa had a cover of deciduous forests and wide, grassy savannahs. Its climate was on the whole tropical, with a warm, rainy season from November to April and a drier, cooler season the rest of the year. Most of the center of the island was high plateau, mixed forest, and grassland, with scattered peaks to 9,000 feet in altitude. Today the face of the land has been greatly changed. Most of the original forests have been cut, and the grasslands have been modified by repeated burning, overgrazing, and consequent erosion.

Spreading over their new homeland, the people began to clear the land and raise crops and livestock. They were divided into a number of different tribes and kingdoms, and they often warred with one another. As the centuries went by, Arabs and Africans also came to Madagascar, and the island's people became a racial mixture. The language, customs, and flavor of the East Indies, however, remained dominant.

The first European to discover Madagascar was a Portuguese sea captain, Diégo Diaz, who came upon it in 1500 on a voyage of exploration around Africa, searching for a route to the fabled East Indies. French, Dutch, and English explorers followed in the wake of the Portuguese, and a number of smaller Indian Ocean islands were soon discovered as well.

Among them were three volcanic islands lying 500 to 900 miles east of Madagascar—Réunion, Mauritius, and Rodriguez. Collectively they were known as the Mascarene Islands, after Pedro Mascarenes, a Portuguese mariner who sighted the first two in 1513 as he sailed past them on his way to India. These islands were the home of the extinct dodo bird and its relatives.

About 250 miles north of Madagascar lies the Aldabra Atoll—three small islands surrounding a central lagoon. The main island, just 20 miles long, is the natural home of the only giant tortoises that survive in the Indian Ocean islands today. A related but different tortoise is found on Madagascar.

Some 200 miles south of Aldabra lie the Comoro Islands, a volcanic group consisting of four main islands in the Mozambique Channel, about halfway between Madagascar and the African mainland. In the coastal waters of these islands living specimens of the coelacanth—a fish thought to be extinct for seventy million years or more—have been taken by local fishermen on a number of different occasions during the past forty years.

Soon after the discovery of Madagascar by Europeans, trading settlements began to appear along its coasts. During the nineteenth century the French became dominant, establishing a protectorate over Madagascar in 1888 and later proclaiming the island a French colony in 1896. This protectorate was supplanted in 1960 by peaceful transition to a republic. The people now control their own destiny as the Malagasy Republic.

Madagascar's Unique Plants and Animals

The early Europeans in Madagascar and the islands of the Indian Ocean marveled at the many strange plants and animals that were unlike those found anywhere else in the world. On the Mascarenes they discovered the unique flightless birds, the dodo and solitaire. Every island they visited also had its unique giant tortoise population.

The huge island of Madagascar, however, boasted the greatest variety of peculiar forms of wildlife. Among these animals were the many species of lemurs—a group of primitive primates that evolved and specialized in many directions during Madagascar's long isolation from Africa. Another group of mammals that evolved in isolation into a bewildering variety of specialized forms were the tenrecs—small, primitive insectivores. The only native predatory mammals were a few meat-eaters of the family Viverridae. Largest was the fossa, a sleek catlike animal with dark chocolate-black fur and a long tail.

Of the birds, an estimated 65 percent of the two hundred or so breeding species are found nowhere else in the world. Madagascar is also the home of three-fourths of the known species of chameleons. Strange as the living animals of Madagascar are today, some that have disappeared, like the elephant bird, were even more striking.

ELEPHANT BIRD, OR AEPYORNIS
Aepyornis maximus

One of the best-known stories of *The Arabian Nights* is the tale of Sinbad, an Arab sailor who is seized in the talons of a giant bird,

Elephant Bird, or Aepyornis

the Roc, or Rukh, and transported to a fabled island. The idea for this tall tale may very well have come from Madagascar. Arab ships and sailors had been touching on the island since the early Middle Ages at least—probably long before—and natives had told them of a giant bird that lived there.

The first French governor of Madagascar, Admiral Étienne de Flacourt, heard about a giant bird too. In his *Histoire de la Grande Isle de Madagascar*, published in 1658, de Flacourt mentions what islanders called the *vouron-patra*, "a giant bird that lays eggs as big as those of an ostrich. . . . The people keep water in the eggs of the vouron-patra." From the way he mentioned the bird, it was evidently still living at that time, although he did not claim to have seen one. Later visitors to Madagascar were told that the eggs were much bigger than ostrich eggs, a fact that was finally substantiated when actual eggs were brought forth and examined.

In 1850 a French seaman, Captain Abadie, secured three such eggs and a number of bones of the giant bird and sent them to Paris. After studying them intensively, the zoologist Geoffroy Saint Hilaire described the elephant bird scientifically and gave it the name *Aepyornis maximus*, literally "largest of the tall birds."

The elephant bird stood between nine and ten feet in height and weighed in the neighborhood of 1,000 pounds, more than three times the weight of the largest bird living today, the African ostrich. The elephant bird had very thick and trunklike legs with three toes, all of them directed forward. The legs were rather short and supported so much weight that *Aepyornis* could not have been a fast runner. Its eggs sometimes measured close to fifteen inches in length and twelve inches in diameter, and they had a liquid capacity of nearly two gallons.

Aepyornis is thought to have survived until the mid-1600s. Man evidently killed it off not only by hunting it and taking its eggs, but by destroying much of the forest habitat in which it lived.

The largest elephant bird was *Aepyornis maximus*, but at least six other related species—differing mainly in size and weight—have been described from skeletal remains.

LEMURS: THE INDRI AND GIANT EXTINCT FORMS
Indri indri

About forty million years ago, the ancestors of lemurs made their way from Africa to Madagascar, evidently rafting to the island on logs or on floating leafy branches. Because of Madagascar's long isolation from the continent, these primitive primates faced little competition from potential rivals such as elephants, large carnivores, hoofed animals, and the more advanced monkeys that would become dominant in Africa. As a result, the lemurs flourished in Madagascar's benign surroundings and evolved into many different forms.

When people reached the island about A.D. 500, at least forty kinds of lemurs lived there—about a dozen of them giants of their kind. One of them, described by zoologist Alison Jolly, a lemur specialist, "rivaled a gorilla in size and was probably earthbound by its great weight." Another was *Paleopropithicus*, weighing about 110 pounds. A slow climber, it used all four limbs and clung to branches suspended like a sloth. Still another was *Megaladapis*, about the size of a small bear. It clung to tree branches like a koala. Shortly after humans arrived on the island, these and all the other giant lemurs became extinct.

All in all, fourteen species of lemurs have disappeared during the past thousand years, victims of humans killing them for food and other uses, and destruction of their natural habitat. Twenty-eight species survive today, many of them in critical danger of imminent extinction.

Largest of all living lemurs, the indri weighs 15 pounds and stands about three feet high when walking on its hind feet, as it sometimes does. Almost tailless, it has a mostly black-and-white coat. All four of its lateral toes are joined together by a weblike membrane, and they work together in opposition to the first toe. A leaf-eater, the indri travels in troops and spends most of its time in the trees. The animal gets its name because the first naturalists who studied the species thought that *indri* was the native name for it. Pointing to the animal, a local guide would cry, *"Indri!"* In the Malagasy language, however, the word means "look." The people themselves call the species *babakota*, "man of the woods."

Strange as the indri's appearance may be, its call or song is even more unusual. In the April 1975 issue of *Defenders of Wildlife*, writer Faith McNulty describes its effect upon her: "Suddenly the strangest, most thrilling music I have ever heard rose from the hills around us. . . . It was a chorus of high voices, not shrill, but silvery, that rose and fell through a series of liquid notes. . . . It was alien and wild. It was a sound echoing from the distant past. Millions of years ago, indri had greeted the dawn of a young world with a song like this."

The indri and all the other surviving lemurs are threatened with extinction in the wild, partly because of hunting, but even more because of habitat destruction. More reserves and stricter protective laws are needed as well as a halt to the wholesale destruction of what remains of the natural environment. The Analamazaotra Reserve on Madagascar's eastern slope shelters an indri population of eighty or less.

Scientists recognize the deadly peril that the lemurs face and are trying in various ways to help them. The Duke University Primate Center in Durham, North Carolina has the world's largest collection of captive lemurs. This flourishing research center is dedicated to the conservation of prosimian (pre-monkey) primates such as lemurs, lorises, and tarsiers. It houses several hundred lemurs of thirteen different species and subspecies. Most of these are breeding in captivity and are the subjects of a number of research projects concerning lemur behavior, social organization, and requirements.

DODO
Raphus cucullatus **and Its Relatives**

Arab sailors had undoubtedly visited Mauritius and Réunion long before their discovery by Europeans, but neither they nor the Portuguese paid them much attention. Small and remote, they remained uninhabited specks of land in the vast ocean until 1598, when Dutch admiral Jacob Corneliszoon van Neck landed on Mauritius and conducted a preliminary exploration of the island. His crewmen marveled at the giant tortoises and strange birds they saw. One chronicler of the expedition recorded, "There are large birds, as big as our swans, but with bigger heads." They were dodos, clumsy birds with stubby flightless wings, thick legs, and great hooked beaks up to nine inches long. Slate-gray in color, they weighed as

Dodo

much as 50 pounds apiece. The Dutch called them *walghvogels*—"nauseous or disgusting birds"—because according to some tastes they were evidently not very good to eat. But there were others who claimed that the bird's breast meat was delicious.

Even though opinions varied as to the dodo's edibility, every passing ship stocked up on the birds, killing and salting them, and storing them aboard as a welcome change from the usual shipboard fare. One seaman, Willem Ysbrandtz, wrote in his journal: "We found there also a quantity of geese, pigeons, grey parrots and other sorts of birds, numbers of tortoises, of which there were sometimes twenty-five under the shade of a tree. We took all these animals as many as we wanted, for they did not run away. There were also some dodos, who had small wings and could not fly. They are so fat that they could hardly move."

Meantime, settlers came to Mauritius, bringing with them pigs, rats, dogs, monkeys, and other exotic species. These animals, together with humans, sealed the doom of the clumsy, flightless dodos, which nested on the ground and were defenseless against such enemies. As early as 1634, an official of the British East India Company visited Mauritius and noted that he had seen "Dodoes, a strange kind of fowle, twice as big as a Goose, that can neither flye nor swymm, being cloven footed." In 1638, just four years later, when he visited the island again, he observed: "We now mett with None."

Once started, the dodo's downfall was swift and complete, and the year 1681 marks the date when the last one was seen alive on Mauritius. The dodo had the unfortunate distinction of being the first documented wildlife species to disappear as the direct result of human activities. Ever since, the dodo has been a symbol of extinction, as the phrase "dead as a dodo" bears witness. And the year 1681 is used by wildlife conservationists today as the reckoning date from which the tragic and ever-lengthening list of animals exterminated at the hands of modern man is recorded.

A similar bird, the white dodo, lived on Réunion. It was much like its Mauritius relative but a lighter color. It evidently became extinct about 1750, although its actual demise was not noted until 1801, when a scientific survey of the island's animals failed to uncover it.

On remote Rodriguez there was another large flightless bird, the Rodriguez solitaire, as described by a fugitive French Huguenot, François Lequat, who lived on Rodriguez from 1690 to 1692. He published his travel journal in 1798, noting: "Of all the Birds in the Island, the most Remarkable is that which goes by the Name of the Solitary, because 'tis very seldom seen in Company, tho' there are abundance of them." This species disappeared sometime during the eighteenth century.

"A craving for the impossible gratification of seeing, touching or hefting the sheltered, innocent bulk of a dodo comes over me strongly in my more whimsied moments," zoologist Archie Carr confessed in his book, *The Land and Wildlife of Africa*. "I suspect it must come over every man with any time to think. I believe our descendants will have more time of that kind. I know they will have a lot more dodos than we have, to yearn to have been allowed to see."

ALDABRAN GIANT TORTOISE
Testudo gigantea

Aldabra Atoll is the last home and breeding grounds of a unique reptile—the Aldabran giant tortoise. The nearest surviving rela-

Aldabran Giant Tortoise

tives of these huge, dignified beasts are the giant land tortoises of the Galápagos Islands, located some 600 miles off the coast of Ecuador, on the other side of the world. Several million years ago, however, giant tortoises were evidently widely distributed over many continents and islands. As recently as a few centuries ago, distinct forms of these reptiles could be found in South America, the Galápagos Islands, Madagascar, the Mascarenes, and on other islands of the Indian Ocean as well, often in great abundance. They all belonged to the genus *Testudo*, with several different species found on different island groups.

Visiting Rodriguez in 1691, François Lequat reported "such a plenty of land turtles in this isle that sometimes you see two or three thousand of them in a flock, so that you may go above a hundred paces on their backs." Yet, as a result of ruthless slaughter, the Rodriguez tortoises were all gone by 1786, less than a century later. Records show that in just one eighteen-month period, ships' crews took about thirty thousand of the huge beasts from the island for fresh meat as a welcome change from the typical diet at sea. The tortoises of Mauritius, Réunion, and the Seychelles were exploited in similar fashion. As a result of such practice, the giant tortoises have long since been exterminated everywhere except for those that live and breed on Aldabra and a few captive specimens.

Portuguese seamen first visited Aldabra Atoll in 1511. In the seventeenth century it became a French dependency, and in 1810 a British colony. Until about a century ago ships made frequent stops at the islands to capture giant tortoises and take them aboard as fresh meat for long ocean voyages to the Far East. Charles Darwin, the celebrated British evolutionist, had been fascinated to see the giant tortoises of the Galápagos in 1835. When there was a movement afoot in 1874 to exploit Aldabra's mangrove timber, he rose in defense of these other tortoise islands and led a movement to set Aldabra aside as a sanctuary for its unique wildlife. By the end of the nineteenth century the tortoise numbers on Aldabra had sunk to their lowest point. About 1910, however, the population slowly began to increase.

Zoologists consider the species the most long-lived of all terrestrial vertebrates. A German expedition to the Seychelle Islands, several hundred miles north of Aldabra, viewed a specimen in 1899 that was said to have been brought from Aldabra a century before. On Saint Helena one tortoise that was said to have been there when the exiled Napoleon arrived in 1815 still survived in 1967.

In the 1960s the British government readied plans to build an airfield and military staging area on the atoll. There was immediate protest from wildlife conservationists, for such development spelled certain doom to the tortoises as well as to various birds that lived and nested there. Aldabra is the home of a rare, flightless rail (a wading bird) and is also the principal breeding grounds for the pink-footed booby and most of the frigate birds of the Indian Ocean. Due to the protests—and perhaps also because it could ill afford the money needed for the development—Britain abandoned the plans for the airfield and designated the atoll a nature reserve.

In 1976 Aldabra became part of Seychelles, a self-ruling republic of Indian Ocean islands within the British Commonwealth. Seychelles continues to protect the tortoises, and has taken steps to control the goats which compete with the tortoises for food on the atoll. Recognizing Aldabra's importance as a unique wild refuge, the United Nations Educational, Scientific, and Cultural Organization (UNESCO) named it a world heritage site in 1982. Judging from current population studies, as many as 150,000 of the tortoises may survive on Aldabra today.

A Heavy Toll of Vanishing Species

Dodos, solitaires, and giant tortoises are not the only species that have disappeared from the islands of the Indian Ocean. The full toll since these islands were settled is staggering. Animals living on small oceanic islands are particularly vulnerable to the changes brought about by humans. In a 1984 paper, "Historic Extinctions: A Rosetta Stone for Understanding Prehistoric Extinctions," population biologist Jared Diamond noted that of 171 species and subspecies of birds that had become extinct since 1600, no fewer than 155 of them were island birds. The species native to Pacific and Indian Ocean islands have been especially victimized. The Mascarenes have what is probably the world's worst record for extinction, with the Hawaiian Islands their only rival.

According to the best estimates, about 90 percent of the birds native to the Mascarenes have become extinct since their settlement. Those species that still survive are threatened with the same ultimate fate because of the inroads people have made—and continue to make—on the islands. Both Réunion and Mauritius have dense human populations. Both have been stripped of their forest cover. As for Rodriguez, practically none of its native vegetation is left. Almost any wildlife species would find survival in such an inhospitable area difficult.

One of the world's poorest countries, Madagascar has an extinction record for wildlife that is tragically similar to that of the Mascarenes. About 85 percent of the island's original forests are now gone, and only 2 percent of the land is protected. The human population, now twelve million, has doubled since 1960, and every year additional natural habitat is destroyed to make room for more cropland to support the ever-increasing number of people.

Little wonder that most of Madagascar's unique flora and fauna are in deadly peril today. Some sanctuaries and nature preserves have been set aside, but many more are needed if some of the earth's most fascinating creatures are to have any chance for survival.

*Situated upon the Equator, and bathed by the tepid
water of the great tropical oceans, this region enjoys a
climate more uniformly hot and moist than almost any
other part of the globe, and teems with natural produc-
tions, which are elsewhere unknown. The richest of
fruits and the most precious of spices are here indige-
nous.*

Alfred Russel Wallace
The Malay Archipelago

6

The Malay Archipelago

Lying between the continental land masses of Asia to the north
and Australia to the south is a watery world of warm seas spotted with some ten thousand islands or more that make up the Malay
Archipelago. Clustered around the equator, these steamy tropical
lands show infinite variety: coastal mangrove swamps and lush jungles; coral atolls and soaring mountain ranges; fiery volcanoes and
lofty summits capped with snow; grassy plateaus and sandy, palm-
fringed beaches. Flanked by the two great land masses, the myriad
islands form a series of stepping-stones over which animals and
plants from both continents have traveled. The islands in the center
provide a meeting place for both Asiatic and Australian forms.

The northernmost group are the Philippines—more than seven
thousand islands, the vast majority of them tiny, uninhabited, and
unnamed. Ninety-five percent of the land is included in eleven
main islands, the two largest being Luzon in the north and Mindanao in the south.

South and east of the Philippines lies the vast and still par-

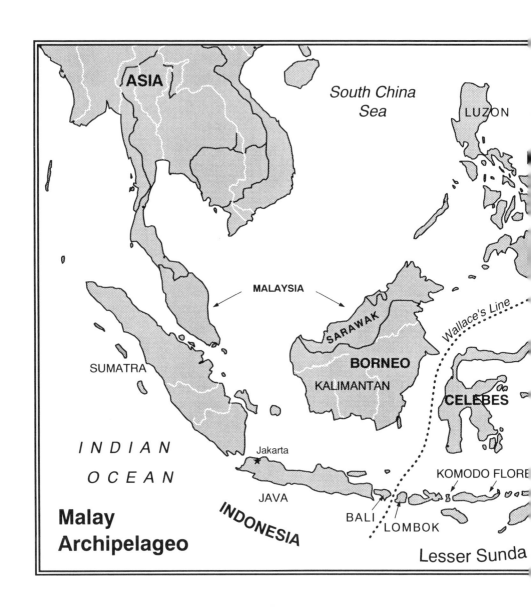

Malay
Archipelageo

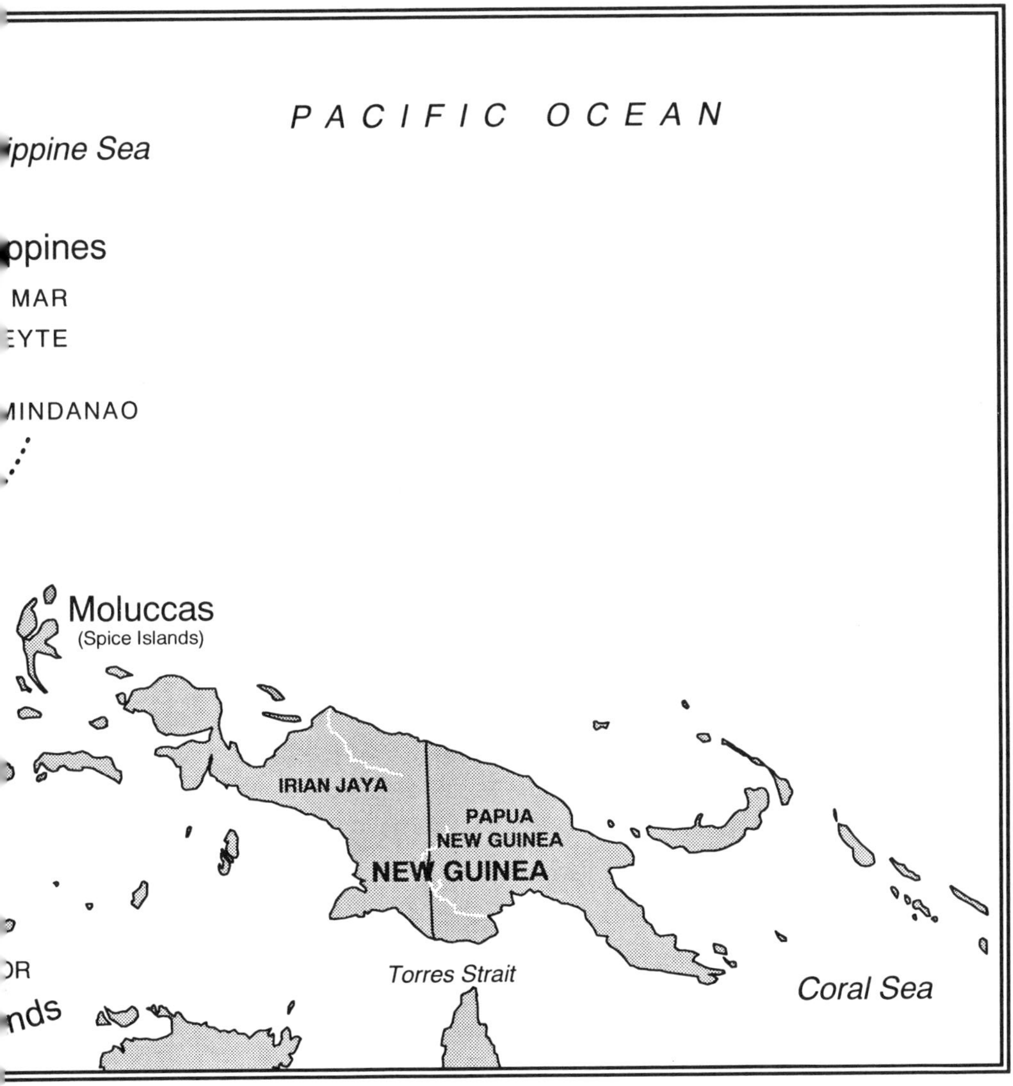

PACIFIC OCEAN

ippine Sea

ppines

MAR

EYTE

MINDANAO

Moluccas
(Spice Islands)

IRIAN JAYA

PAPUA
NEW GUINEA

NEW GUINEA

OR

nds

Torres Strait

Coral Sea

tially unexplored island of New Guinea, a mysterious land fringed by dense equatorial jungles and impenetrable coastal swamps, with a backbone of mountains soaring as high as 16,000 feet. After Greenland, it is the world's second largest island, stretching 1,500 miles from east to west through the western Pacific.

Reaching in a great 3,000 mile arc westward from New Guinea lie the East Indies—some thirteen hundred islands in all. Farthest toward the setting sun is Sumatra, which flanks the coast of the Malayan Peninsula like a huge finger pointing across the Bay of Bengal toward India.

Sumatra, Java, Celebes, and Borneo make up the Greater Sunda Islands, one of the two major island groups of the East Indies. The other group, the Lesser Sundas, consists of a number of much smaller islands—Bali, Lombok, Timor, and many others— that stretch eastward from Java. A smaller but important group of islands lies between New Guinea and Celebes—the Moluccas, or Spice Islands. The treasured spices grown on these islands were what brought about much of the early trade between the East and West, which stimulated the search for a new route to the Indies, which launched the great voyages of exploration undertaken by Vasco da Gama, Christopher Columbus, and Ferdinand Magellan.

Once part of the continent of Asia, the East Indies were separated from the mainland during the Pleistocene, when the great ice caps and glaciers melted and the levels of the seas rose. New Guinea, which had been linked to Australia, was separated from that southern continent in the same way.

A Mix of People

The native peoples of the Malay Archipelago are a beguiling and bewildering mix, the result of different races that successfully migrated from Asia during and after the Pleistocene. The first to come were the most primitive groups. They were pushed out by more advanced peoples and forced either to move on to other islands or to retreat deep into the jungles or high onto the slopes of rugged mountains. Most of the natives of New Guinea are dark-skinned Melanesians. Many of them until several generations ago lived as primitive hunters. Pygmy Negritos still live high in the mountains of the island's interior.

The earliest inhabitants of the Philippines were also Negritos. They were followed by Malayans and other more advanced groups from Asia. But as recently as 1970 a small group called the Tasaday was discovered deep in the rain forests of Mindanao, living a Stone Age existence. Fewer than one hundred in number, the Tasaday were food gatherers and hunters, with no knowledge of agriculture or working with metals. As with other endangered groups, the Tasaday will probably disappear as a result of their discovery and exploitation by modern technological man.

As succeeding groups of human beings populated the East Indies, a complex mixture gradually resulted. Melanesians mixed with Malayans, and yellow, brown, and white races added their genes to the pool. Hindus from India invaded Java and Sumatra sometime during the past two thousand years, and Moslems conquered Java in the fifteenth century. The Arabs, of course, had been trading with India and the Far East for many centuries before that time.

The Lure of the Spice Islands

Before the sixteenth century, however, this whole vast region of some ten thousand islands—the Malay Archipelago—was practically unknown to Europeans. Marco Polo touched at Java and Sumatra in the year 1292, when he was on his way home after serving the Great Khan, and told a little about life on these islands in his writings. Various products of the East Indies were also known in Europe at that time—especially the highly prized spices that reached the continent over ancient caravan routes or through trade with the Arabs.

All of the spices—but especially clove, cinnamon, nutmeg, mace, and pepper—were treasured articles of commerce. "They were a part of life in both the European and Asiatic worlds," historian Samuel Elliot Morison observes. "They flavored all kinds of cooked food. They were used in perfumes and (like myrrh) for embalming. Spices were among the most important ingredients of *materia medica*."

Spices stimulated many voyages of exploration during the late fifteenth and early sixteenth centuries in traders' efforts to find new and easier routes to the Indies. The idea of a western route across the Atlantic from Europe to the Spice Islands prompted the Spanish monarchs, Isabella and Ferdinand, to back Christopher Columbus in his epochal voyages of exploration.

New Routes to the Indies

On his first voyage in 1492, and on subsequent voyages as well, Columbus found that a western route to the East Indies posed many difficulties. His main idea was correct, but instead of the Spice Islands he discovered a New World—North and South America— that blocked his way to the Pacific and the East Indies.

Heading southward from Portugal in 1497, the mariner Vasco da Gama successfully demonstrated that sailing to the Indies by an eastern route was possible. He was the first European to take his ships around Africa's southern tip and eastward across the Indian Ocean to Calicut on the Malabar Coast of India. From that point the sail is a short one, comparatively speaking, to the East Indies. Following him in quick succession, many other European navigators reached the East Indies by traveling the same route.

Columbus had been blocked by the New World in the west, but Ferdinand Magellan, sailing for Spain a generation later, finally did find the western route to the Indies. Leaving Europe in 1519, he sailed westward through the straits that are named for him, and onward through the great South Sea, which was so calm and benign that he named it "Pacific."

Reaching the island of Mactan in the Philippines in March 1519, Magellan found not savages but people with an advanced culture and social system. Wishing to gain favor with the local sultan, he made the mistake of getting mixed up in local politics and backing his host in warfare with a neighboring ruler. Magellan paid for that mistake with his life on April 27, killed in a battle off Mactan.

His companions sailed on to Borneo and then to the Spice Islands, where they were ceremoniously welcomed by the Sultan of

Tidore, who gave them two bird-of-paradise skins to take back as gifts to the Spanish monarchs.

Portuguese mariners had visited the Spice Islands a few years earlier, however. They soon returned and subdued the garrison that the Spaniards had left behind. From that time on the East Indies became pawns in a colonial power struggle among many European nations: Spain and Portugal at first, the Dutch and English soon thereafter, and finally the French and Germans.

By 1601 the Dutch were firmly entrenched at the Cape of Good Hope. From this strategic point they controlled the eastern route to the Indies and as a result had already mounted at least fifteen expeditions to the East Indies. The Dutch East India Company was formed, and soon the Netherlands claimed most of the East Indies as their colonial empire. The Portuguese kept a toehold in the Far East at Timor. The British and then the Germans staked out protectorates in New Guinea. The Spanish, driven from the Indies by the Dutch, took over the Philippine Islands until 1898 when they were ousted by the United States.

Wallace's Line

Alfred Russel Wallace, a British naturalist, traveled and collected zoological specimens in New Guinea and the East Indies from 1854 to 1862. In 1869, he described his experiences in a classic book of natural history, *The Malay Archipelago.* A careful observer and thinker, Wallace visited many islands of the East Indies and was struck by the fact that neighboring islands often supported very different kinds of plants and animals.

On the islands west of a certain imaginary line he noted that the fauna was largely Asian in origin. East of that line the Australian influence was dominant. After long thought and observation, Wallace established the line of demarcation—known ever since as Wallace's Line—between what he said were the Indo-Malaysian and Austro-Malaysian zoogeographical regions.

Today zoogeographers recognize that line as separating two great faunal areas—the Oriental and the Australian. Going from north to south (as shown on the map, pages 124–125), Wallace's

Line passes below the Philippines, then turns southward between Celebes and Borneo, and through the narrow passage between Bali and Lombok. These last two tiny islands are just a few miles apart, but each supports a very different and distinct fauna. All of the islands to the north and west of Wallace's Line have predominantly Asiatic animals. All to the south and east have animals that are typically Australian. There are some islands close to either side that support a mixture of the two.

New Nations

Since World War II the islands of the Malay Archipelago have been largely freed from colonialism and now pursue their destinies as independent nations. The Philippines were granted their freedom by the United States in 1946. The states of Sarawak and Sabah in northern Borneo are today part of the independent nation of Malaysia, while Kalimantan, the larger southern portion of the island, is now part of the Republic of Indonesia.

Indonesia, a teeming country of three thousand islands and 200 million people, includes all of the old Dutch East Indies as well as the western half of New Guinea, which is now known as Irian Jaya, or West Irian. The eastern half of the island, known as Papua New Guinea, is one of the newest of all independent nations. Made up of former German, British, and Australian colonies and protectorates, it was granted its independence in 1975. Many of its population of 4.2 million people are still struggling to emerge from a primitive way of life.

For each of these new nations, the problems of feeding the population and the strenuous efforts being launched to advance the country's economy have taken up most of the people's efforts. Little time is spent on conservation, but old preserves are still guarded and many other areas of natural habitat are largely untouched. With each passing year, however, the situation is changing—usually for the worse.

JAVAN AND SUMATRAN RHINOCEROSES
Rhinoceros sondaicus and *Didermocerus sumatrensis*

Stopping at the islands of Java and Sumatra in the year 1292, Marco Polo noted that in the kingdom of Pasei: "There are wild

Javan Rhinoceros

elephants in the country, and numerous unicorns, which are very nearly as big. They have hair like that of a buffalo, feet like those of an elephant, and a horn in the middle of the forehead, which is black and very thick . . . ."

These "unicorns" of which he spoke were none other than one-horned Javan rhinoceroses. This species, however, is almost hairless, while the Sumatran rhino is the hairy one. The intrepid Venetian traveler must have seen—or heard about—both species.

The Javan, or lesser, one-horned rhinoceros is somewhat smaller than the great Indian rhinoceros, and has armor-plated skin that is similarly folded but without the round rivet marks of its larger relative. It once was found on the Asian mainland from Burma to Malaya and ranged through Java, Sumatra, and Borneo as well. Until the mid-nineteenth century it was quite abundant in many of these areas. Like the Indian rhinoceros, however, it was hunted mercilessly. Colonial sportsmen often hunted the Javan rhinoceros merely for fun during the nineteenth and early twentieth centuries, and poachers would go to almost any lengths to kill it for its valuable horn and other parts.

As the inevitable result, the Javan rhino had disappeared almost everywhere by 1900. An estimated fifty of them survived in

Java, and perhaps a dozen or so remained in Sumatra. There were also a few hundred stragglers on the mainland, but they soon disappeared. The Sumatran remnant vanished as well, and western Java seemed to be the only area where the Javan rhinoceros survived.

In a determined effort to protect the species, Dutch officials in Java established the 117-square-mile Ujung Kulon Nature Reserve in 1921 on the western tip of the island. Later made a national park, this wild area helped to protect other threatened species such as the Javan tiger, the wild ox or banteng, the rusa deer, the chevrotain (a small, deer-like animal), various gibbons and hornbills, and the green peafowl, as well as the Javan rhinoceros.

Today, about fifty Javan rhinos survive in Ujung Kulon. The recent discovery of footprints and other evidence in Vietnam's Cat Tien National Park indicate that an additional ten or fifteen of them still live on the Asian mainland. These two populations—about sixty-five animals in all—are the only surviving Javan rhinoceroses.

In 1991 the Indonesian government announced tentative plans to capture some of the rhinos in the Ujung Kulon Reserve for a captive breeding program, but many conservationists had strong misgivings about the success of any such effort. Field biologist Mike Griffiths, who had been studying the species for two years in Ujung Kulon, observed: "When you know you have a growing population, then you can consider taking two or three animals away." The captive breeding program was shelved.

The Sumatran two-horned or hairy rhinoceros once ranged through much of southeastern Asia, from Assam in northeastern India and Bangladesh through the Malay Peninsula to Sumatra and Borneo. Smallest of the rhinos, its hide is not pleated like that of its two Asian relatives, but is covered with considerably more hair.

Once abundant in the Mekong Delta of southern Indochina, common throughout most of its range in the early years of the twentieth century, the Sumatran rhinoceros has in the years since been killed off nearly everywhere. Today the entire population numbers perhaps five hundred animals in small scattered populations in Sumatra, Borneo, and the Malay Peninsula. In 1994 there were twenty-two of them held in captive facilities in Malayasia, Sabah (North Borneo), Indonesia, England, and the United States. All attempts to breed them in captivity, however, have failed.

MALAY TAPIR
Tapirus indicus

Tapirs, along with horses and rhinos, are grouped in the order Perissodactyla—hoofed animals that have an odd number of toes. The Malay tapir is the largest of the four living species of tapirs, and the only Old World representative. The other three—the Brazilian, Baird's, and mountain or woolly tapir—inhabit the forests of Latin America, from southern Mexico to Argentina.

All the tapirs have stocky bodies with short legs that have four toes on the front feet and three on the hind, all ending in small hoofs. The nose and upper lip are prolonged to form a short proboscis. All of them live in heavily forested jungle habitat, usually near swamps or streams. Their food consists of forest vegetation and fallen fruit.

The Malay tapir, which may weigh as much as 700 pounds, is blackish brown with a white blanket or saddle extending from its shoulders to its hips. Some call it the saddle-backed tapir. The coat of the young is marked with white or yellowish streaks which fade and disappear by the time it is four to six months old.

The species once ranged from Burma and eastern Thailand through the Malay Peninsula and Sumatra, but has long since disappeared from much of this region. It is almost extinct in Burma, and its future in Thailand and Sumatra is bleak. Isolated family groups survive in Thailand, and the total population in Sumatra, where reserves have been established for its protection, is no more than forty or fifty animals.

ORANGUTAN
Pongo pygmaeus

A troop of gibbons swings through the treetops like circus acrobats, their whoops echoing far and wide through the Bornean forest. A big, helmeted hornbill flies past them, heading for the tree where his mate incubates eggs in a nest cavity. A huge red ape appears, carefully walking along a high branch with arms outspread like a tightrope walker. Squatting on the limb, the orangutan seizes a nearby cluster of fruit and begins to eat.

One of the four kinds of great ape—the others are the gorilla, chimpanzee, and the gibbon—the orangutan ranged widely throughout suitable forest habitat in southeastern Asia during the Pleistocene era. Within historic times, however, it has been limited to the islands of Borneo and Sumatra and was first made known to Western science in the mid-seventeenth century by William Bontius, a Dutch doctor in Borneo. The first detailed description of the species in its natural habitat was written little more than a century ago by the English naturalist Alfred Russel Wallace.

Largest of all mammals that spend most of their lives in trees, adult male orangutans may weigh nearly 200 pounds while females commonly weigh half that amount. Zoo specimens often weigh a great deal more, for they are more sedentary. A big male seldom stands taller than four feet, two inches, but his long arms, spread from side to side, may span nearly eight feet. The coat of both sexes ranges from a warm red color to dark brown. Most mature males develop wide, leathery cheek pads, as well as a throat or laryngeal sac, and an old male may grow a beard. The expression *orangutan* means "man of the forest" in Malayan, a very suitable name for this great ape.

Unlike the social chimpanzee and gorilla, the orangutan is a solitary species. It lives a nomadic existence, wandering through the lowland rain forests and swampy wooded areas alone, except at mating time. An excellent mother, the female cares for her young one until it is five or six years old. The chief food is fruit, such as figs and durian, a large pulpy fruit with a prickly rind. At nightfall, all orangutans except the largest and heaviest males make sleeping nests for themselves in the trees, drawing limbs together within a fork and fashioning a mattress of leaves and branches. During wet weather they sometimes construct a sheltering roof over the nest.

During World War II the homeland of the orangutan suffered severe upheavals as both Borneo and Sumatra were captured by the Japanese, then retaken by Allied armies. Even more unrest followed when the Indonesians forced the Dutch colonials out of Sumatra and southern Borneo (Kalimantan). For a number of years afterward there was sporadic fighting between the forces of Indonesia and Malaysia—both newly independent countries—for control of Sarawak and Sabah in northern Borneo. In addition, much natural habitat was destroyed through deforestation, and many orangs were killed or captured for sale to zoos or to individuals who wanted exotic pets. As a result, the population of this great ape has dwindled steadily during the past fifty years.

Today, the orangutan is legally protected in both Borneo and Sumatra, and some 12,000 square miles of its vital rain forest habitat are being preserved within Gunung Leusser National Park in Sumatra and in Tanjung Puting National Park and two other reserves in Kalimantan, Borneo. Illegal hunting and smuggling of live species still goes on. A young orang may sell for $5,000 or more, and for that kind of money many poachers are willing to take plenty of risks. The usual methods involve the shooting of an adult female with a baby, and then capturing the youngster. Captive young are smuggled out to Singapore, Hong Kong, or Taiwan, where they are supplied with forged papers and certificates so that they may be sold abroad. For every captured young orang that survives in captivity, an estimated seven or eight others die.

In Sarawak during the 1960s Mrs. Barbara Harrisson, wife of the director of the Sarawak Museum, started a rehabilitation center where young orangs seized from poachers could be cared for and prepared for eventual release into their native habitat. A similar program was later instituted by the Forest Department in Sabah, which set up an orangutan rehabilitation center in the Sepilok Forest Reserve.

At the initiative of Mrs. Harrisson, the hunting and trading of orangs in Indonesian Borneo and in Sumatra were sharply reduced in 1968 when an agreement was negotiated between Indonesia's conservation authorities and the Survival Service Commission of the International Union for the Conservation of Nature and Natural Resources (IUCN). Under the provisions of this agreement no orangs could be exported from Indonesia without SSC clearance and papers. In 1969 the world's bona fide zoos willingly agreed to this restriction. In the years since, the Indonesian Forestry Service has established one rehabilitation center for confiscated orangs in the Tanjung Puting Reserve in Kalimantan as well as similar centers in northern Sumatra.

In 1971 Biruté F. Goldikas, the so-called "Ape Lady of Borneo," began her lengthy study of wild orangutans at Tanjung Puting. Recruited by Louis Leakey, who had already started Jane Goodall in her study of chimpanzees, and Dian Fossey in her study of mountain gorillas, Biruté Goldikas established a Camp Leakey in the park, and for the next quarter of a century lived with the big red apes, following them in their solitary wanderings through the forests, and gathering hitherto unknown information on their daily habits, foraging abilities, mating behavior, and reproductive cycles. As one of her activities, she established a halfway house at Camp Leakey for orangutans liberated from illegal captivity. Here they were fed and cared for until they could be reintroduced into the wild. In 1986 she established an Orangutan Foundation to help raise money to promote conservation of the species, and raise the public's awareness of its endangered status.

Her tireless zeal in behalf of orangutans inevitably rubbed many government officials the wrong way. In a *New York Times Magazine* article in 1992 Mark Starowics, who produced a documentary on her for the Canadian Broadcasting Company in 1991, noted, "Her advocacy for protection of orangs has placed her in conflict with some of the most powerful people and economic interest groups in Indonesia, where she cannot work without government approval." She still spends part of each year in Borneo, however, and also teaches at Simon Fraser University in Vancouver, British Columbia.

Today, best estimates of orangutan numbers indicate a wild population of twenty thousand or more. There are nearly seven hundred of them in zoos worldwide, more than five hundred of them born and bred in captivity.

PHILIPPINE MONKEY-EATING EAGLE
Pithecophaga jefferyi

Exploring the Philippine island of Samar in 1896, the English naturalist John Whitehead collected an eagle then unknown to science. In his notes, Whitehead remarked: "He is well known to the natives as a robber of their poultry and small pigs, but chiefly as a destroyer of monkeys which are the only animals sufficiently abundant to support such a large bird."

Philippine Monkey-eating Eagle

Largest of the eagles, and one of the most magnificent of the world's feathered species, the monkey-eating eagle has a wingspread of eight feet or more. Its sleek plumage is a combination of dark brown and cinnamon with some black markings, with underparts that are mostly white. It has fierce gray eyes, a shaggy crest, and a huge, sharply hooked beak. Its former range included the islands of Mindanao, Luzon, Samar, and Leyte. It nests in huge kapok and mahogany trees, high on the forested mountain slopes, and raises only one young each year. The prey of the species includes squirrels, monkeys, and colugos, or "flying lemurs," unique gliding mammals that are placed in an order of their own, the Dermoptera, or "skin wings."

Never plentiful, the monkey-eating eagle was a prized trophy for hunters, as well as a valuable addition to any zoo collection. Natives of the Philippines once killed it as a menace to their poultry. Forestry operations and agricultural clearing that destroyed much of its needed habitat also contributed to the eagle's decline. In 1969, for example, the *Philippine Free Press* reported that deforestation in Mindanao was occurring at the incredible rate of two-and-a-half acres every three minutes. Whether those figures were reliable or not, they illustrated the vast changes that have been taking place on the island. In 1976, the human population of the Philippines was about forty-two million people. In 1996, just twenty years later, it was seventy million.

As a result of all these adverse factors, the monkey-eating eagle has long been one of the world's rarest birds. By 1970 it was believed to be extinct on Samar and Leyte. Luzon had only a few surviving individuals. The last stronghold of the species was Mindanao, and the total population was less than one hundred birds. The Philippine government passed laws protecting the species, but enforcement was very lax.

Because of its spectacular size and regal bearing, the monkey-eating eagle had always been a prized zoo exhibit. Recognizing the danger of its imminent extinction in the wild, however, the American Association of Zoological Parks and Aquariums established a boycott of illegal trade in the species in 1962. In spite of that, six Philippine eagles were exported the next year. In 1967 the same organization passed a resolution prohibiting any of its members from selling, trading, capturing, or accepting a monkey-eating eagle as a gift, with the exception of those made available by governments or conservation organizations.

In 1992 there were very few captive monkey-eating eagles in zoological collections around the world. None had ever been bred successfully in captivity, although several experimental programs had been initiated in several leading zoos. In June of that year, however, the *International Zoo News* reported the following: "The Philippine Eagle Conservation Program Foundation (PECPF) has hatched its first chick—conceived by artificial insemination and hatched by a 22-year-old female. Only 35 eagles survive, of which 13, including the new arrival, are at PECPF's headquarters in Davao City [Mindanao]. There are no plans to release any birds in the wild because their habitat has been so devastated that survival would be unlikely."

That news item records a triumph of veterinary science, but a tragedy for the Philippine eagle's wild ecosystem.

KOMODO MONITOR
Varanus komodensis

Off the western tip of Flores, one of the Lesser Sunda Islands, lie three tiny islands—Komodo, Rinca, and Gilimotang. Komodo, the largest of the three, is about 25 miles long by 12 miles wide. These islands are the home of the giant lizard known as the Komodo monitor, or Komodo dragon.

In 1912 a pioneering Dutch aviator from Java made a forced landing on Komodo, an island that was then practically unknown even to the Dutch who ruled over it by colonial claim. There, much to his astonishment, the airman saw what looked like huge dragons, some of them measuring ten feet or more in length. He carried tales of these fearsome creatures back to Java with him and, after further investigation, the director of the zoological museum in Buitenzorg (now Bogor, south of Jakarta, in western Java), published a description of this Komodo dragon.

Male Komodo monitors may measure ten feet in length and weigh more than 300 pounds. Some early observers reported specimens nearly thirteen feet in length and correspondingly heavier. Females are smaller than the males, seldom measuring more than eight feet. The adults have a tough beaded skin that varies from a dull grayish brown to black. Many platelets embedded in the skin make it almost useless in the hide trade. Chinese hunters killed the monitor in the old days, nevertheless, and sold "dragon's tail oil" as a remedy for burns and other ailments.

The adult monitors are too heavy to climb trees, but the young are active climbers. About sixteen inches long when they hatch, the young are much more brightly marked than the adults, with an orange throat and belly and golden spots dotting the gray-black back. Whatever its age, every Komodo monitor is equipped with a long forked tongue, which it uses as a sense organ for touching and smelling food. Adults are mainly scavengers and eat such carrion as the carcasses of deer, goats, pigs, and other smaller animals. On occasion they also stalk and kill live prey. They are voracious eaters, and one investigator who spent a year studying the species on Komodo reported that a female monitor eight-and-a-half feet long and weighing about 100 pounds ate all of a 90 pound pig at one time. Given the opportunity, they will occasionally attack human beings. In recent years about ten people have been killed or injured.

From December through March of each year the "islands of the thousand dragons" have monsoon rains. They are quite dry during the rest of the year, and the monitors retreat into burrows to protect themselves from the hot sun and high temperatures.

The Indonesian government has declared the islands as reserves for the species, and perhaps four or five thousand monitors survive on the three islands today. There are 2,571 on Komodo, 795 on Rinca, and 100 on Gilimotang, according to David Quammen, a recent visitor to the islands and author of *The Song of the Dodo: Island Biogeography in an Age of Extinction.* There are also about 130 on the western tip of Flores. The government strictly controls the number of Komodo monitors that may be collected for scientific studies or exhibition. It also caters to the tourist trade. The thousands of curious travelers who come to see the monitors every year are treated to a controversial biweekly public feeding show in which a goat is killed and then tossed to the monitors. They obligingly cluster about the carcass and rip it apart.

In 1990 the National Zoo in Washington, D.C., received a pair of young adult Komodo monitors from the Indonesian government. Two years later they were observed mating. The female laid a clutch of large eggs which were placed in a high-temperature incubator. Nine months later, as reported in the *New York Times* for March 1, 1994, "a dozen babies slashed through their leathery egg shells and began wolfing down baby mice." Since then, clutch after clutch has yielded about thirty live babies. Many of these have been sent to other U.S. zoos.

Queen Alexandra's Birdwing (male)

BIRDWING BUTTERFLIES
Ornithoptera **species**

The Ornithoptera or birdwing butterflies of the Indo-Australian region include the world's largest butterflies among its members. The various species range from Malaysia to Borneo, New Guinea, and the Solomon Islands, with one species inhabiting tropical northern Australia.

Most of the males have wings that are a deep, velvety black, with broad bands or splashes of iridescent green, blue, or gold, and bodies that are marked with crimson or yellow. Expanded, their wings measure six or seven inches from tip to tip. The females are considerably larger. Their wings span ten inches or more, but lack the bright iridescent colors of the males. Birdwing caterpillars feed on the leaves of various species of the worldwide plant family Aristolochiaceae—woody vines such as the Dutchman's pipe and snakeroot in America. From the leaves they acquire very distasteful properties, which the adults retain, and which gives them effective protection from predators.

As long as they have been known to science, however, birdwing butterflies have been eagerly pursued as prized trophies by collectors who sometimes sold them for hundreds of dollars a pair. Today, such collecting of specimens from the wild is illegal over much of the birdwings' range, but a legal cottage industry of butterfly farming—raising the adults from eggs under controlled and supervised conditions—has been established in some areas. The butterfly farming does not affect the wild population and is an effective contribution to the local economy.

Largest of all these butterflies is Queen Alexandra's birdwing, which ranges across the island of New Guinea. The female has a wingspread measuring nearly a foot. The species has been legally protected in Papua New Guinea since 1966, but its habitat is increasingly threatened by logging and the rapid spread of oil palm plantations. As reported in the July 1994 issue of *Oryx*, the publication of the British-based Fauna and Flora Preservation Society, Angus Hutton, "who pioneered the butterfly farming industry in Papua New Guinea, has been appointed Conservation/Naturalist Consultant for a five-year research and conservation project." Hutton's field studies have shown that the range of Queen Alexandra's birdwing is three times more extensive than had previously been thought. He also found healthy populations of the world's second largest butterfly, the Goliath birdwing. A moratorium on logging was directly declared in the area.

Butterfly farming is also practiced in some areas in Irian Jaya. With support from the World Wildlife Fund for Nature, natives living in the Arfak Mountains of northwestern New Guinea raise birdwing butterflies in the mountain gardens, then mount and dry the adults and sell them abroad for as much as $350 a pair.

Similar methods of butterfly farming are being practiced in various Central and South American countries to satisfy the demand for the brilliant iridescent blue morphos and other brightly colored tropical species.

Other Animals of the East Indies

In 1945 zoologist Francis Harper listed eleven species of animals that were vanishing in the Malay Archipelago, among them the orangutan, the Sumatran elephant, the Javan and Sumatran rhinos, the babirussa, or wild pig, and various species of wild oxen—anoas, the tamarau, and the banteng. All of these animals are still threatened today, but none has vanished completely.

The tamarau is one of the smallest wild cattle, and also one of the most endangered. Found only on Mindoro, the Philippine Islands, its estimated population is no more than 150 to 200 animals. Celebes, one of the Greater Sunda Islands, is the home of the lowland and mountain anoas. Hunted for their meat, much of their wild habitat being destroyed by human activities, both are facing extinction. The banteng still survives in scattered populations on the Malay Peninsula, Borneo, and Java, but its numbers are decreasing for the same reasons.

The Bali tiger has long since vanished, and the Javan tiger may now be extinct as well. In Sumatra, the beautiful golden cat is now rare and may soon disappear entirely on the islands. The same can be said of the proboscis monkey of Borneo and the beautiful Javan, or green, peafowl.

In New Guinea, the dominant mammalian species are the tree kangaroos, cuscuses, and the peculiar long-beaked echidna. All of them—and many smaller species as well—are hunted by the people for food. The introduction of modern shotguns and the destruction of forest habitat contribute to the dwindling fortunes of many of these mammals and to those of the cassowary, a huge flightless bird, as well. The New Guinea harpy eagle, closest living relative of the Philippine monkey-eating eagle, is being taken as a hunting trophy, and New Guinea crocodiles are prized for their skins.

The Australian continent has been described as a colossal natural history museum stocked with living fossils.

Ellis Troughton
The Furred Animals of Australia

7

AUSTRALIA AND NEW ZEALAND
Strange Lands Down Under

Although European geographers of the Middle Ages and before had no reliable reports to back them up, they spoke of a great unknown southern continent—*Terra Australis Incognito*, "the Unknown Southland"—that they concluded must exist somewhere in the southern hemisphere as a counterbalance to the great land masses of the northern hemisphere. Long before the Middle Ages, however, the ancient Chinese and other highly civilized peoples of southeastern Asia and the Malay Archipelago knew something of this great land to the south. Although there are no records to confirm the facts, their trading junks and sailboats doubtless came within sight of its northern shores, and their ships' crews probably landed at one spot or another. But the Western world did not learn about this land down under until it was encountered by European explorers and adventurers.

The first vague facts about this southern continent were reported by Portuguese and Spanish explorers in the sixteenth century as they charted their ways through unknown seas, seeking new routes to the Spice Islands. In 1606 the Spanish navigator, Luis de Torres, sailed through the narrow strait that now bears his name, between New Guinea and Australia, and from 1610 on various Dutch mariners sighted or touched on the western coast of Australia, which they called New Holland, as they sailed to the Spice Islands by way of Cape Horn and the Indian Ocean.

Early Exploration

In 1642 Anton Van Dieman, governor general of the Dutch East Indies, sent Dutch mariner Abel Tasman on a voyage of exploration, the object being to take advantage of the west-blowing trade winds and find a southern route to South America. Sailing westward from Batavia, Java, across the Indian Ocean, Tasman touched at Mauritius, then sailed southeast until he reached Tasmania, which he named Van Dieman's land in honor of the governor general. Later, he discovered New Zealand some 1,000 miles farther east. Satisfied that a clear route to South America lay open across the Pacific from there, he turned north and returned to Java by passing to the north of New Guinea. Along the way he discovered the Tonga and Fiji Islands. In ten months Tasman had sailed completely around the continent of Australia without actually finding out much about it. In some measure, however, he had charted the extent of the great southern continent.

Captain Cook Discovers Botany Bay

Coming along more than a century after Tasman, Captain James Cook, the famous English mariner and explorer, was the first European to explore and describe the eastern coast of Australia and to chart the coasts of New Zealand, eastern Australia, and New Guinea. Cook made three voyages to the Pacific between 1768 and 1778 before being killed on Hawaii in a fight with natives over a stolen boat.

In April 1770, Captain Cook sailed to the east coast of Australia and anchored at Botany Bay, which is surrounded today by high-rise apartments in the suburbs of Sydney. Cook and his men explored the green wilderness around the bay and marveled at the strange animals and plants they saw. Heading northward, Cook a few weeks later beached his ship *Endeavor* for repairs on the coast of the great peninsula that he christened Cape York. There he saw his first kangaroo, which he describes in his journal: "It was of a light mouse Colour and the full size of a Grey Hound. . . . Its progression is by Hopping or Jumping seven or eight feet at each hop upon its hind legs only. . . . It bears no sort of resemblance to any European animals I ever saw; it is said to bear much resemblance to the Jerboa, excepting in size, the Jerboa being no larger than a common rat."

On Cape York Captain Cook also saw and remarked upon another animal, the flying fox, a huge bat with a foxlike face and a wingspread of three feet or more: "It was a most peculiar animal about the bigness of, and much like, a one-gallon keg. It was as black as the Devil, and had wings; indeed, I took it for the Devil, or I might easily have catched it, for it crawled slowly through the grass."

Finally Cook reached the northern tip of the continent and Torres Strait. There, on August 22, 1770, he "hoisted the English colors, and in the name of His Majesty King George the Third took possession of the whole eastern coast," giving it the name of New South Wales.

Cook had words of high praise for this new land he was claiming for England: "In this extensive country, it can never be doubted but what most sorts of grain, fruit, roots, etc. of every kind would flourish here were they once brought hither, planted, and cultivated by the hands of industry; and here are provender [provisions] for more cattle, at all seasons of the year, than ever can be brought into the country."

Encouraged by Cook's glowing words, England began to settle the east coast of Australia in 1788, when a group of convicts debarked at Botany Bay. Each year thereafter the rich eastern and southern coasts received more settlers, and the transformation of Australia, after an isolation of many millions of years, was well launched. In 1803, Matthew Flinders charted and surveyed much of the coastline of the continent, and later in the nineteenth century the interior was finally explored.

Land of the Aborigines

The entire continent is smaller than the United States. Its northern tip, Cape York, thrusts into the tropics, just a few miles from the southern coast of New Guinea. Its eastern and southern coasts have a temperate climate, with rich grasslands and eucalyptus forests—a pleasant region, much like England in many ways. The eastern forests and farmlands rise into highlands and mountain ranges, separating the green coastal areas from the drier and more sparsely settled western half of the continent. The heartland of Australia is a forbidding desert, which endures long periods of drought and searing heat. Few people, animals, or plants inhabit this great area.

European settlers coming to Australia found that it was inhabited by slim, dark-skinned people who led a nomadic way of life and whose Stone Age culture satisfied their needs. Living intimately with nature, the aborigines left little mark upon the land, using what they found without changing it. "In reality they are far more happy than we Europeans, being wholly unacquainted not only with the superfluous but with the necessary conveniences so much sought after in Europe," wrote Captain Cook approvingly in his journal. "They are happy in not knowing the use of them."

The aborigines are thought to have arrived in Australia from islands to the north some twenty to thirty thousand years ago. There were probably no more than 400 thousand of them when Europeans came to stay two hundred years ago. Today they have been reduced to half that number. "Wherever the European has trod," remarked Charles Darwin after his visit to Australia in 1836, "death seems to pursue the aboriginal."

Australia's Remarkable Wildlife

Most of the animals the Europeans found were quite different from those in other portions of the world. Australia had been separated from Asia near the end of the Age of Reptiles. Mammals were just

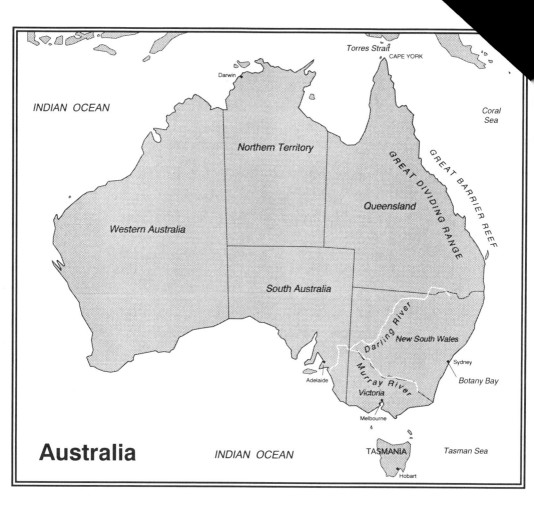

INDIAN OCEAN

Coral Sea

Torres Strait

CAPE YORK

Darwin

Northern Territory

GREAT DIVIDING RANGE

GREAT BARRIER REEF

Queensland

Western Australia

South Australia

Darling River

New South Wales

Sydney

Adelaide

Murray River

Botany Bay

Victoria

Melbourne

Australia

INDIAN OCEAN

TASMANIA

Tasman Sea

Hobart

getting their start at that ancient time, and primitive forms still dominated.

In Australia, primitive pouched mammals were the predominant forms at the time of Australia's separation from Asia, and the southern continent's long isolation from the rest of the world allowed these remarkable mammals to flourish and evolve without competition from more advanced forms. Specializing and adapting in many different ways, these pouched marsupials occupied all of the different ecological habitats that Australia had to offer.

Wolflike and catlike carnivorous marsupials took over the role

ıredators; kangaroos, wallabies, and a host of smaller forms be-
ne grazers and browsers; pouched moles, anteaters, mice, and
rats appeared. "Australia may be regarded as the natural home of
marsupials," Australian naturalist Ellis Troughton noted, writing in
1947. "They come to us as a natural heritage from the past, born
of our continent's age-old isolation, woven on the loom of evolution,
and as characteristic of the land as are the birds, gumtrees, and
wattles [Australian trees of the genus *Acacia*] so beloved by Australians as emblematic of their country."

Along with the pouched mammals, two forms of even more
primitive mammals survived: the egg-laying platypus and the
echidna. The only advanced, or placental, mammals already established in Australia when the aborigines arrived were bats and small
rodents, which probably arrived on storm-driven logs or other floating platforms. The aborigines are thought to have brought with them
the dingo, or wild dog. This advanced predator began immediately
to make inroads on the defenseless native marsupials. But the
dingo represented only the beginning.

Introduced Animals

When European settlers came to Australia just over two hundred
years ago, they brought with them domestic stock and many kinds
of Western plants, as well as such familiar wild animals of Europe
as the rabbit, the fox, the stoat (weasel), and many others. The
effect that these new species had on the native Australian fauna
proved devastating. Many of the smaller marsupials disappeared
even before they could be studied and described. As the paleontologist W. K. Gregory observed in 1924, "Late in the eighteenth
century there arrived in Australia by far the most destructive placental mammal the world has ever seen, *Homo sapiens*, variety *eu-
ropaeus*, who has devastated the continent and is now completing
the work of destruction."

Part of this devastation was the result of the unequal competition between the native pouched mammals and the more advanced
placental mammals. Part was due to the wholesale destruction of
the natural environment in many areas, almost wholly caused by
modern man and the animals and plants he brought with him.

As Captain Cook had predicted, the land was good for stock, and sheep raising became the national industry. Millions of sheep changed the fertile grasslands to near deserts through overgrazing. And rabbits accelerated the process after their introduction to the continent in 1859.

Multiplying in incredible numbers in this new and virgin territory, with few of the natural checks and enemies that had kept them under control in Europe, rabbits were soon the scourge of the continent. In 1882, nine million rabbits were killed and their skins exported in efforts to control them; in 1927, some thirty million. Not until 1950 did an introduced viral disease, myxomatosis, provide partial control.

Stockmen fought the rabbit fiercely—and they still do—for rabbits have contributed greatly to the devastation of the land. In Australia there is not enough grass to go around, when divided between sheep and rabbits—both of which overgraze the land— and native kangaroos, which have been cropping their share of the vegetation for millions of years without harm. Many ranchers kill off kangaroos as well as rabbits every chance they get. They also hunt the hated dingo, which they regard as a sheep killer. Hundreds of millions of dollars have been spent in the dingo war, using guns, traps, poisons, and a 5,000 mile fence erected across the continent in an effort to keep them out of the sheep country.

The real losers in all of these unequal struggles and sheep wars, however, have been the native flora and fauna.

KANGAROOS
Family Macropodidae

The most-familiar of all the marsupials, kangaroos are the symbol of Australia—both of the continent and the nation. Their likeness is featured on coins and stamps and on the nation's coat of arms. Kangaroos are found only in Australia and New Guinea, and there they have evolved into many species of various sizes and habits to take advantage of different habitats. In size they range from the little rat kangaroo to the red and great gray, the males of which may stand five to seven feet high and weigh as much as 200 pounds. Between these two forms are a host of others of varying sizes and

Red Kangaroo

colors, known by such names as tree kangaroos, rock wallabies, and wallaroos. Altogether the family Macropodidae includes fifty species or more. All of them have the same general form, with enlarged hind feet (*Macropus* means "big foot"), small forelimbs, and a long tail that acts as a balancer when hopping or as a third foot when stopping to eat.

The best-known species—those recognized everywhere as kangaroos—are the big ones: the red kangaroo (*Macropus rufus*) of the interior plains and ranching country; the eastern gray, or forester, kangaroo (*Macropus giganteus*); the western gray (*Macropus fuliginosus*); and the Euro kangaroo, or wallaroo (*Macropus robustus*), which lives in rocky country. These giants of the family have become familiar sights in Australia ever since its settlement. The mature male is called a "buck" or "boomer," the adult female is known as a "doe," immature females are called "fliers," and baby kangaroos are known as "joeys." Most Australians view them with toleration and affection, but not the ranchers and sheepherders. The latter consider kangaroos pests, rivals for valuable grass and water needed by their domestic flocks.

The settling of the country has affected the kangaroo family in two different ways. Land clearing and the environmental changes brought about by ranching have worked against smaller species of kangaroos by depriving them of natural cover and food. The fox and other introduced predators have also reduced their numbers so much that several of them are in danger of disappearing. But the clearing of land for ranching and the creation of artificial water holes in dry country has, in some instances, been advantageous to several of the larger kangaroos. The red kangaroo, for example, thrives in open country and, in fact, increased its population during the first half of the twentieth century.

As a result, most ranch owners had long urged kangaroo control by any available means. Many hunters needed no urging, however; they went after kangaroos for profit. The skins are used extensively in the manufacture of all sorts of leather products, and the soft fur is featured in children's toys and as souvenir trophies. Kangaroo meat is processed as pet food and for human consumption. Kangaroo-tail soup is still a popular Australian delicacy.

Because of these multiple onslaughts, Australia's annual kangaroo kill increased steadily, reaching a high of nearly two million annually during the 1950s and 1960s. For the next fifteen years between one and two million animals were killed for export alone each year, the United States being the chief buyer of kangaroo products during that period.

Conservationists all over the world and many Australians were justifiably alarmed by such slaughter. Controversy simmered between supporters of the kangaroo and commercial stockmen, the leather industry, and hunters. The United States market provided hunters—both legal shooters and poachers—with the major economic incentive for kangaroo killing. The uproar against the slaughter grew to such proportions by 1970 that stricter limits and controls were imposed. These laws reduced the legal take to approximately one million animals yearly.

At this point several Australian wildlife-management organizations started to promote a philosophy of managing kangaroos and harvesting them for profit on a sustained-yield basis. They claimed that the largest kangaroos have increased in numbers with improvements in their habitat since stocking with sheep began. Building on this base, they tried to convince farmers that kangaroos should be managed and cropped along with such domestic stock as sheep and cattle and that such harvesting would be economically worth their while.

Meanwhile, rampant poaching continued and even increased. Criticism of government policy became so great that in the spring of 1973 Australia banned the export of all kangaroo products and began a crackdown on illegal kills. Sheepmen opposed such a policy and fought back vigorously, claiming that kangaroo populations had increased greatly during 1973. The following year they proposed that a million animals should be killed by poisoning water holes. The poisoning program was never implemented. Best estimates at that time put the total number of big kangaroos in Australia at as many as twenty million animals.

The whole history of the kangaroo question has been heavily overlaid with elements of human politics, prejudices, and profit motives, not only in Australia but also in the United States. In January, 1975, the U.S. Fish and Wildlife Service placed the red, the eastern gray, and the western gray kangaroos on their "threatened" list and banned the import of their products into the United States for commercial purposes. However, a loophole was left in the regulations. If Australia certified that any of its states had developed an effective sustained-yield program for kangaroos, skins from that state would be allowed into the United States.

In the years since, both the Commonwealth and the individual Australian states have developed kangaroo conservation and management plans that have proved very effective. Kangaroos are taken on a sustained-yield management system with closely monitored harvest quotas. If the kangaroo population drops in any given area, the quota for that area is diminished accordingly. By 1988, as noted in the February issue of *National Geographic*, devoted to Australia, kangaroo hunters "kill as many as 2.8 million a year for meat, skins, and fur." That is a huge toll, but as wildlife writer Terry Dawson observed in *Natural History* magazine in 1995, seven years later, "Regulated harvesting of red kangaroos has had little effect on their numbers."

That same year the U.S. Fish and Wildlife Service removed

the red and gray kangaroos from its list of wild species that are threatened or endangered, stating that "the kangaroo population today may well exceed that present before Australia was settled by Europeans."

HAIRY-NOSED WOMBAT
Lasiorhinus latifrons

Charting the strait between Australia and Tasmania at the end of the eighteenth century, explorers George Bass and Matthew Flinders observed some strange animals on several islands. Writing in 1801, Flinders remarked: "The new animal, called Wombat by the natives . . . has the appearance of a little bear. It eats grass and other vegetable substances, and its flesh something resembles tough mutton. The animal is about the size of a turnspit dog, but there is not too much meat upon it for three or four people to eat in a day."

This early account does not really shed much light on one of Australia's most interesting animals. The wombat is beaverlike in size and appearance, except that it is practically tailless. An exclusive vegetarian, it has teeth like those of a rodent, with a single pair of constantly growing incisor, or gnawing, teeth in each jaw. Equipped with powerful forelimbs and stout claws, it is an expert burrower and is notorious for digging lengthy tunnels and burrows. Like its arboreal relative the koala, the wombat has a backward-opening pouch—one with an entrance away from the head rather than toward it, as is true of kangaroos. It usually give birth to just one young at a time.

The several species of wombats are usually divided into two groups: naked-nosed wombats, which generally live in coastal country, and hairy-nosed wombats, which inhabit inland areas. At one time wombats could be found in the eastern part of the continent from northern Queensland to Victoria and South Australia, as well as in Tasmania. Today they have disappeared completely over vast stretches of former range and are threatened in their remaining areas.

Ranchers destroy wombats because they compete with livestock for food. Also, their burrows provide convenient shelters for pestiferous rabbits, and the entrance holes make hazardous footing for livestock. As a consequence, naked-nosed wombats are greatly reduced throughout their range; the Queensland hairy-nosed wombat is found in only one small area of mideastern Queensland, where it is now protected. One of the largest marsupials, it is also one of the rarest. In 1992 only about seventy of them remained. The southern hairy-nosed wombat apparently survives only in a few isolated colonies in semiarid regions of South Australia.

THYLACINE
Thylacinus cynocephalus

Very doglike in appearance, the thylacine, if it still survives, is the largest meat-eating marsupial. Standing two feet high at the shoulder, it has a body nearly four feet long and a twenty-inch tail. The coat of short brown hair is interrupted across the back and sides with sixteen dark stripes. Hunting alone or in pairs, the thylacine runs down its prey like a dog, seizing and killing it with its fanglike canine teeth. The newborn young are carried in the mother's backward-opening pouch. Later they are housed in an underground den.

Also known as the Tasmanian tiger because of its stripes, the

thylacine has another common name, the marsupial wolf, which
suits it better. The scientific name means "pouched dog with a wolf
head."

Fossil remains show that the thylacine once inhabited the
Australian mainland. It disappeared from that continent many thousands of years ago, in all probability soon after the dingo, the Australian wild dog, invaded the continent. The dingo never reached
Tasmania, however, and the thylacine survived there. When Europeans arrived in Tasmania in the nineteenth century, the thylacine
was a common animal over much of the island. As the land became
settled, the population of small native marsupials and rodents—the
thylacine's natural prey—became scarcer; as a result, the pouched
meat-eaters turned to poultry and sheep, which were easy to kill.

The settlers fought the thylacine with guns, traps, and poisons.
As early as 1840 the Van Diemen's Land Company offered a six-
shilling bounty for every thylacine scalp brought in for collection.
In 1888, the government started paying a bounty of one pound ster-
ling for every adult thylacine and ten shillings for every immature
specimen. When the last government bounty was paid in 1909,
records showed that hunters had collected bounties on 2,268 animals, but many more were probably killed. Thylacines were becoming uncommon by this time, and soon there was a further rapid

decline in their numbers. Some people thought that this decline was caused by an epidemic disease such as distemper that swept through the wild population.

By the 1920s the thylacine was rare everywhere. In 1930 a farmer shot a young one, the last recorded wild victim. Three years later a living tiger was caught in a trapper's snare. The only specimen surviving in captivity, it died in 1936 in the Hobart Zoo in Tasmania. The species seemed to be gone for good, but the government gave belated protection to it, with the hope that a few individuals might survive.

The thylacine certainly appeared to be extinct, but during the next twenty-five years there were repeated rumors and unverified reports of sightings of the animal. Numerous professionals and amateurs have searched for it, and the respected Australian scientist David Fleay reported finding its tracks in the 1940s. He did not find a specimen, however.

In 1961 a young male thylacine was killed at Sandy Cape on the west coast of Tasmania, proof that the animal still survived. Two years later tracks and droppings were found in another area, and in 1966 a thylacine lair showing signs of recent occupation was discovered. Early in the same year the government set aside as a game reserve a total of 1.6 million acres in the southwest district of Tasmania. Dogs, cats, and guns were prohibited in the area, and if any thylacines survived, some of them were sure to be in this wilderness refuge. The preserve also served to protect spiny anteaters, or echidnas, platypuses, and the rare Tasmanian ground parrot. Meanwhile, the search for proof of the survival of the thylacine continues to this day, with group after group seeking to find, photograph, and study it. There have been more than three hundred alleged sightings since the 1930s, but none by a trained naturalist until 1982, when an experienced ranger with the National Parks and Wildlife Service sighted one in northwestern Tasmania and described it in detail.

More than a century ago the eminent English naturalist and bird painter John Gould visited Tasmania and collected many zoological specimens there. Writing of the thylacine, he prophesied: "When the comparatively small island of Tasmania becomes more densely populated and its primitive forests are intersected with roads from the Eastern and Western coasts, the numbers of this singular animal will speedily diminish. Extermination will have full sway and it will then, like the wolf in England and Scotland, be recorded as an animal of the past." A remarkably clear-sighted judgment, it might yet be proven false with strict protective laws and expanded reserves.

Australia Today

Smallest of all the continents, Australia was the last to be discovered and is by far the most sparsely settled. About eighteen million people live there today, a mere handful as compared to other continents or to the total world population of nearly 5.5 billion people. The United States (exclusive of Alaska) is just slightly bigger than Australia but has a population of 260 million, about fourteen times as many as live on the continent down under. And such teeming countries as India and China have population densities that are many times greater.

In spite of Australia's sparse population and brief human history, its land and native wildlife have felt the deteriorating effects of modern man more severely in many areas than in practically any other region of the world. Most of the human population is concentrated in a pleasant temperate strip on the eastern and southern coasts. The human effect on this region has, therefore, been intensified, and the forests and grasslands have borne the brunt of the mistreatment. The vast interior of the continent is too hot and arid to support a great deal of life, but marginal semiarid lands have been used far beyond their capacity. As a result of this misuse, they have deteriorated even more. Some people believe that the whole western two-thirds of the continent, between the Darling River and the Indian Ocean, are on the verge of changing from merely arid to true desert land. In such dry areas, the effects of overgrazing and the impact on the native fauna of rabbits, dingoes, foxes, and other introduced animals are doubly devastating. At present, at least twenty-five of Australia's 120 species of marsupials are considered to be in immediate danger of extinction. The populations of many others are also dwindling.

There are hopeful signs for wildlife in Australia, however, for the conservation consciousness of the nation has been raised in recent years. Many programs to protect and conserve wildlife are being put into effect, and additional nature reserves and parks are being created.

New Zealand: Land of Flightless Birds

Roughly 1,200 miles to the east of Australia and Tasmania, New Zealand is a rugged, mountainous land with numerous volcanoes, glaciers, and large areas of lush, forested wilderness. Geologists believe that New Zealand has been isolated from all other lands for at least seventy million years. Until the last thousand years, it has been without human inhabitants. It consists of two main land masses—North Island and South Island, separated from each other by 16-mile-wide Cook Strait—with countless smaller islands scattered along their rugged coastlines.

Stretching over 1,000 miles of ocean, from 35 to 48 degrees of south latitude, New Zealand has a pleasant, temperate climate. With hot springs and fertile valleys, North Island hints of the tropics; with snow-capped peaks, glaciers, and forbidding rocky coasts, South Island reaches toward polar seas.

Isolated for such a long period of time, New Zealand developed its own distinctive fauna. With no predatory animals to threaten them, many flightless birds evolved. Dominant among them were the moas, a group of ostrichlike birds that varied from small, goose-sized species to giants twelve feet tall. There were no native mammals except two bats and perhaps a small rodent or two. These latter, however, may have arrived as stowaways with the first people who came to New Zealand.

Settlement

Humans first came to New Zealand about one thousand years ago, when a few Polynesians landed, perhaps driven to the islands by chance when their outrigger canoes were blown off course during a storm. Not until about the year 1300, however, did the main invasion come. This time, as their descendants record it, a great fleet of

New Zealand

Polynesian long canoes arrived at "the land under the long white clouds," a colonizing force that was deliberately seeking a new home away from the crowded ancestral home islands to the east. These new arrivals were Maoris, a warlike group of Polynesians, who quickly defeated and assimilated the earlier inhabitants. They were well entrenched when Westerners first found the islands some three hundred years later.

The European discoverer of New Zealand was the Dutch explorer Abel Tasman who landed on the islands in 1642 and named them after one of the regions of his native Holland. Captain Cook explored the islands in 1769 and returned on several subsequent voyages. Once it was known, New Zealand became a popular place for both missionaries and whalers to visit. In the 1840s it became a crown colony of the British Empire, but not without prolonged and determined opposition from the proud Maoris who resented this modern invasion of their land. From 1861 until 1871 the Maoris fought the British invaders, often very effectively. Superior arms finally won out, but the Maoris were granted a considerable degree of autonomy.

As had happened in Australia, the exotic animals introduced by white settlers flourished in New Zealand—in many cases far too well. Rabbits multiplied at an amazing rate, and wars of extermination were quickly declared against them. The European red deer was introduced in the mid-nineteenth century, and many other antlered species soon followed—North American white-tailed deer and wapiti, English fallow deer, Asiatic sika deer, and various others. The deer flourished in the virgin lands, and for the past half century or more some species have been so abundant that the government has had to employ professional hunters and poisoners to keep them under control.

Rabbits, deer, sheep, and other introduced animals have caused extensive envionmental damage in New Zealand, and their effect on native animals, especially the flightless birds, has been devastating. Man alone, however, was probably responsible for the disappearance of the moas.

MOAS
Family Dinornithidae

The moas are known today only by their bones and bits of other, mostly fossilized, remains. To date, more than twenty different species have been described and named. A number of them were still living in New Zealand when the Polynesians first came to the islands, and several forms may even have survived until the close of the eighteenth century. It is quite safe to say that humans—the Maoris in this particular instance—caused this unique family of birds to disappear when it did. White explorers and settlers first learned about moas only through stories told to them by Maoris.

Great Moa

Later they began to uncover more tangible proof of the birds' existence.

In 1839 an English traveler in New Zealand obtained the thigh bone of a huge creature, which he sent to the English anatomist Richard Owen. Upon first examining it, Owen thought it was merely an ox bone. After more complete study he determined that it had come from a huge ostrichlike bird. At about this time two missionaries sent Owen a box full of similar bones.

After much study the noted anatomist described the birds from which the bones had come and gave them the generic name *Dinornis*, or "terrible bird." He also determined that at least five different forms were represented by the remains he had examined.

Between 1847 and 1850 Walter Mantell, a New Zealand government official whose father was a noted geologist and paleontologist, collected over one thousand moa bones, bone fragments, and pieces of eggshell during extensive travels about the country. He sent the material to England for further examination and classification.

Various studies since that time confirmed the view that the moa family included many species—some large, some small. In

1949 excavations in Pyramid Valley, a swampy area some hundred miles from the northeast coast of South Island, unearthed virtually complete skeletons of about 140 specimens. At least a third were remains of the great moa (*Dinornis maximus*), which stood twelve feet tall. Pollen-dating methods demonstrated that the birds had been mired in the swamp over a period of many centuries, starting about A.D. 500. Sophisticated carbon-14 dating of the stomach contents of some of the largest remains showed an age of about 670 years. In other words, the great moa evidently was still living in the year 1200, a century before the legendary great fleet of the Maoris arrived in New Zealand.

Climatic changes may have been a contributing factor in the disappearance of the various moa species, but most students believe that humans were the primary agent of extermination. The Maoris hunted the big flightless birds for food and had evidently killed most of them by the time Captain Cook visited New Zealand in the last quarter of the eighteenth century. A few moas may have survived until that time, however.

In 1844 an old Maori named Haumatangi came forward when questioned to say that he remembered Captain Cook's second visit in 1773. He further claimed that the last moa in his part of New Zealand had been seen just two years before Cook's visit. Another venerable native, one Kawana Paipai, said that when he was a boy—about 1790—he had actually taken part in moa hunts. The Maori hunters, he related, surrounded the defenseless birds and killed them with spears.

Further evidence of the existence of moas until comparatively recent times was uncovered in 1859, when a group of miners discovered a Maori tomb in which sat a complete human skeleton holding in its cupped finger bones an enormous moa egg, ten inches long by nearly eight inches in diameter.

One of the most tantalizing moa reports was recounted by Sir George Gray, governor of New Zealand in 1868. He declared that the natives had told him of the recent killing of a small moa, "describing with much spirit its capture out of a drove of six or seven." Were the natives telling the truth, or merely embroidering a tall tale about the killing of some flightless bird in order to please the governor? One is inclined to think that the latter is the case. Strong evidence points to the probability of a few moas still surviving to the latter years of the eighteenth century. Possibly a few may have survived in the hidden wilderness areas for another seventy-five years or more.

Other Endangered Species

Some authorities estimate that over forty birds have become extinct on New Zealand and nearby islands since the Polynesians first settled on the main islands about a thousand years ago. A large number of them, of course, were the flightless moas. Others were two flightless geese, two ducks, a swan, several flightless rails, and many passerines, or perching birds. At least nine birds have been exterminated since Europeans invaded the land two hundred years ago. Among them are the New Zealand quail, the New Zealand fruit pigeon, and the North Island laughing owl.

Two species that are threatened with the same fate are the takahé, a chicken-sized flightless rail with red legs and bill, and the kakapo, an owl parrot. Both are found only in a few scattered valleys of Fiordland, in the southwestern section of South Island.

The takahé was first described from bones gathered in 1847 by Walter Mantell, the collector of moa bones, and was considered an extinct species. A living takahé was collected in 1849, however, as were three other specimens during the next forty-nine years. During the next half century no other living birds turned up, and once again the takahé was relegated to the extinct category. In 1948, however, a whole colony of them was found in a small hidden valley in Fiordland. The New Zealand government promptly closed a huge area as a protected sanctuary for the species. Today about 185 of them, perhaps more, survive there. In 1990 a successful program of breeding takahés was established at Mount Bruce, with the aim of starting new populations in other areas.

The kakapo is a fairly large bird, about two feet in length. Its back and wings are mossy green, interrupted with brown and black mottling. Although practically flightless, it does climb trees in search of berries, and has been observed "flying" earthward after feeding, using its stubby degenerate wings to help cushion its fall. Easy prey for introduced predators such as dogs, cats, weasels, and rats, it had almost disappeared and seemed doomed to extinction. Twenty-two kakapos were captured in 1982 and released on Little Barrier Island, which was free of predators, with the hope that they would flourish there and reproduce. The program met with no success, however, until 1990 when two eggs were laid and a single chick hatched. It died five days later. The total population of the kakapo at that time was just forty-three birds. A Kakapo Recovery Team, under the leadership of Don Merton of the New Zealand Department of Conservation's Threatened Species Unit, continues its efforts to save the kakapo.

The list of other birds that are threatened with extinction is lengthy. Fortunately, New Zealanders have come to appreciate their unique fauna and are today making strenuous efforts to save the endangered forms.

Deer, Conies, Hares and fowls . . . in incredible abun-
dance. . . . The soil is the most plentiful, sweete, fruit-
full and wholesome of all the world.

Arthur Barlowe
letter to Sir Walter Raleigh, 1584

8

NORTH AMERICA
The Conquest of a New World

At four different times during the million or more years of the
Ice Age, great sheets of ice thousands of feet thick covered
much of the northern hemisphere. Vast quantities of water were
locked up in the frozen depths during these glacial ages, lowering
the oceans and exposing a broad land bridge connecting Asia and
North America. Free of ice, this wide grassy plain was the route by
which many Old World animals traveled to North America, and
many New World animals passed them, on the way to Asia.

Some twelve thousand years ago the ice caps of the last glacial
age began to melt, causing the oceans to rise and cover the land
bridge. Modern man, *Homo sapiens,* was one of the last Old World
species to come to America before the land link was submerged.
The time? Perhaps fifteen thousand years ago, perhaps two or three
times that long in the past.

The first pioneering bands of early humans were followed by
others, but for many centuries their travels to the south were

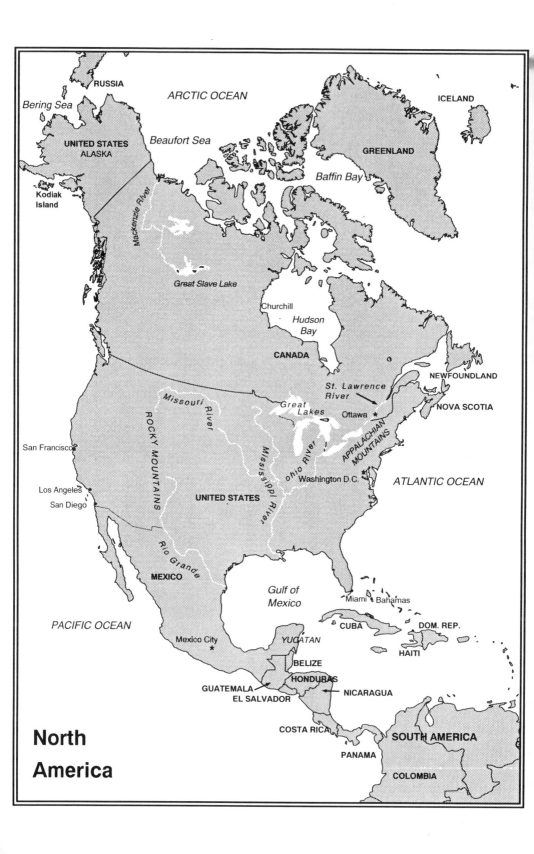

blocked by vast glaciers. As the climate grew warmer, the final melting eventually opened up an ice-free corridor to the rest of North America. Forging southward, humans gradually fanned out across the broad land. After many hundreds of generations they had spread over the entire continent. Some used crude boats to reach the islands of the Caribbean and settle there. Others ventured across the Isthmus of Panama and traveled onward through South America.

The Face of North America

All of these first people lived off the land, foraging for seeds, bulbs, and fruit in the fields and forests, and hunting the animals that lived there too. To the south and east, the primitive hunters found North America, a land of varied and spectacular landscapes. In the East were tree-covered mountains and endless primeval forests— the home of deer, many fur-bearing animals, and lumbering mastodons as well. In the center of the continent the forests gradually gave way to flat, treeless prairies, a kingdom of grass that furnished food for great herds of giant bison and strange prongbucks with four horns. Toward the setting sun, the prairies gave way to high plains and a great chain of craggy, snow-capped mountains that stretched north and south for thousands of miles. In the far Southwest, these early Americans found a parched land, a great American desert with deep, sculptured canyons and towering cliffs of red and yellow rock. South of the desert was a rugged land of mountains, and high plateaus that gradually blended into the lush tropical forests of Central America.

Adapting to all of these contrasting areas, the early Americans separated into many tribes with a multitude of different cultures, languages, and ways of life. Wherever they settled, they hunted the animals they found living around them, killing them for food, for hides, for the bones and horns that they could fashion into tools and weapons.

Early Man, the Hunter

In the Far North they pursued caribou and musk-oxen with Stone Age weapons. They killed seals for their blubber and stalked the great white bear of the Arctic for its flesh and warm fur. Whenever they would find a woolly mammoth trapped in a bog or rocky ravine they would kill it with stones and crude spears. Then the whole tribe would celebrate as they feasted for days on the monster's flesh. Along the coasts the people became fishermen, spearing and netting salmon, and gathering other food from the sea. In the prairies and plains they hunted giant bison and other hoofed animals as well as mastodons and huge ground sloths. They battled cave bears and other Ice Age giants—huge lions, saber-toothed cats, and fierce dire wolves.

Most of these big Ice Age animals had lived in North America for hundreds of thousands of years, but after modern man arrived they all became extinct within several thousand years. The giant lion disappeared about ten thousand years ago; the mastodon, the mammoth, and the dire wolf followed about two thousand years later. During that same brief period of time, a host of other large Ice Age mammals also vanished in North America—giant bison and tapirs, huge armadillos, ground sloths, saber-toothed cats, and many others.

Could early man have had anything to do with their disappearance? Many scientists believe so. "A great wave of extinction hit North America's megafauna, or big animals, as the Pleistocene ended," one writer observed in the book *Our Continent: A Natural History of North America.* "Seventy percent of the genera—including animals a million years on earth—vanished within a few millenia. They had survived the rigors of the Ice Age, to fail with the coming of a continental spring. Though science withholds a verdict, the time and pattern of the great dying coincide with the advance of hunting man."

Early Civilizations in America

After the great dying, the remaining wildlife in North America was much as it is today. The native Americans hunted and used that wildlife as they had hunted and used the larger forms that had vanished. Many centuries and millenia went by, and the various tribes of humans developed ever more sophisticated cultures, customs, and traditions. In the parched Southwest, some of the ancient ones built apartment cliff homes of sun-baked clay in sheltered canyons and tended fields of maize, beans, and melons. By A.D. 1500 the five nations of the Iroquois—the Cayuga, Mohawk, Oneida, Onondaga, and Seneca peoples—were beginning to forge a tightly knit military alliance or confederacy. In Mexico two other groups of early Americans, the Maya and the Aztec, had already achieved highly developed civilizations.

The Maya were the Greeks of the New World, developing advanced civilizations in both the Yucatán peninsula and Guatemala. They practiced an agricultural economy based on corn and other crops, created a calendar, were far advanced in astronomy and mathematics, kept written records in hieroglyphic writings, and developed engineering, architecture, and the arts to a remarkable degree.

As the Romans built upon the Greek civilization, the Aztec built upon the Mayan, and refined their military arts and political structure. Aztec power was at its peak as the fifteenth century drew to a close. It was then that another invader came to America— European man.

Spanish Explorers and Conquerers

The date was October 11, 1492, and Christopher Columbus was on the eve of a momentous discovery. He had sailed from Spain more than two months before to find a westward passage to India and the fabled Spice Islands of the Far East. He never did find a passage to the Indies, but he did stumble upon the island of San Salvador in the Caribbean Sea—the gateway to a whole new world. On this and three subsequent voyages Columbus explored the extent of the Caribbean and initiated the conquest of both North and South America by the nations of Europe.

In the wake of his discoveries, Spanish explorers by the hundreds followed Columbus to the Caribbean. Soon there were Spanish settlements on many of the islands. "We came here for the service of God," one conquistador claimed, "and also to get rich."

Cuba was one of the first islands to be settled and plundered.

Soon the work performed by the enslaved inhabitants proved inadequate to the expectations of the Spaniards, and black slaves were brought in from Africa to do field work and other manual labor. The numerous islands just off the coast of Central America were also raided for more Indian slaves. Exploratory expeditions under Juan Ponce de León and Francisco Hernández de Cordoba left Havana to explore Florida and Yucatán on the North American mainland.

In 1513 the conquistador Vasco Núñez de Balboa crossed the Isthmus of Panama and, from a mountain peak, gazed at the Great South Sea, the Pacific Ocean. He promptly laid claim to it for the greater glory of Spain. By then the Spaniards were well on their way to consolidating their hold over much of the Americas.

Sailing from Cuba in 1519, conquistador Hernán Cortés landed in Mexico with an army of 550 men and sixteen horses and set out to explore and conquer the country. By November 8, 1519, his little group of soldiers had advanced to the outskirts of Tenochtitlán, the imperial city of the Aztecs, in central Mexico. Built on an island in a lake, Tenochtitlán was a city of some 200 thousand people, with wide paved streets, canals and causeways, powerful fortresses, massive pyramids, and other architectural wonders. "It was like the enchantments," historian Bernal Díaz del Castillo, one of the company, wrote, "on account of the great towers and temples and buildings rising from the water . . . things never heard of, nor seen, nor even dreamed."

The Spaniards were greeted by Montezuma, the Aztec ruler. Misunderstandings and mutual distrust blossomed into open hostilities, during which Montezuma was fatally injured. The aroused Indians drove the Spaniards away, inflicting many casualties. But Cortés returned the next year and conquered the city. Soon all of Mexico had fallen to the conquistadors. During the next two decades, Hernando de Soto, Francisco Coronado, and other conquistadors led exploratory expeditions northward from Mexico, as far as Kansas and Arizona. It wasn't long until Spanish outposts and settlements sprang up in what are now Florida, South Carolina, Texas, New Mexico, and California.

France and England Vie for Empire

Further north, other European nations were staking out their own claims to empire. For many years, English and French fishermen had been sailing to the Grand Banks off Newfoundland to harvest the riches of the sea. John Cabot explored the coasts of Newfoundland in 1497, and in 1534 Jacques Cartier, a French explorer, ventured into the St. Lawrence River, the northern gateway to the interior of the continent. Year after year, the French pressed ever more deeply into the northern forests and waterways. By 1603 they had established trading posts in the Great Lakes region and beyond. At the same time, the English were busy exploring the east coast of North America for favorable areas in which to establish settlements, but they were also vying with the French for control of Canada. In 1670 they chartered the Hudson's Bay Company to compete with the French in the northern fur trade.

Further south, the Dutch created New Amsterdam along the Hudson River, and English settlers founded Jamestown, Virginia, and Plymouth Plantation on the shores of Cape Cod. By 1664 the English had also wrested New Amsterdam from the Dutch and renamed it New York. From their coastal settlements they began to move inland, and from Massachusetts to Georgia the wilderness slowly gave way to pioneer settlements.

The French, meanwhile, were aiming to take possession of the center of the continent. Forging southward from the Great Lakes, they discovered and explored the Mississippi River and staked their claim to the lands drained by that river and the Ohio. England claimed the Ohio region as well, and from 1755 to 1763 the two European empires waged a long and bloody war known as the French and Indian Wars, with Canada and the western lands the prize. England was the final winner of that contest. In the Treaty of Paris, which ended the long struggle in 1763, France was forced to surrender Canada to England, and her vast Louisiana Territory—all the western lands drained by the Mississippi and Missouri rivers—to Spain. In 1800, however, Napoleon forced Spain to return Louisiana to France.

Throwing off the Colonial Yoke

Below the St. Lawrence, Britain's thirteen colonies soon tired of Mother England's dominion over them, and declared their independence in 1776. Having gained their freedom after a long and bitter conflict, the colonists faced westward. They scaled the Appalachians and traveled down the Ohio toward the Mississippi River. As they advanced they either purchased the western lands they occupied by signing treaties with the Indians—empty promises which they seldom honored—or took possession of them by force.

In 1803 President Thomas Jefferson negotiated the Louisiana Purchase with France, and in one stroke the young United States gained the vast territory stretching between the Mississippi River and the Rocky Mountains. Soon the lucrative fur trade lured mountain men into the western wilderness, and other hardy adventurers and settlers followed in their wake. The California gold strike of 1848 quickened the rush westward, as thousands of pioneers headed for California and Oregon with dreams of making their fortunes or settling on rich farmlands.

In 1821 Mexico had rebelled against Spanish rule—as the thirteen colonies had rebelled against England in 1776—and won its independence. In turn, Texas settlers, many of them English, declared their independence from Mexican rule in 1836, and gold-seeking fortune hunters declared California an independent republic in 1848. Both Texas and California then joined the United States. When the United States purchased Alaska from Russia in 1867, the main territories of the nation, except for Hawaii, were complete.

With westward expansion at full swing after the California gold rush, the native American tribes were subdued, one by one, and exiled to reservations. At last the exploitation and plunder of all the rich natural resources of the continent could switch into high gear.

"The United States in the 1800s was a nation on the move," conservationist historian James B. Trefethen noted in his book *Crusade for Wildlife*, "a lusty young giant concerned more with the pleasures of the present than with the security of the future.

Blessed with a birthright of natural wealth greater than that of any nation on earth, it seemed bent on squandering its riches in a single massive binge. The American wilderness was not only being tamed; it, almost literally, was being beaten to death."

Something had to give before such pressures. What gave were the forests, the rich prairie soil, the watersheds, the wetlands—and the wildlife. Some species, such as the Carolina parakeet and the passenger pigeon—the latter the most abundant bird species on the continent—became extinct. Others were slaughtered so merci- lessly—for market, for fur, for sport—that they were threatened with extinction. Two of these were the American bison and the griz- zly bear.

BISON
Bison bison

When the first European settlers came to North America, bison, or "buffalo" as the English called them, ranged over a great part of the continent, from the Great Slave Lake wilderness of Canada southward to Mexico, and from Oregon eastward to New York, Pennsylvania, and Georgia. Some zoologists estimate that there were sixty million or more of the humped wild cattle at that time, roaming in vast herds across the plains and prairies.

An imposing animal, a big bull bison may weigh a ton or more, and stand nearly six feet tall at the shoulder hump. His head is bearded, and both head and shoulders are covered with a shaggy mane of hair. Cows are considerably smaller. The reddish brown calves are born in the spring, nine months after the fall mating season. Two races are recognized: the plains bison (*Bison b. bison*) and the slightly larger and darker wood bison (*Bison b. athabascae*), which is found in Canada. The bison that roamed from New York to Georgia in colonial days may have been a third subspecies, now extinct. Very dark in color, it had little or no hump, and its horns flared upward like the horns of Ayrshire cattle. On this hearsay description, Colonel H. W. Shoemaker, a twentieth-century chronicler of Pennsylvania history and folklore, gave the eastern bison the subspecific name *pennsylvanicus.*

The first Europeans to see bison were probably Cortés and his band of conquistadors. After conquering the Aztecs in 1520, they visited the menageries of Montezuma, the Aztec ruler. There, as a chronicler of the conquest recorded, they encountered "the Mexican Bull; a wonderful composition of divers Animals. It has crooked shoulders, with a Bunch on its back like a camel; its Neck covered with hair like a lion. It is cloven footed, its Head armed like that of a Bull, which it resembles in Fierceness, with no less strength and Agility."

Twenty years later, Francisco Coronado and his soldiers explored the lands north of Mexico and saw vast herds of bison, "like fish in the sea," on the Texas plains. For the next three hundred years the great herds of plains bison remained unaffected by European hunters until westward expansion was in full swing after the Civil War.

In the eastern part of the continent, however, pioneer hunters and settlers began killing off the bison at a much earlier date. By 1799 there was just one last herd of about four hundred animals in Pennsylvania. They wintered that year in the Seven Mountain area of Union County. The winter of 1799–1800 was a severe one, and in December the bison came down from the hills to the settlements, desperate for food. As told by Shoemaker, they invaded the barnyard of one pioneer and began to devour a haystack. Panicked by shots from the settlers, the bison stampeded. Crazed with fear, they broke down the door of a log cabin and crowded in, as many as could, crushing and stamping to death a pioneer wife and her children. After this, they retreated to the mountains. The aroused settlers quickly organized a bison hunt and tracked the herd to a hollow near the present town of Weikert. The animals were floundering neck-deep in snowdrifts, and the settlers killed practically all of them. That was almost the end of the Pennsylvania bison. Three were seen and one shot the next year, and a bull was killed a year later. That, as far as anyone knows, was the last bison ever seen in Pennsylvania.

In less settled states, some eastern bison may have survived for a few more years. By 1830, however, bison had disappeared east of the Mississippi River. The great herds still roamed the western prairies and plains, but their time would come, as well.

For centuries the Plains Indians—the Sioux, Cheyenne, Crow, Blackfeet, Comanche, Kiowa, and many other tribes—had hunted bison, but with little effect on their total numbers. The whole way of life of these "buffalo Indians" was based on the comings and goings of the countless hordes of wild cattle. Buffalo meat was eaten raw or cooked. Cut into strips, it was dried in the sun. Mixed with dried berries and fat, it was pounded into pemmican, a nourishing food that could be stored for winter use, or taken along on hunting or war parties, when no campfires were wanted. Tanned buffalo hides were used to make leggings and other clothing, as well as summer coverings for beds. Scraped hides were stitched together to make coverings for tepees. The thick woolly robes were used as winter blankets. Rawhide was useful for making storage boxes and cooking pots, as well as rope. Spoons and ladles were fashioned from the horns, and tools from the bones. Nothing was wasted. The Plains Indians could not have lived as they did without the seemingly inexhaustible herds of bison.

In his book *The American Bison,* Martin Garretson retells an ancient native American legend in which the Great Spirit descended to the Kiowas, saying: "Here are the buffalo. They shall be your food and raiment, but in the day you shall see them perish from off the face of the Earth, then know that the end of the Kiowa is near—and the sun set."

Before the Plains Indians had horses, they hunted buffalo on foot, and killed them with spears and arrows. Hunters often draped themselves in animal skins and crept close to a herd undetected. Sometimes a whole herd was surrounded and stampeded over a cliff. Once the Indians gained the horse, starting with strays that had escaped from the conquistadors, they could gallop right into the midst of a herd of buffalo and shoot them with ease.

The Indians continued their traditional buffalo hunts through the first half of the nineteenth century with little thought to the few white men who were beginning to trickle west of the Mississippi to trap beaver or explore the unknown lands stretching to the Pacific. But the discovery of gold in California in 1848 swelled the trickle of western pioneers and adventurers to a torrent. After the Civil War, the invasion of the West increased, and the immigrants set out to tame and conquer the land, including all the buffalo and the Indians that were there.

Railroads began to advance westward through buffalo and Indian country in the 1870s, bringing professional hide hunters who fanned out across the plains and began to slaughter buffalo by the hundreds of thousands. Stripping off the hides, which sold for $1.25 apiece, and cutting out the tongue, which might sell for a quarter, the hunters would leave the rest of the carcass to rot, or be eaten by wolves, coyotes, and vultures. Many hunters were hired by the railroads to kill buffalo to supply the railroad workers with meat. "Buffalo Bill" Cody got his start that way. Working for the Kansas Pacific Railroad, he killed 4,120 buffalo in a little over a year as food for the construction crews. Passenger trains brought crowds of "sportsmen" to the western plains, too. Swarming out of the cars, they shot and killed buffalo indiscriminately, just for the fun of it.

Under ruthless attack on every side, the great herds on the southern plains were killed off by the 1870s. Then the hide hunters concentrated on the northern herds in the Dakotas and Yellowstone region. In their wake came bone collectors, gathering the bleaching bones and shipping them east by the trainload to be ground up for fertilizer.

The Indians naturally resented the invasion of their lands in violation of many solemn treaties and the slaughter of the buffalo, their staff of life. Desperately trying to stem the tide, they fought a series of bloody battles with U.S. Army troops that had been sent west to subdue the Indians and protect the invading hunters and fortune-seekers. In 1876 the Sioux leaders Sitting Bull and Crazy Horse united the northern tribes to annihilate General George Custer and most of his command in the famous battle of the Little Bighorn in Wyoming. It was a hollow victory, however, for within a year most of the scattered tribes were subdued and herded onto reservations. At last the hide hunters and settlers were free to kill off the remaining bison as quickly as they could.

"Every buffalo dead is an Indian gone," Major General Phil Sheridan, famous Union cavalry leader during the Civil War, and equally famous Indian fighter after the war, had declared in 1869. How prophetic that statement proved to be!

In 1883 the last big herd of bison, some seventy-five thousand strong, was annihilated by professional hunters in the Yellowstone area. After that, only scattered remnants of the once-great herds remained to be killed. By 1890 only several hundred wild bison survived in the United States, and the powerless Indians danced their ghost dances on the reservations and prayed in vain to the Great Spirit to bring back the buffalo.

By 1894 only twenty or twenty-one bison remained in the Yellowstone area—the last wild bison in the country, except for an equally small band in Lost Park, Colorado. It was only then that Congress finally passed a law making it illegal to kill bison in Yellowstone National Park. By 1897 the Colorado bison had all been killed, and the species' fortunes in North America had reached their lowest ebb.

Several hundred bison survived in small private herds, however, fenced in and protected by conservation-minded ranchers. There were several hundred wood bison still living in the Great Slave Lake area of Canada, as well. By now the public was aroused to help protect the remaining animals, and in 1906 the American Bison Society was founded, with the stated purpose of saving them. William Temple Hornaday, a former hunter turned wildlife conservationist, and the director of the New York Zoological Park (Bronx Zoo), which had forty bison in its zoological collections, was its president. In 1907 fifteen of these zoo animals were sent to the newly created Wichita Forest and Game Reserve in Oklahoma as a nucleus herd. The next year the Society arranged for thirty-four animals to be sent to the National Bison Range in western Montana. During the next few years, other herds were started at Wind Cave National Park in South Dakota and several other government reserves.

Canada did its part for the preservation of buffalo, too. In 1906 it purchased a privately owned Montana herd and took the animals to Wainright, Alberta, where they flourished under protection. By the 1920s, the herd numbered eight thousand or more. Between 1925 and 1928 about six thousand of these were transported to a wilderness area south of Great Slave Lake and released there. By this time the wood bison herd had increased to about two thousand and the government had officially designated their range as Wood Buffalo National Park. The transplanted Plains buffalo interbred with the wood buffalo, and by the 1940s the pure strain of wood bison was considered extinct. In 1957, however, a band of about two hundred pure wood bison was found near the northern border of the park, and some of these were transported to a new area known as the Mackenzie Bison Sanctuary, north of Great Slave Lake. They have fared well there, and now number more than two thousand.

At the present time an estimated 200 thousand bison roam national parks, wildlife ranges, and Indian reservations in Canada and the United States, and hundreds of ranches and other private reserves as well. Bison are flourishing so well that some are killed and sold for meat every year to keep their numbers in proportion to the available range. Many people argue that bison should also be reintroduced into many national forests and other public lands.

During the first half of this century Yellowstone National Park Service rangers limited the park herd of bison to about five hundred animals—a manageable number for the park's size—by sale and slaughter. In the 1960s the policy was changed to one of letting nature take its course. As a result, the herd grew bigger and bigger (in 1996 it was about four thousand animals), and some bison began roaming outside the park boundaries to find better pasture during winter. Cattlemen objected, for they feared that the bison might infect their cattle with brucellosis, a disease that affects cattle, bison, elk, and other hoofed stock and can infect humans with undulant fever. During the 1980s the Montana ranchers and the state government had spent nearly $30 million getting their state certified brucellosis-free. Understandably, they wanted no threat of having their cattle infected by wandering bison. The state therefore initiated a policy of shooting any found outside the park. During the winter of 1996–97 game wardens had shot more than 700 bison by January and were gunning for more. All in all, several thousand have been killed in recent years.

As might be expected, there is vigorous disagreement about the value of the program. Some experts say the threat of brucellosis infection is virtually nonexistent. "There's never been a proven case of bison transmitting brucellosis to cattle in the wild," asserts Marsha Karle, a park official. But "the park's bison should be managed so they remain compatible with the habitat inside Yellowstone," declares Ron Aasheim, a spokesman for the Montana Department of Fish, Wildlife, and Parks, the state agency responsible for bison control.

Meanwhile, animal rights activists and organizations have raised a protest at the killing of the bison, and the state finally asked a federal court to intervene and rule on the conflicting policies of the National Park Service and the U.S. Department of Agriculture, which issues brucellosis eradication directives. In early 1997 no agreement had been reached. The killing continued.

Bison will never roam the western plains and prairies in unnumbered millions, as they once did. But thanks to protective measures taken in the nick of time, their survival is assured.

GRIZZLIES AND ALASKAN BROWN BEARS
Ursus arctos subspecies

Brown bears evolved millions of years ago in Asia. Spreading to Europe, they gave rise to the huge cave bear of the Ice Age and the European brown bear. Some of these Old World bears migrated to North America during the Ice Age and spread through much of the continent. Today most mammalogists consider all American and Eurasian present-day brown bears—including Alaskan brown bears and grizzlies—as one species, *Ursos arctos*, with a number of subspecies.

Alaskan Brown Bear

When Europeans first arrived in North America, the big brown bears ranged over most of the western part of the continent, from Alaska to northern Mexico, and as far east as the Dakotas and Minnesota. In those days there may have been as many as fifty to one hundred thousand grizzlies in the American West. Today there are fewer than one thousand of them south of the Canadian border.

A formidable wilderness monarch, an adult grizzly weighs anywhere from 500 to 1,000 pounds or more. It has fearsome teeth and claws and an unpredictable temper. The shaggy fur varies in color from pale yellow to almost black, and frequently has a grizzly frosting, giving rise to the bear's nickname, "Silvertip." When Lewis and Clark made their epochal expedition to explore the region drained by the Missouri River and find a route to the Pacific Ocean, they had many exciting confrontations with grizzly bears. In his journal, Meriwether Lewis recorded that "the wonderful power of life which these animals possess renders them dreadful . . . we had rather encounter two Indians than meet a single brown bear."

During the next half-century, gold-seekers, farmers, and intrepid travelers of every kind flocked westward in ever-increasing numbers. These hardy pioneers did not want dangerous animals such as grizzly bears around their settlements, and waged relentless warfare on them. Countless bears were killed during the California Gold Rush. Forty-niners found the grizzly's flesh good eating, and its tanned hide and fur good bedding.

In the old Southwest, groups of Spanish cowboys, or *vaqueros*, with an urge to live dangerously, sometimes lassoed grizzlies and captured them alive. With ropes secured around each of its legs, the bear was spread-eagled and immobilized. Then it was trussed up and carried triumphantly to town, where it was often chained to a stout post in an arena and subjected to the cruel sport of bear baiting—a contest to the death with a long-horned fighting bull.

Grizzly Adams, a Massachusetts shoemaker who went west at the time of the Gold Rush and set up a hunting camp in the Sierra Nevada of California, had many exciting adventures with grizzlies. A fearless hunter, he killed many, but what's more interesting, he captured and tamed several young cubs. As his first cub, Lady Washington, grew up, he taught her to carry packs on her back and accompany him on hunting trips. Another pet, Ben Franklin, he affectionately called "the flower of his race, my firmest friend, the boon companion of my after-years." Ben Franklin once helped to save Adams's life by tackling a wild grizzly that had attacked his master.

As cattle and sheep began to populate the west, some grizzlies turned to killing livestock. One of these renegade bears was Old Mose, a Colorado grizzly that terrorized a wide range of mountain country for nearly thirty-five years. Two missing toes identified Old Mose, and during his long reign of destruction he was accused of killing at least eight hundred head of cattle, many horses and sheep, and five men. He eluded hunter after hunter out to collect the $1,000 bounty on his head until 1904, when one hunter with his dogs finally cornered Old Mose and pumped eight bullets into him.

Hated and feared by ranchers and other settlers, grizzlies continued to be hunted relentlessly during the last half of the nineteenth century and the first half of the twentieth. Their numbers steadily dwindled everywhere throughout their range. California, which features the grizzly on its state flag and seal, recorded its last grizzly kill in 1922, and the last sighting of one, in Sequoia National Park, two years later. Arizona and New Mexico saw their last grizzlies about the same time. In Colorado, grizzlies vanished in the early 1950s.

By the late 1950s the Mexican grizzly (*Ursus a. nelsoni*), a smaller, light-colored race, had also been exterminated, except for a small population of perhaps thirty or forty that survived in the Sierra del Nido, some 50 miles north of the city of Chihuahua. The Mexican government placed these on its list of protected species in 1959, but in remote regions the legal safeguards were unenforceable. In 1961 a rancher commenced unrestricted warfare on the bears, claiming that he had lost cattle to them. When Dr. Karl Koford, a zoologist with the University of California in Berkeley, went to the area in 1968, he found no evidence of any grizzlies surviving there since 1962. More recent investigations indicate that the Mexican grizzly is indeed extinct.

By mid-century grizzlies were gone nearly everywhere south of the Canadian border. Since then, logging, clearing of land for agriculture, and other habitat destruction have reduced suitable grizzly territory in the lower forty-eight states to about one percent of what it once had been. The few grizzlies that are left are making their last stand in the wild country around Yellowstone and Glacier National Parks. Today there may be three hundred grizzlies in and around Yellowstone, and as many as five hundred to seven hundred in the Glacier National Park ecosystem and northwest Montana. For some years Montana has permitted fourteen grizzlies to be killed yearly, from all causes. Between 1981 and 1991 eighty bears were legally shot in the state.

Although considered extinct in Colorado since the early 1950s, a grizzly was killed in the San Juan Mountains in the southwest corner of the state in 1979. In the years since, there have been reports of grizzly tracks in the region and several unverified sightings, indicating the possibility that a few Colorado grizzlies may still survive.

Grizzlies once roamed the Selway-Bitterroot wilderness system—the nation's largest roadless area south of Alaska, on the Montana-Idaho border—but disappeared there about fifty years ago. At the present time the Fish and Wildlife Service is making plans to reintroduce the species into the region by translocating five or six Canadian grizzlies annually for five years.

In Canada and Alaska, grizzlies and big brown bears still have very healthy populations. Best estimates indicate eleven thousand to eighteen thousand of them in Canada, and eight thousand to ten thousand in Alaska. These northern lands still have large wilderness areas, and that is what grizzlies and big brown bears need above all. In some of British Columbia's and Alaska's wild country, however, bear habitat is being threatened by logging operations and other development. The same cycle of human activity that destroyed much grizzly habitat in the lower forty-eight states is being repeated in these northern areas which boast the continent's largest bear populations. Grizzly habitat in British Columbia is being destroyed by "clear-cut slaughter," Peter McAllister, the founder of Victoria's Raincoast Conservation Society, has declared. "The number of bears appears to be plunging."

The big brown bears of coastal Alaska and its islands look very much like inland grizzlies, but are even larger. Record specimens have weighed as much as 1,600 pounds. They seem to be in no serious present danger, although vast lumbering operations there, as in British Columbia, threaten some of their wilderness range.

The Kodiak bear (*Ursus a. middendorffi*) is the biggest of all the big Alaskan brownies. Kodiak Island National Wildlife Refuge, 1.8 million acres of wilderness domain on Kodiak and Afognak islands when originally established in 1941, provides more than 90 percent of the giant predator's habitat. Some fifteen hundred bears roam the refuge, and each year hunters have been permitted to shoot an allotted number to keep the population in balance with the suitable habitat.

The Alaska Native Claims Settlement Act passed by Congress in 1971 gave native corporations the right to select and own some 320,000 acres in some of the refuge's prime wildlife habitat. Many of these inholdings have been threatened with development or sale to private investors, because the native corporations or individuals who own the land cannot afford to pay property taxes. In 1992 the World Wildlife Fund, together with various Alaskan native organizations and several environmental organizations, started an active program of helping native owners of inholdings to solve their financial difficulties and preserve the bear habitat in its undeveloped state.

The U.S. Department of the Interior has been working on the same problem as well. In May 1995, Secretary of the Interior Bruce Babbitt signed an agreement with two native corporations that will preserve 150,000 acres of native holdings in the Kodiak Island refuge from development. Six months later he signed a second agreement with another Alaska native regional corporation, adding an additional 60,000 acres to be preserved. More than 80 percent of native parcels on Kodiak have now been protected from damaging development.

POLAR BEAR
Ursus maritimus

Known to some of the Eskimos who hunt it as "Nanook," the great white bear of the polar regions is the biggest land meat-eater in the Arctic. Adult female bears usually weigh no more than 650 pounds, but males average 900 or 1,000 pounds. One record-breaking specimen weighed slightly more than 1,700 pounds. The bear's coat is white, sometimes with a faint yellowish cast in summer.

Nanook's head seems small for the massive body, and looks rather weasel-like. The nose is long and straight, the ears small, and the sharp eyes a glistening black. The shaggy fur is underlaid with a protective layer of fat, which keeps the bear warm in below-zero temperatures. The broad feet have thick pads with fur between them, which give a nonslip grip as it moves over the ice.

The polar bear ranges across the polar seas all around the globe, and the Norwegians call it *isbjorn*, or "ice bear," for it is usually found on the arctic ice pack or close to it. Not a marine mammal in the strictest sense, it is often considered one because it inhabits a marine environment for most of its life and gets practically all of its food from the sea. It usually comes ashore only during the brief arctic summer or when it dens up to give birth to cubs.

For most of the year the polar bear dines on seals. Sometimes an infant walrus is taken if the bear can snatch it without rousing the mother walrus. Keen eyesight and smell help the bear in its hunt. So does its white coat, which serves to conceal the meat-eater as it stalks its prey across the ice.

In summer, when the ice floes break up, the bear may head for land for several months, during which time it eats berries, grasses, eggs, and whatever other food it finds.

Late winter and early spring, from February to April, is mating time for polar bears. The pregnant female then has all summer to eat and gain weight and store up a thick layer of fat to help sustain her during the winter to come. In the fall, the prospective mother heads for land. There she digs out a den for herself on a snowy slope before the arrival of the long cold season. A roomy shelter, the den usually has a passageway of six feet or more that leads to either one or two large chambers. The entrance, often facing south, is usually a sheltered spot under a bank of earth or a ledge of rock. Covered with several feet of snow and ice, this bear-fashioned igloo has a small air hole in the roof. Temperatures inside the den are many degrees warmer than the arctic temperatures outside. The young are born in December or January. By late March or early April they are well furred out and weigh about 15 pounds apiece. Now they are ready to emerge from the den with their mother and explore the springtime landscape.

In former days, the killing of a polar bear was a great feat for the natives of the Far North. Accompanied only by his sled dogs, and armed with just a knife and spear, the Eskimo hunter some-times trailed the bear for several days. When the encounter came, either the bear or the man was usually slain. If the hunter was successful, the bear's fur was made into a warm robe and the meat was eaten by both the Eskimo's family and his dogs.

In the late seventeenth century, Western explorers and whal-ing men began to venture into the Arctic. There they encountered the ice bear and began to hunt it with more effective and powerful weapons than those of the Eskimos. The invasion of the Arctic was intensified during the eighteenth and nineteenth centuries, and the polar bear kill increased in proportion, along with the kill of other animals of the Far North.

In the twentieth century, polar bears became popular big game trophies. After World War II, American "sportsmen" often hunted the bears by searching for them in light planes—sometimes with two planes flying as a team—that easily tracked the big animals down in the snowy wastes. Landing near the quarry, trophy hunters stepped out of the plane, took aim, and shot the bear. Each year some two hundred to four hundred bears were killed in Alaska in this way.

The five nations that have populations of polar bears in their Arctic territories are the United States, Canada, Denmark (in Greenland), Norway, and Russia. The first nation to take decisive action to conserve the species was the Soviet Union, which gave complete protection to it in 1956. Several years later the USSR designated Wrangle Island, which faces Alaska's northwest coast across the Chukchi Sea and is an important denning area for preg-nant females, a polar bear preserve.

In the early 1960s, the hunting of polar bears in Alaska was regulated by the state, not by the federal government. Disturbed by the polar bear kill there, Senator Bob Bartlett of Alaska organized and convened an international polar bear conference at Fairbanks in 1965. Experts from all five countries that had polar bear popula-tions within their borders met there to pool their knowledge and exchange views. A second conference was held in Switzerland in 1968, sponsored this time by the International Union for the Con-servation of Nature and Natural Resources (IUCN). At this conference a polar bear specialist group was formed. It meets periodically and keeps a close watch on what is happening to polar bears throughout the Arctic.

Norway stopped the hunting of polar bears in its territories in 1971, and in 1973 placed a five-year moratorium on all killing of the species. Denmark permitted only Inuits or permanent residents using traditional methods to kill polar bears in Greenland. Canada barred most hunting after 1968, but still allowed certain coastal Indians and Inuits to hunt the bears under a quota system.

Management of the polar bears in Alaska was returned to the federal government by provisions of the Marine Mammal Protection Act in 1972. The hunting of the bears by planes was prohibited, and the U. S. Fish and Wildlife Service has limited the kill to coastal native hunters. "The greatest threat to these bears," observes the Fish and Wildlife Service, "is posed by oil and gas exploration, drilling and extraction on the North Slope of Alaska." Oil spills and human activities near denning areas are also cited as distinct threats.

In 1973, at another international polar bear conference held in Oslo, Norway, the five nations concerned finally negotiated a detailed agreement on the conservation of polar bears that became formally effective in May 1976. Regulated and limited hunts by native peoples are still permitted, but among other matters the agreement generally prohibits any other hunting of polar bears except for bona fide scientific or conservation purposes, and bans all hunting with aircraft or large motorized vehicles. All the nations agreed to continue research on the polar bear and the practices that threaten its well-being.

Churchill, Manitoba, a small town on the southwest coast of Hudson Bay, has dubbed itself "the polar bear capital of the world"—and with good reason. Every summer, polar bears— mostly males and young bears—leave the melting ice packs in Hudson Bay in July and come ashore, then travel northward by land. They usually reach the vicinity of Churchill between mid-October and early November, where they are joined by females and their cubs who have spent the previous winter in denning sites on the western shores of Hudson Bay. For a few exciting and exhilarating weeks the citizens of Churchill welcome the coming of the bears and advise the flocks of tourists to exercise caution and common sense. By November most of the bears have moved out onto the freezing ice packs and headed northward on their own annual tour.

Today, estimates of the world population of polar bears range from twenty to forty thousand, and the species seems to be thriving under international surveillance. With the international cooperation and research that have been undertaken, there is every reason to believe that the survival of the polar bear has been assured.

The Status of Other North American Giants

That other American bear, the black bear (*Ursus americanus*), ranges across suitable territory from Alaska to northern Mexico. Its population, estimated at 450,000, is more than the populations of all other species of bears throughout the world, combined. Like all of its relatives, the black bear is hunted and killed illegally for its gall bladder, which is highly prized in oriental medicines.

America's largest cat, the mountain lion, or cougar, once ranged over most of North America, from northwestern Canada to the Isthmus of Panama, and from ocean to ocean. Relentlessly hunted as a livestock killer, it had largely disappeared from eastern North America by 1900. By 1950, with a bounty on its head, it was fast disappearing in the West as well. Today, protected in most states, or regarded as a game animal, it has repopulated most of its former range. An estimated sixteen thousand of the big cats now roam the American West. On the other side of the continent, the Florida race of mountain lion barely survives, with an estimated population of perhaps forty animals. The eastern race has been considered extinct for most of the past century. In recent years, however, there have been many sightings and reports of tracks, indicating that it almost certainly survives in wild areas of New England, the Adirondacks, and the Appalachian Mountains.

The moose, largest of the deer family, ranges across Alaska and most of Canada, southward through the Rocky Mountain states and northern New England in flourishing populations. The Alaska moose is the giant of all the world's deer.

The next largest American deer is the elk, or wapiti. The eastern elk was killed off more than a century ago, and by 1900 the only sizeable elk herds remaining in North America were in Wyoming and Montana—the Rocky Mountain race. These herds increased under protection, and through the years many were trapped and translocated to other areas. Today, nearly a million elk roam the American West.

Barren Ground Caribou

Barren Ground caribou still wander across the tundra of northern Canada and Alaska in herds totalling hundreds of thousands, but the numbers of the more southern woodland caribou have shrunk drastically in recent years. They once ranged through forest regions of Canada and a number of northern states, from Maine to Washington. During the past century, however, they have disappeared entirely from many areas. At the present time the only woodland caribou in the United States are a tiny band that wanders back and forth from Canada to the Selkirk Mountains of northern Idaho.

Some nineteen million white-tailed, mule, and black-tailed deer roam the United States these days, perhaps more than in pioneer times. Hunters regularly harvest two million or more of them every year. In many areas deer are so plentiful that they are considered pests.

The pronghorn antelope is the only surviving member of a unique family of hoofed animals—the Antilocapridae—which evolved in North America. Its original population probably numbered many millions. Hunted and killed as the buffalo was during the nineteenth century, its population had dropped to only twenty thousand or so by the early years of the twentieth century. Protected at last, its numbers increased. Today about a million pronghorns roam through western North America, nearly half of them in Wyoming and Montana. Hunters harvest fifty thousand or more of them yearly in these states. The only endangered race is the Sonora pronghorn. About five hundred of them live in the Sonoran deserts of southern Arizona, New Mexico, and northern Mexico.

America's largest birds—the trumpeter swan, whooping crane, California condor, and the bald and golden eagles—have had varying fortunes through the years. After centuries of persecution and destruction of their nesting and wintering habitats, the first three had almost disappeared by the 1940s.

The trumpeter swan, which once ranged over most of interior North America, is the world's largest waterfowl. It has recovered most encouragingly under management and protection. By the 1970s, its continental population was five thousand or more, and increasing.

The whooping crane, our largest wading bird, had sunk to its lowest point in 1942 when only fifteen birds survived. In 1945 the U.S. Fish and Wildlife Service, the Canadian Wildlife Service, and the National Audubon Society organized an all-out research program to try to save the species. In 1954 previously unknown nesting grounds in Wood Buffalo National Park were discovered; and in 1967 eggs were removed from nests (the whoopers would lay others in their place) and placed in incubators at Patuxent Wildlife Research Center in Laurel, Maryland. A captive flock was established. Several of these captive birds mated and laid eggs. A second generation of captive young was raised—some the product of artificial insemination. In recent years several new flocks of whooping cranes have been established in the wild, the last a group released in 1993 in protected prairie habitat in south-central Florida. At the present time the population has increased to more than two hundred and fifty whooping cranes, in both wild and captive flocks.

The California condor has gone through a similar intensive and all-out effort to keep it from becoming extinct. Only about sixty of these giant birds survived in the 1960s, in mountainous areas of Los Padres National Forest, some 70 miles northeast of Los Angeles. By 1984 their numbers had dwindled to fifteen wild birds, plus several in captivity. A last-ditch effort to save the species from extinction led to the capture of all the remaining wild birds. A captive breeding program proved so successful that by 1992 the condor population had increased to sixty-four. By 1996, twenty-seven captive birds, after being conditioned for life in the wild, had been released in California. In late fall of that year, the total condor population had increased to 104 birds in captivity and seventeen in the wild, and biologists announced plans to release some of the captive-bred birds in the Vermillion Cliffs area just north of the Grand Canyon in Arizona. The goal is to establish a self-sustaining population of at least 150 birds in this area.

The two next largest North American birds of prey, the bald and golden eagles, have always been the target of trigger-happy "sportsmen" who consider all birds of prey as trash or "varmints." Indeed, the territorial government of Alaska paid bounties on about 128,000 bald eagles killed there from 1917 to 1952.

Hunting is just one of the dangers that have plagued eagles. Another is the way human beings have changed the land, not only with ax and saw and bulldozers but also with pesticides and poisons. The bald eagle population in the lower forty-eight states took a precipitous plunge after World War II, when DDT was used extensively as a pesticide. DDT proved deadly to the reproductive success of fish-eating birds, such as pelicans and bald eagles. By 1968 only 2,772 eagles were counted south of Canada, and breeding pairs had disappeared in many states. The next year the use of DDT was restricted in the United States, and banned completely three years later. A long, slow period of recovery began, aided by a program of transferring fertile eggs from the nests of eagles still successfully breeding in Wisconsin and other states to nests of eagles

Bald Eagle

that were breeding without any success in a number of eastern states. As a result, the winter census of bald eagles in the lower forty-eight states had risen to 13,574 birds in 1991. Besides these, an estimated 15,000 pairs of bald eagles live in Alaska. There are many in Canada as well.

The golden eagle, condemned by ranchers as a lamb-killer, was shot and killed by the thousands in the Southwest for many years. By 1960 its U.S. population had dwindled to no more than 10,000—perhaps as low as 3,000. Conservationists persuaded Congress to protect the species in 1962. Today, its population is estimated at between 100,000 and 200,000, and relatively stable.

The alligator, North America's largest reptile, originally ranged from North Carolina to eastern Texas. By the 1960s it had disappeared from great portions of this range, principally because of unremitting persecution for its hide. In one ten-year period, from 1929 through 1938, records show that 1.47 million alligator skins were taken in Florida alone. The southern states eventually awakened to the fact that the species was fast disappearing. Florida outlawed all alligator hunting, and in 1961 most of the southern states quickly followed suit. After the federal government declared the alligator an endangered species in 1967, fully protected everywhere, alligator populations began to increase. By the 1990s populations had recovered completely, and the alligator was no longer endangered. Several states once again permit limited and strictly regulated alligator hunts.

The North American crocodile has always been a much rarer animal. In the United States it survives only in southern Florida and the Keys, with a population of perhaps three hundred to five hundred. Other remnant populations can be found on several Caribbean islands, on the Gulf coast of Mexico as far south as Colombia, and along the Pacific coast to Ecuador. The species is endangered not only in the United States but throughout its entire range.

Today most North American countries prize their native wildlife and are working actively to protect and preserve it. In the United States, the Endangered Species Act of 1973 protects all our endangered and threatened wildlife. Many individuals, as well as industrial and commercial organizations, attack the Act as too restrictive—a law that critics claim costs American jobs. Up for renewal every four years, the Endangered Species Act is in serious danger of being weakened or gutted by these critics.

*. . . what we may rightly call a New World . . . a
continent more densely peopled and abounding in animals than our Europe or Asia or Africa.*

Amerigo Vespucci

9

SOUTH AMERICA
Land of Contrasts

The great southern continent, South America, is a land of startling geographical contrasts and an extraordinarily diverse
fauna. More than 80 percent of South America's native mammals
are species found nowhere else. About 36 percent of all the known
species of birds in the entire world—3,500 of 9,670 species—are
native to the lands from central Mexico to Tierra del Fuego. As for
reptiles and amphibians, South America boasts the largest snakes
in the world, seven different kinds of crocodilians, many large lizards, and many brightly colored frogs. South America also has more
kinds of fish—some 2,500 species—and known species of insects
than any other continent.

This extraordinary biodiversity is the result of a couple of vital
prehistorical and geographical happenstances: first, for many millions of years South America was isolated, separated from North
America, allowing its unique wildlife to evolve and multiply without
competition from more advanced species from North America; and

ISTHMUS OF
PANAMA

VENEZUELA

GUYANA

SURINAM

FRENCH
GUIANA

Orinoco River

COLOMBIA

Magdalena River

★ Quito

ECUADOR

Rio Napo

Rio Negro

Amazon River

PERU

ANDES MOUNTAINS

Rio Madeira

BRAZIL

Lake Titicaca

BOLIVIA

MATO GROSSO

GRAN CHACO

PARAGUAY

Rio de Janeiro

PACIFIC
OCEAN

CHILE

ARGENTINA

★ Santiago

Buenos Aires

URUGUAY

Rio de la Plata

ANDES MOUNTAINS

PATAGONIA

ATLANTIC OCEAN

Falkland Islands

Strait of
Magellan

TIERRA DEL FUEGO

South
America

second, the continent provides a great diversity of ecosystems for its plants and animals. One of the most important of these was the luxurious greenbelt of rain forests that cover most of the northern half of the continent.

"The rain forests were and are of crucial importance as reservoirs of diversity," zoologist Edward O. Wilson declared in his autobiography, *Naturalist* (1994). "They teem with the greatest variety of all the world's ecosystems."

Rain Forests of the Amazon

The lands drained by the Amazon River include the largest expanse of tropical rain forest in the world—vast areas of dense jungle that sometimes extend unbroken for hundreds of miles. They stretch from the Atlantic Ocean to the slopes of the Andes and encompass most of the northern half of South America. The Amazon itself—more than 3,000 miles long, fed by over 1,000 tributaries—is one of the world's mightiest rivers. Its mouth is 150 miles wide and 200 feet deep. For most of its length it is at least 5 miles wide. Until recent years, human beings settled only along the banks of the great river and its tributaries, except for bands of Stone Age Indians who lived in the unknown interior. Sixty or more inches of rain fall yearly in the Amazon basin, and during the rainy season, from November to May, much of the region is flooded.

The rain forest of the Amazon is made up of a succession of different layers, from the tea-colored waters of the rivers and swamps to the ever-shaded lower trees and underbrush, the intermittently lighted middle level of vegetation, and finally the sun-drenched crowns of the forest giants that tower as high as 200 or more feet into the sky.

Blue morpho butterflies sail above the evergreen crowns of the trees while brightly colored parrots, macaws, toucans, and other birds, together with troops of monkeys, inhabit the middle layers of the forest. Below them lives a host of other animals. Slow-moving sloths cling to the branches of cecropia trees, and nimble marmosets leap from branch to branch. Here also are prehensile-tailed anteaters, porcupines, and opossums. Beneath them, in the shaded areas of the forest floor, roam jaguars and tapirs, deer, and many smaller animals. At every level of the jungle there are insects.

Mountains and Deserts

West of the Amazon rain forests rises the longest chain of mountains in the world, the Andes. They stretch from Panama and Venezuela southward 4,500 miles to the Strait of Magellan, forming a rugged, snowcapped continental spine that looks over the Pacific coast of the continent. Included in that spine are forty-two peaks higher than Mount McKinley, the highest mountain in North America.

The Andes Cordillera (*cordel* is the Spanish word for rope) forms a high barrier between various extremes of climate and vegetation, varying from the dry coastal deserts of Peru and Chile to the humid cloud forests that drain into the steamy jungles of the Amazon Basin. In Bolivia, two spurs of the range enclose a large stretch of high plateau.

The coasts of Colombia and Equador are humid tropical lowlands, but the coasts of Peru and northern Chile are hugged by windswept deserts. Farther south are coastal forested areas that merge into a sparkling land of lakes and fjords that reach toward Patagonia.

The coastal deserts of Chile and Peru are the result of the cold Humboldt current that sweeps northward from the Antarctic. The current is a great oceanic river that stirs up rich minerals from the depths of the Pacific. The cold waters swarm with plankton that provide abundant food for many kinds of fish and seabirds.

South of the Amazon rain forests, the jungle gives way to a transitional zone, the Gran Chaco, a mixture of dry subtropical forest, open areas, and swamps. These lands in turn change into the fertile and almost treeless pampas, the vast grasslands of South America. Stretching southward from the pampas to the Strait of Magellan are the barren and windswept plateaus of Patagonia. The southernmost tip of the continent is Tierra del Fuego, which means "land of fire." It is so-named because of the warning signals that Indians lighted on the beaches in 1520 when Magellan and his companions sailed through the Strait on their way to the Pacific, the Great South Sea.

The Evolution of South American Wildlife

Much of the wildlife of the great southern continent is strikingly different from the wildlife found in North America. Many species can be found on both continents, but a number of others are unlike animals found anywhere else in the world, as young Charles Darwin, naturalist on board the HMS *Beagle*, observed in 1833, when on a collecting trip along the Argentine coast at Punta Alta. On one small area of the beach he found a rich vein of natural wonders, including the fossil remains of many giant prehistoric mammals. Among them were the bones of an extinct horse, several different kinds of giant ground sloths, the remains of a huge animal with an armored covering like an armadillo, as well as "a huge beast with a long neck like a camel." He also found the bones of a giant hoofed animal, *Toxodon*, "perhaps one of the strangest animals ever discovered: in size it equalled an elephant."

After reflecting upon his finds, Darwin reasoned that these strange prehistoric beasts must have developed in relative isolation: the isthmus connecting North and South America must have once been submerged.

Darwin's reasoning was correct. Before the isthmus was submerged, however, South America and North America had been connected, and during that ancient period various primitive marsupials, or pouched mammals, and some early placental mammals, that nourished their young internally, spread into the southern continent. Then, more than seventy million years ago, during the dawn of the Age of Mammals, South America was cut off from North America. Freed from having to compete with the more advanced placental mammals that developed in the northern hemisphere, these primitive South American mammals flourished and multiplied.

The marsupials evolved into many strange forms, just as they did in Australia, which had become isolated from Asia at an even earlier date. There were opossumlike marsupials, rodentlike marsupials, and carnivorous marsupials. Some of the latter resembled weasels; others looked like hyenas. One had long stabbing canine teeth, like those of the placental saber-toothed tiger that flourished in North America during the Ice Age.

South America's primitive placental mammals branched out in equally strange ways during the many millions of years of isolation. The great southern continent gave rise to the first primitive edentates, an order of toothless mammals. These were the ancestors of our present-day sloths, anteaters, and armadillos. Ancient herbivores of many sizes and shapes roamed the grasslands and forests, and huge, meat-eating flightless birds pursued their prey across the southern plains.

Several new groups of mammals—monkeys and certain rodents among them—succeeded in reaching South America at various times during the long period of isolation. Probably they arrived by making their way from island to island as helpless passengers on logs or other floating debris.

Two or three million years ago, before the beginning of the Pleistocene, or Ice Age, South America gradually became reconnected with North America as the present Central American land corridor became established. Once this connection was made, some of the greatest animal migrations in earth's history took place.

Animal Migrations between North and South America

Early camels—ancestors of South America's vicuña, guanaco, llama, and alpaca—spread southward from the northern continent. Tapirs, peccaries, and the ancestors of our familiar white-tailed deer took the same route south. Bears had invaded North America from their original Eurasian homeland, and one kind made its way to South America, where its descendants survive today. Horses, which had evolved in North America, migrated to both South America and Asia, as the early camels were doing. The horse eventually died out in the Americas, but spread throughout the Old World and flourished there. In the early 1500s, Spanish conquistadors re-introduced it to the New World. Many placental carnivores made their way to the southern continent too—raccoons, wild dogs, weasels, and cats—including *Smilodon*, the saber-toothed tiger of the Ice Age.

As one consequence of this invasion, many of the ancient inhabitants of South America quickly died out. They could not compete with the invaders from the north. But a few of the opossumlike marsupials survived: one opossum, indeed, invaded North America, where it has flourished and spread. Several of the giant sloths made their way north too, among them the giant *Megatherium*, as large as an elephant, and *Mylodon*, whose remains Darwin found in Argentina.

The Spanish and Portuguese Conquest

In 1498, on his third voyage to the New World, Columbus skirted the southern shore of Trinidad and then sailed on into the Pearl Coast of Venezuela, on the South American mainland.

Spain and Portugal were the two European nations most active in this Golden Age of Exploration. In 1494, to forestall any disputes that might arise as a result of this natural rivalry, they signed the Treaty of Tordesillas, based on a papal ruling, dividing the unexplored regions of the world between them. Spain was to have all the new lands to be found west of a north-south line drawn through the western hemisphere some 370 leagues (about 1,100 miles) west of the Cape Verde Islands; all the lands to the east of the line were Portugal's. As a result, Portugal was entitled to what is now Brazil, and Spain could claim the right to explore and conquer all the rest of the New World.

Sailing for Portugal in 1501, Amerigo Vespucci, an Italian, made a landfall on the Brazilian coast and was impressed with what he saw. "How shall I enumerate the infinite variety of wild animals, lions, panthers, cats (not like those of Spain but of the antipodes), such as wolves, stags and monkeys of every sort, and many of them very big?" he asked. On a second voyage to Brazil in 1503 and 1504, Vespucci claimed that he had found "a New World," even though he had been far from first on the scene. Subsequently, a German professor of geography, Martin Waldseemüller, who published Vespucci's accounts of his travels in 1507, gave the name "America" to this New World.

Pizarro and the Incas

Francisco Pizarro, a lieutenant of the explorer Balboa, settled in Panama in 1519 and soon began a series of voyages down the west coast of South America, to discover what new treasures might be gathered there. His first two efforts were unproductive, but on a third voyage in 1531 Pizarro was more successful. Landing on the coast of what is now Ecuador, with 183 men and 37 horses, he claimed the lands for Spain. Before the next year was out, he had conquered the heart of the vast Inca empire.

The Incas were an Indian nation that had risen from obscurity three hundred years before to become the rulers of a mighty mountain empire that was just reaching its zenith when the Spaniards came and destroyed it. The lands of the Incas stretched from southern Colombia to central Argentina, a region more than 2,000 miles long and from 100 to 400 miles wide. The Incas called their kingdom *Tahuantinsuyu*, "the Four Quarters of the World." They had no written language, but they did have a highly organized civil and military government that ruled and administered conquered territories by means of a sophisticated road system linking together all the remote areas of the empire. They proved curiously powerless, however, against Pizarro's tiny band of conquistadors, very probably because they misinterpreted the true intent of the Spaniards. Within six years the Spaniards had extended their rule to all the lands of the Inca empire and had begun to strip it as quickly as possible of all the gold and silver and other riches that they could find.

It wasn't long before the two Europeans powers, Spain and Portugal, had extended their rule over the rest of South America, and for nearly three hundred years their colonial exploitation of the continent continued.

Throwing off the Colonial Yoke

In the early years of the nineteenth century, however, the native peoples of South America, following the lead of the North American colonies, began their struggle for freedom. Argentine colonists won their independence from nearly three centuries of Spanish rule in

1816. Chile, after eight years of struggle, became an independent republic in 1818. Brazil proclaimed its independence from Portugal in 1822, and for more than a century was in turn an independent kingdom, a republic, a dictatorship, and finally a democracy. Simón Bolívar, a revolutionary leader known throughout South America as "The Liberator," led Venezuela and Colombia to freedom in 1818 and 1819, then marched south to help Peru cast off the Spanish rule in 1824, and establish in 1825 a new nation named after him, Bolivia.

Today, all of these nations of South America are struggling to develop their economies and take advantage of their natural riches. They are a century behind the United States in exploitation of their natural resources, but are following the same pattern: cutting down rain forests, clearing the land for crops, destroying natural ecosystems. While doing so, they are killing off or endangering many wildlife species found nowhere else in the world.

JAGUAR
Panthera onca

A flock of parrots rises in raucous flight as a capybara—the world's largest rodent—bursts out of the underbrush and heads for a stream. Close behind it sounds a deep, throaty cough, and then a jaguar bounds out in pursuit. In a moment it has struck down its victim and killed it. Latin Americans know the big cat as *el tigre.*

Ranging to eight feet in length and from 125 to 280 pounds in weight, the jaguar is the largest of all the New World cats. Its stocky, muscled body, short legs, and massive chest make the jaguar a powerful and efficient hunter, unafraid of any other animals within its territory, dangerous to livestock and sometimes even to people. Just as handsome as its slightly smaller relative, the Old World leopard, the jaguar has a spotted coat with a background color varying from pale yellow to cinnamon buff. The underparts are mainly white, but the back and sides are decorated with large black rosettes, many of them with smaller spots in the center. Albino individuals are known, and in some areas melanistic, or black, animals are not uncommon.

Although the jungles of Brazil form the center of the jaguar's homeland, the species inhabits a vast range that once stretched from Arizona and New Mexico southward as far as northern Argentina. Although jaguars may sometimes roam hundreds of miles, they are seldom seen north of the Mexican border these days. Mountain man John Adams (Grizzly Adams) observed and trailed a pair of the big, spotted cats in the Tehachapi Mountains of California, north of Los Angeles, in 1855. The last recorded California specimen was killed near Palm Springs in 1869. More recently, one jaguar was shot in southern Texas in 1946, and two others in Arizona—the first in 1949, and the second in the 1980s. In March 1996, another jaguar was seen in Arizona.

Throughout its range, the jaguar adapts to many habitats, from tropical rain forests and swampy areas to scrublands and grasslands. It is a good climber but does most of its hunting on the ground. Deer and tapir are frequent victims; so are the peccary, the capybara, and smaller game. The big cat sometimes pursues caimans and crocodiles in jungle streams and is fond of fish. Naturalist Alfred Russel Wallace, in his book, *A Narrative of Travel on the Amazon and Rio Negro*, notes:

> The jaguar, say the Indians, is the most cunning animal
> in the forest; he can imitate the voice of almost every

bird and animal exactly, as to draw them toward him; he
fishes in the rivers, lashing the water with his tail to imi-
tate falling fruit, and when the fish approach, hooks them
with his claws. He catches and eats turtles, and I myself
have found the unbroken shells, which he has cleaned
completely out with his claws; he even attacks the cowfish [manatee] in its own element, and an eyewitness assured me that he watched one dragging out of the water
this bulky animal, weighing as much as a large ox.

Jaguars are hated in ranching country because of their toll on
livestock, and they are feared close to settlements because of their
threat to human life. They are therefore killed at every opportunity,
just as most big cats are anywhere in the world. George Schaller,
who studied jaguars in the Pantanal region of southwest Brazil in
1977, reports that "one hunter shot thirty-seven jaguars on one
ranch in a twelve-year period and another sixty-eight on a different
ranch during an eight-year period." During pioneer days in the
southern pampas, daring vaqueros sometimes pursued the big cats
on horseback and lassoed them. One famous jaguar hunter of the
twentieth century was a man named Sasha Siemel. He often tracked
them with dogs and spears and is said to have killed three hundred
jaguars during a long and exciting career.

Jaguars have always been prized for their beautiful spotted
coats. For many years, thousands of Brazilian jaguar skins were
exported annually to the fur markets of the world. In the mid-
1960s, an estimated fifteen thousand jaguars were taken every year
in the Brazilian Amazon, but after the government enacted laws to
protect them in 1967, the kill was greatly reduced.

In spite of such nominal protection, jaguars had disappeared
from many parts of their old range by the 1970s because of hunting
pressures. They had vanished from coastal Brazil and from all of
Uruguay and Paraguay. Probably no more than two hundred of the
big cats survived in Argentina, and only a few remained in southern
Mexico.

Many South American countries now protect the jaguar, but
the big cat can still be legally hunted in others, even where it has

already almost disappeared. In the Amazon Basin, its last stronghold, it is threatened today not only by hunting but by the loss of suitable habitat as the rain forest is being opened up to lumbering, farming, livestock raising, and other human activities. Although listed for protection by the 1973 Convention on International Trade in Endangered Species (CITES), the jaguar is still a flourishing item of trade in countries where illegal poaching and smuggling are prevalent.

One of *el tigre's* last strongholds is in the tropical rain forests of the little Central American country, Belize. During the early 1980s, field biologist Alan Rabinowitz of the New York Zoological Society studied the big cats there, and in 1984 persuaded the government to declare an area known as the Cockscomb Basin in southern Belize as a protected reserve for jaguars and other wildlife. In 1990 the Cockscomb Basin Wildlife Sanctuary—the only jaguar reserve on earth—was enlarged to more than 100,000 acres. In 1996 the sanctuary was home to an estimated fifty jaguars—the greatest concentration of the species anywhere in the Americas.

GIANT OTTER
Pteronura brasiliensis

The tea-colored waters of the jungle river run slowly between the banks. Half a dozen giant otters laze on shore, sunning themselves.

One splashes into the shallows, then comes up with a crayfish, which it carries ashore to eat. Two others dive into the river and begin to play with one another, twisting and turning and rolling over and over in the water.

Largest of the world's otters, the giant otter usually measures five to six feet in length; a big male may reach seven feet or more. Its thick, lustrous pelt is chocolate brown, with a large cream-colored or pale orange spot or spots on the throat and chest. The nose is completely haired between the nostrils, and the feet are more webbed than are those of most river otters. The long, thick tail is flattened at the end into a thin paddle, and it has a distinct ridge, or keel, along each side.

Giant otters are social and vocal animals, often living together in family groups or bands of as many as twelve or fifteen. Their preferred habitat is slow-moving streams. Usually most active by day, they hunt for fish, mollusks, and crustaceans. At night they sleep in a communal den or campsite along the riverbank.

The original range of the giant otter extended from the Amazon and Orinoco rivers drainage system southward to northern Argentina. Once familiar throughout this region, the animal has disappeared entirely in many areas and is very rare in others because it has long been hunted for its pelt, prized by the fur industry. It is a particularly vulnerable species because its social habits, curiosity, and fearlessness of human beings make it easy prey for hunters. In 1967, one investigator reported that more than 61,000 pelts had been imported in nine years from the Brazilian state of Amazonas alone. The trade declined markedly in the early 1970s, however, after otter hunting was banned.

Today, the species is legally protected everywhere, but enforcement is very lax if not impossible in remote jungle regions where skins are still taken and smuggled out to the fur trade. Thus the species is becoming increasingly rare throughout its range and is considered one of South America's most endangered mammals, with a total population of perhaps twenty-five hundred animals. A hundred or more of them live in Peru's Manú Biosphere Reserve. The Pantanal region of southern Brazil shelters another protected population. In 1995 the Nature Conservancy and its Brazilian partner, Ectotropica, acquired 81,510 acres there for a refuge.

GIANT CHACOAN PECCARY OR TAGUA
Catagonus wagneri

The giant Chacoan peccary was first discovered by scientists as a living species in 1972, although in 1930, it had been described as a fossil form after examination of some bones. The living animal is the largest of the three species of piglike peccaries, which are found only in the New World, ranging from the southwestern United States to Argentina.

The giant peccary is a gray-brown color with a faint collar of lighter hair across the shoulders. It sometimes weighs as much as 90 pounds. It lives in the Gran Chaco, the dry, thorny scrub country of Paraguay, southeastern Bolivia, and northeastern Argentina. Active during daylight hours, the giant peccary travels in family groups as it forages for food. The total population is probably only several thousand animals and is declining because of human hunting and loss of natural habitat.

In an effort to preserve the species, a captive breeding colony of the giant peccary was established at Toledo, Paraguay, in the heart of the preferred habitat, with the help and backing of the San Diego and Lincoln Park (Chicago) zoological societies. In 1992 there were more than forty giant peccaries in the colony, most of them captive-bred.

GIANT ANTEATER
Myrmecophaga tridactyla

The order Edentata, or toothless mammals, includes some of the most interesting animals in the world—the anteaters, armadillos, and sloths. Of these, only the anteaters are really toothless; the others have no canine or incisor teeth, but do have primitive, peg-like, grinding teeth. The Edentata evolved in South America during its many millions of years of isolation and gave rise to many strange forms—giant ground sloths, armored armadillos called glyptodonts, and huge anteaters. Some made their way as far north as the southern United States during the Ice Age, and their fossil remains have aroused the curiosity of scientists, including Charles Darwin, wherever they have been found.

Only three species of anteaters survive today, all of them inhabitants of Central or South America. By far the largest is the giant anteater, which stands about two feet high at the shoulder and has a total length of about seven or eight feet, half of it a bushy tail. The giant anteater's long coarse hair is grizzled gray, and a broad black stripe extends like a collar from the throat over the shoulders and back on either side. The beast's long, narrow head is shaped somewhat like a nozzle; the mouth is a tiny circular opening no bigger in cross section than a pencil.

A ground-dwelling animal, the giant anteater sleeps in some sheltered spot, its bushy tail wrapped about its curled-up body.

Active during the day or early evening, it comes out to look for food, shuffling along on the outer part of each forefoot, with the big claws curled under.

Ants and termites are the chief food of the giant anteater. After discovering a termite nest, the anteater tears it apart with its hook-like claws. When the insects begin to stream out, the anteater extends its long, wormlike tongue as much as ten inches to trap the tiny victims on its sticky surface. The tongue darts rapidly in and out, bringing in countless numbers of insects in a very short time; a single individual often consumes many thousands in a day.

Ranging through open lowland forest and grasslands from Guatemala to northern Argentina, the giant anteater bears just a single offspring, which the female carries about with her on her back, even when swimming across streams and rivers. Although inoffensive and seemingly defenseless, the giant anteater can and does defend itself very effectively when necessary with the powerful claws on its forefeet.

The giant anteater's meat and skin have no commercial value, but the species is frequently killed by humans as a trophy, or because the hunter is afraid that this strange creature will injure dogs or domestic stock with its powerful claws. The main threat to its survival, however, is loss of suitable habitat because of human colonization and clearing of land for agricultural purposes. As a result, the giant anteater has disappeared from large areas where it once lived and is becoming increasingly rare everywhere.

GIANT ARMADILLO
Priodontes maximus (= giganteus)

Armadillos, like anteaters and sloths, are members of the order Edentata, but they differ from the others in both structure and way of life. Despite their classification as "toothless," armadillos have many primitive peglike teeth and are protected by a tough armor-like shell. "The armadillo," observed Sir Walter Raleigh, after seeing it in Guiana almost four hundred years ago, "is a beast which seemeth to be all barred over with small plates, somewhat like a *Renocero*."

In Spanish, the word *armadillo* means "little armored thing."

The animal's shell is composed of thick, tough scales that are joined together into a number of bony plates, or bands, that are set in the skin and may or may not be movable.

The armadillos of today are modern cousins of the giant glyptodonts—some measuring as much as fourteen feet in length—that lived millions of years ago. Glyptodonts were protected by a thick, unhinged coat of armor, and some were armed with a tail that ended in a spiked club.

Armadillos evolved in the New World and are found nowhere else; the center of their present population is South America, where a number of species still survive. One of them, the nine-banded armadillo, has ranged as far north as Texas, Florida, and several other southern states.

The giant armadillo is the largest of all present-day species. With a body three feet long and a tail half that length, it sometimes weighs as much as 120 or 130 pounds. On the middle finger of each forefoot, it has a powerful, oversize claw. About four inches long and one and one-half inches across at the base, this sickle-shaped weapon is an effective instrument for tearing into termite or ant nests or for protection against predators. Largely nocturnal, the armadillo also uses its claws to dig burrows in which it takes shelter during daylight hours.

The generic name (*Priodontes*) of this giant means "saw-toothed." Zoologist William Beebe noted that one he captured in

British Guiana (now Guyana) had sixty-eight peg-like teeth. Also, the tongue which extended five inches beyond the creature's lips, was "covered with an infinite number of minute teeth, each a semi-circle of horn split into three to seven points."

The giant armadillo was once widespread in eastern South America from Venezuela to northern Argentina, in forest as well as in brushy or open land. It is intolerant of disturbance, however, and has long since disappeared from much of its former range and is greatly reduced in the rest, due to human destruction of suitable habitat. It is also hunted for its flesh, which is prized in many areas by humans.

GIANT GROUND SLOTH
Mylodon **and Its Relatives**

In the 1890s a German captain named Eberhardt retired to a ranch in southern Patagonia. One day in 1898, while exploring a large cave, he found a rolled-up piece of animal hide about five feet long and half that wide. Nearly three-quarters of an inch thick, the hide had remnants of long reddish fur on it; embedded in the skin were numerous small bean-sized bones. This curious hide was still supple and seemed reasonably fresh, with remanants of sinew and muscle still attached to it.

A piece of this hide eventually was sent to Professor Floren-

tino Ameghino, a paleontologist with the museum at Bueno Aires.
The professor identified it as the skin of a giant ground sloth, pre-
sumably one closely related to *Mylodon*, an Ice Age species whose
bones had been discovered at various localities in Argentina. The
possibility that this skin had come from an animal killed during
recent times was supported by the experience of one of Ameghino's
friends, a politician named Ramon Lista who had once been governor of Santa Cruz province in southern Argentina. While exploring
in Patagonia some years before, according to Lista, he and his party
had seen a huge armadillo-like animal covered with long hair; even
though the animal was shot, it had run away, seemingly uninjured.
Had it been protected by small bones in its skin? Had it been a
living giant ground sloth?

There was certainly plenty of evidence to show that giant
ground sloths had once lived in Patagonia. Darwin had collected
their bones in 1835. Before Darwin, other giant bones had been
uncovered near Buenos Aires and sent to Europe, where the renowned French zoologist Baron Georges Cuvier classified them as
belonging to a gigantic ground sloth more than a dozen feet long.
He named the beast *Megatherium*. Reconstruction of the skeletons
of giant ground sloths showed that they were lumbering, long-tailed
beasts armed with immense curved claws, which they evidently
used to hold onto limbs and drag them within reach for feeding on
the leaves.

Further exploration of the cave in which Eberhardt had found
the skin in the first place revealed beyond doubt that human beings
and giant ground sloths had lived at the same time. The cave revealed other remains of ground sloths, as well as man-made walls
resembling stony corrals in which ground sloths could have been
imprisoned. There were heaps of sloth dung in the cave, and grassy
fodder that scientists speculated could have been cut by people
and kept as food for the imprisoned beasts. All of this evidence
seemed to show that early inhabitants of the region had kept giant
ground sloths in the cave. Perhaps they were domestic animals, but
more probably they were imprisoned so that they could be slaughtered for their flesh as needed.

Thus, giant ground sloths certainly still lived in Patagonia when the first human beings entered the area. Perhaps a few of them survived until historic or modern times, although there is no certain evidence to prove this supposition.

The only sloths that survive today are two species of small tree sloths—the two-toed sloth and the three-toed sloth. These curious, porcupine-sized beasts live almost their entire life hanging from the branches of trees in tropical New World forests and eating leaves and buds, especially those of the cecropia tree. Covered with long gray hair, these modern sloths have flat blunt faces and almost no external ears or tail.

Hyacinth Macaw

MACAWS
Family Psittacidae

"From their large size, the length of their tails and the gorgeous tints of blue, red, and yellow adorning their plumage, the macaws are the most showy and conspicuous of all the parrots," English naturalist Richard Lydekker declared a century ago. Ornithologists, aviculturists, and all who have ever observed these spectacular birds would agree.

All parrots are popular cage birds, but the macaws are particularly prized by aviculturists, who may pay $10,000 or more for a single specimen. Some of these bird fanciers have succeeded in breeding and rearing macaws in captivity, and the sale of these captive-bred birds is legal. Capturing wild macaws for export and sale, however, is against the law in most if not all the countries where they are found. In spite of protective laws, the illegal trade continues to flourish throughout South America. The captured birds are smuggled out of their native lands and shipped by air to foreign countries where they are sold under false or forged papers. In shipment, the birds are often so crowded and poorly cared for that many die before reaching their destination.

Fifteen or sixteen species of macaw survive today, ranging in the wild from Mexico to Argentina. At least nine of these are in serious danger, and several are on the verge of extinction, as the following examples demonstrate.

The hyacinth macaw (*Anodorhynchus hyacinthinus*), measuring almost three feet from beak to tip of tail, is said to be the largest parrot in the world. Cobalt blue in color, it has a patch of yellow skin around each eye. Its powerful black beak can easily crush thick-shelled palm or Brazil nuts to a pulp. Evidently never a common species, it ranges through the dry forests of Central Brazil and the adjacent Pantanal region of eastern Bolivia and northeastern Paraguay. Today, an estimated three thousand survive.

The Lear's or Indigo macaw (*Anodorhynchus leari*) survives only in two cliff-nesting colonies, one in Brazil, one in northeastern Bolivia—probably no more than 140 birds in all. It faces imminent extinction because of the destruction and disturbance of the licuri palm stands that are its feeding habitat, and also because it has been hunted for food and for the pet trade.

The glaucus macaw (*Anodorhynchus glaucus*), which once ranged throughout southeastern Brazil and portions of Paraguay and Argentina, has not been sighted in the wild for some years, and is now considered almost certainly extinct. Like all the other macaw species, it suffered from such human activities as forest destruction, agricultural practices, and hunting.

The Spix's macaw (*Cyanopsitta spixii*), a small blue species, was known for more than a century only from specimens that were trapped for the cage bird trade "somewhere in Brazil." It was not until the 1980s that its wild habitat was traced to woodland near Rio São Francisco in the state of Bahia, eastern Brazil. Only three birds were seen, and these disappeared in 1987 and 1988; it was believed they were captured for illegal trade.

In 1989 the Brazilian environmental authority IBAMA formed a permanent committee for the recovery of the Spix's macaw, with the idea of trying to save the species from extinction. Their best hope—perhaps their only hope—was in the thirty-nine Spix's macaws that still survived in captivity, twenty-eight of them captive-bred.

In 1990 a single wild male of the species was spotted in the woodland habitat along the Rio São Francisco, and was sighted again several times in subsequent years. In early 1995 the committee for the recovery of the species released a captive female in the vicinity with the hope that the two might find each other. In the spring of 1996 David Wilcove, an ecologist, reported in the magazine *Wildlife Conservation* that the female had paired with the lone wild male. "If all goes well," he wrote, "the pair will nest early this year."

There are no macaws living in the West Indies today, but in 1492 there were. Christopher Columbus's son Ferdinand recorded that "red parrots as big as chickens," called *guacamagos* by Carib Indians, were sighted on Guadaloupe in April, 1496. Other red macaws inhabited Martinique and Cuba and possibly Jamaica as well. The Cuban red macaw (*Ara tricolor*) survived until the 1880s, although the last one recorded as shot was taken in 1864. Jamaica had two macaws—a yellow-and-blue species and a green-and-yellow one. Another green-and-yellow macaw inhabited Dominica. All of these birds have long since disappeared, victims of collectors, hunters, and destruction of their natural habitat.

GIANT RIVER TURTLE
Podocnemis expansa

Largest of the world's freshwater turtles, the giant Amazon river turtle sometimes reaches 150 pounds in weight and has a shell three feet in length and two feet wide. Inhabiting the main rivers and tributaries of the Amazon and Orinoco river systems, it was found in incredible numbers during the first half of the nineteenth century. Naturalist explorers Alexander von Humboldt, Alfred Rus-

Giant River Turtle

sel Wallace, and Henry Walter Bates all remarked on the abundance of the species and its importance to the people of the Amazon Basin, who harvested the turtles and their eggs by the millions for food, meat, oil, and fat.

At the start of the dry season each year, the pregnant female turtles would leave their inland pools and waterways and congregate in the rivers. There they sought out sand banks and islands where they deposited their eggs. Congregating at these nesting spots by the thousands, the turtles laid their eggs at night. A female dug a three-foot-deep hole in the sand, then laid 120 to 150 round white eggs in the cavity, eggs about as large as those of a bantam hen. Other female turtles laid successive layers of eggs on top of them until the hole was practically full. Finally the nest was topped with sand, and the tracks of many turtles crawling over the site erased all traces of its use as a nest. But so many turtles laid their eggs on these beaches that sometimes the whole area was underlaid with thousands of eggs in place for hatching—or for harvesting.

Then the people of the area would congregate on the beaches and dig out the eggs, sometimes heaping them up in great mounds many feet deep. Piled into canoes, the eggs were mashed up with hard instruments or, sometimes, by people jumping up and down on them with their bare feet. The resultant mess was mixed with water and allowed to heat in the sun until the oil had risen to the surface. This oil was then skimmed off, boiled, and stored in large three-gallon jars, to be used for lighting, cooking, and other purposes.

Henry Bates tried to figure out the total number of eggs that were taken just from the region on the upper Amazon where he was making his zoological collections. Each year some 6,000 jars of turtle oil were exported from the area, and another 2,000 jars were kept by the people for their own household use. "Now it takes at least twelve basketsful of eggs, or about 6,000, by the wasteful process followed, to make one jar of oil," Bates declared in his book *The Naturalist on the Amazons* (1884). "The total number of eggs annually destroyed amounts, therefore, to 48,000,000."

The newly hatched turtles, if they managed to avoid this human harvest, faced a gauntlet of other enemies in their first few days and weeks of life. Vultures, storks, and other wading birds found them tasty morsels. Jaguars fed on them, and so did alligators and caimans. Those little turtles that made it into the water often fell victim to piranhas, giant catfish, or other big fish. "People also collect new young by the thousands to eat," Bates noted.

Somewhat older turtles, from a foot to eighteen inches long, were considered a delicacy too. The Indians captured them by shooting them in the water with a bow and arrow. In addition, adult turtles were collected as a food reserve for hard times. "Every house has a little pond called a *curral* [pen], in the backyard to hold a stock of the animals through the season of dearth," Bates noted. "I lived almost exclusively on them for several months. . . . Roasted in the shell, they form a most appetising dish." But Bates also admitted that there could be too much of a good thing. "I became so sick of turtle in the course of two years that I could not bear the smell of it, although at the same time nothing else was to be had, and I was suffering actual hunger."

Whatever his opinion of the turtle as a food resource, Bates recognized the value of the species and pondered its eventual fate. "The Indians say that formerly the waters teemed as thickly with turtles as the air now does with mosquitoes. The universal opinion of the settlers on the upper Amazon is, that the turtle has very greatly decreased in numbers, and is still annually decreasing."

Those words were written more than a century ago, and every year since then the population of the species has probably declined. Today the giant river turtle is a rare species on the upper

Amazon. It has disappeared entirely in many areas and exists only in small remnant populations nearly everywhere else. One of the two largest remaining breeding beaches for river turtles is located on the Orinoco River in Venezuela. The other is on the Rio Trombetas, a tributary of the Amazon, which the Brazilian government has protected since the 1950s.

The turtles are legally protected everywhere in Brazil, Venezuela, Colombia, and Peru, but such protection does little good unless the breeding beaches are actively guarded during the nesting and hatching times. Very few are, especially on the upper Amazon. But if the eggs and young turtles ever can be protected effectively, the species in time may once again become a valuable and renewable food resource for the people of Amazonia.

GIANT GALÁPAGOS TORTOISES
Testudo (Geochelone) elephantopus

Located in the Pacific Ocean some 600 miles west of Ecuador, straddling the equator, the Galápagos Archipelago consists of fourteen large volcanic islands and many smaller ones. They were discovered in 1535 by Fray Tomas de Berlanga, the adventurous bishop of Panama, and his companions, when they were blown off course on a voyage to Peru. As he gazed at the strange and desolate landscape, Berlanga remarked that it looked as if "God had showered stones on it." A unique lost world, the Galápagos Archipelago shows many jumbled masses of rocky outcrops, lofty volcanic peaks, cinder cones, and beds of hardened lava. It is home to strange animals like none found anywhere else on earth: big land iguanas and dragonlike marine iguanas that scuttle over the rocks, and giant tortoises that lumber up and down the slopes. Sometimes called the Dragon Islands, or Islas Encantadas (Enchanted Islands), the archipelago is best known as the Galápagos Islands (*galápagos* is the Spanish word for "giant tortoise").

During the sixteenth and seventeenth centuries, the archipelago became a favorite outpost and victualing spot for pirates and buccaneers, who could hide their ships in any one of innumerable bays and coves while they stocked up on fresh meat. Penguins and flightless cormorants were taken; so were the giant tortoises, which could be kept alive on shipboard and killed as needed for food.

During the eighteenth and nineteenth centuries, the islands became a frequent stopping place for whaling vessels for much the same reasons, and the tortoises were taken by the thousands. One authority estimates that as many as 300 thousand of them were slaughtered from the seventeenth century until the 1930s. Little wonder that the populations of tortoises on the various islands dwindled drastically over the centuries.

When HMS *Beagle* visited the Galápagos in September 1835, young Charles Darwin, as naturalist on board, was fascinated by the strange animals and plants he found there. Isolated from enemies for thousands of years, the birds and other animals had little fear of people and no defenses against predators.

That defenselessness worked against the native wildlife of the Galápagos when it had to compete with the animals that humans brought to the islands. Goats and pigs, introduced to provide fresh meat for the crews of visiting ships, lived off the land and occupied space needed by the native species. Goats, in particular, competed directly with the tortoises for food; they overbrowsed the scanty vegetation and eventually caused the tortoises to die out on some of the islands because of starvation. Pigs destroyed the eggs and young of both tortoises and iguanas wherever they found them. Dogs and cats were also released on various islands, where they became free-breeding meat-eaters that preyed on the native animals. Rats invaded the islands from visiting ships. Both the young and adults of many of the birds were defenseless against such competitors. So were newly hatched iguanas and tortoises.

At the time of Darwin's visit, there were still many giant tortoises to be seen on Isla San Cristóbal (Chatham Island). "These huge reptiles, surrounded by the black lava, the leafless shrubs and the large cacti, seemed to my fancy like some antediluvian animals," Darwin wrote, after he had observed them. One of the government administrators for the islands told Darwin that the tortoises on the different islands were distinct and that he could tell their origin by looking at them. The shape of the tortoise carapace, or shell, differed from one island to another, and the neck and other organs were often distinct as well.

At one time, each of these different tortoises was classified as a unique species, but today all of them are considered subspecies, or races, of just one species. Several of those races are now extinct, and all except three races have been reduced from tens of thousands to probably less than a thousand individuals each. All of these surviving races are classed as endangered, with populations ranging from a few hundred to one lone individual.

Today the total tortoise population for all the islands is about ten or eleven thousand, with perhaps two thousand of one race on Isla Santa Cruz (Indefatigable Island), and five thousand of another race on the slopes of Volcán Alcedo, the middle peak of five different volcanoes on Isla Isabela (Albemarle), the largest of the islands. Each of the other four volcanoes also has its own distinct tortoise.

The tortoises roam about their island homes, feeding on the sparse vegetation, which has almost been destroyed in some areas by goats or pigs. The round eggs, each about two and a half inches in diameter, are deposited in holes in the ground. Newly hatched young are frequent victims of hawks as well as of cats, pigs, and rats. Those that do survive may reach a weight of 150 pounds by age fifteen and possibly 500 pounds in adulthood. They may live for a century or more.

In order to protect the islands' remaining tortoises and other wildlife species, Ecuador declared all the uninhabited areas a national park in 1959 and made it illegal to harm or remove tortoises and many other species. That same year, the Charles Darwin Foundation for the Galápagos Islands was founded under the auspices of UNESCO and IUCN. The aims of the foundation were to conserve the unique fauna and flora of the islands and also to study them.

In 1964, just five years later, the foundation opened the Charles Darwin Research Station on Isla Santa Cruz. A laboratory and facilities where scientists could carry on their work with the unique inhabitants of the islands were constructed.

In 1969 a Galápagos Tortoise Breeding Station was also built on Santa Cruz, in conjunction with the research station, with funds provided by a grant from the San Diego Zoological Society. Several races of the tortoises are being raised there at the present time. One of the station's most successful projects was the return of a group of twenty tortoises—hatched from eggs taken in 1965—to their native Isla Pinzón (Duncan Island). Since that time a number of young turtles of various races hatched and reared at the station have been returned to their home islands.

In 1986 about 21,000 square miles of ocean surrounding the Galápagos Islands were designated a Marine Resources Reserve; four years later, the inland waters of the archipelago were declared an international whale sanctuary. All of the measures taken so far were designed to protect and conserve the wildlife and plants of the islands and the waters surrounding them. New threats to the fragile ecosystems were appearing, however: a burgeoning tourism and an increasing human population on the islands that was demanding more local administrative control and reduced protection for the natural ecosystems.

Every year, the Galápagos Islands were becoming more popular with tourists from all around the world who wanted to observe the unique plants and animals found there. From about one thousand tourists yearly in the early 1960s, the flow had increased to about fifty thousand in 1994 alone. In spite of strict regulations as to where visitors could go and what they could do, the park administrators were having a hard time enforcing protective measures. Another problem was the growing population of permanent island residents, most of them settling there to promote tourism and provide services for visitors. In 1970 about two thousand people lived on the islands. Today there are fifteen thousand, and the total grows larger every year. Many of these people chaff under the restrictive measures that the Ecuadorean government has instituted to protect the fragile ecosystem and are demanding local control. In 1995, under increasing pressure, the National Congress did pass a bill shifting administrative power to the residents, but the president of Ecuador vetoed it. Enraged, a crowd of protesters seized the Charles Darwin Research Station. The government sent in troops to restore order, but agreed to more talks.

In December 1995 tensions rose again when the government closed the lucrative fishery for sea cucumbers—an echinoderm prized for use in Asian cooking—in the waters surrounding the islands, after legal quotas had been vastly exceeded. Fishermen were also camping illegally on some islands and killing a number of tortoises for food. The government had also banned shark fishing, because the fishermen cut off the fins, prized as an oriental delicacy, and left the rest of the shark to rot. Protesters seized the research station once again and held it temporarily.

In early 1996 the government was still talking with the islanders about providing more economic advantages, but the protesters were threatening violence unless their demands were met. How the matter is finally resolved will determine the future of the Galápagos Islands, as either a protected natural wonderland or a degraded and lost world.

Besides the tortoises that survive in their native islands, there are more than two hundred Galápagos tortoises of several races living in some forty different zoological collections around the world. Both the San Diego and Honolulu zoos have successfully hatched and reared Galápagos tortoises in captivity.

Other Endangered South American Wildlife

South America was mostly wilderness when Darwin visited the continent in 1833 and 1834. It was still comparatively sparsely populated at the dawn of the twentieth century, except for a few coastal cities and settlements. In recent years, however, the human population of South America has exploded, for it has one of the highest birthrates in the world. The population actually tripled in size between 1930 and 1970. At present it totals about 400 million people and is still rising rapidly.

As a result, the countries of South America are striving as never before to develop their lands and provide their growing populations with a standard of living that will begin to approach that of the advanced industrial nations. Venezuela is capitalizing on the wealth it gains from its rich oil fields. Argentina is taming her vast grasslands for agriculture and industry. Brazil, the largest country in South America and potentially the richest, is opening its vast interior to settlement and development as quickly as possible. In the process it is destroying the world's largest rain forest. If adequate safeguards are not observed, this program of development poses grave threats to the plants, the wildlife, and the tribes that live in the country's interior. The primitive Indians that make their home in the vast forested jungles of the Amazon region once numbered perhaps three million people. Today they have been reduced to perhaps 100 thousand—or fewer—as a result of the destruction of their natural territory, their ways of life, and their very persons. When there is a conflict between the rights of primitive societies and the demands of advancing civilization, the latter usually wins.

In the same way, the wildlife of the continent is the loser as well. Many other large wildlife species, as well as countless smaller forms, are also endangered because of human activities.

South America's only bear, the spectacled bear, inhabits forested slopes of the Andes as high as 10,000 feet, from western Venezuela to northern Bolivia. Never common, it has long been hunted for its flesh and furry hide. Ranchers usually consider it a menace to livestock and kill it wherever they find it. As a result, it is threatened with extermination in many regions.

Baird's tapir, largest of the three species of tapirs found in the Americas, ranges from southern Mexico to Ecuador and Colombia, west of the Andes. A rare animal everywhere, it has disappeared completely from many of its old haunts because of the destruction of its natural habitat and excessive hunting. The rare mountain tapir roams the slopes of the Andes, generally at elevations from 7,000 to 12,000 feet in Colombia, Equador, and Peru. Hunted for food and facing loss of habitat to deforestation, its numbers have dwindled steadily. Today it is classed as an endangered species. No one knows how many survive, but estimates range from a few hundred to several thousand.

Other threatened mammals include several species of river otters that are disappearing, as the giant otter is, because of the demand for their hides. The once abundant Amazon manatee—the *peixe boi* of the Portuguese, the *vaca marina* of the Spaniards—is now becoming scarce nearly everywhere. Since time immemorial, it has been hunted for its tender, veal-like flesh, its oil, and its hide.

Over the years, many hundreds of thousands of New World monkeys have been captured and exported for medical research and for the zoo and pet trade. In 1968 alone, more than seventy thousand New World monkeys were shipped out; just one species, the squirrel monkey, accounted for about forty-five thousand of these. Today, fortunately, the export traffic in monkeys is much less than it used to be. The reduction reflects not only the growing scarcity of primates nearly everywhere in the world, but the increased protection being given to those that survive in the wild.

Two of South America's largest birds have dwindled alarmingly in numbers in recent years, and face uncertain futures. These are the puna rhea and the Andean condor. The ostrichlike puna rhea was once common in the *puna* region of the Andes (a treeless basin), from southern Peru to Patagonia. Today only a small number survive, and the species faces extinction. The population of the Andean condor, largest South American flying bird, has also dwindled alarmingly during the past half-century, but not so drastically as its northern relative, the California condor.

In the 1960s nine Andean condors were captured in the Andes Mountains of Argentina and taken to the Patuxent research center in Maryland, where the U.S. Fish and Wildlife Service held them for captive breeding experiments, as practice for similar experiments with the California condor. By 1978 nine young Andean condors had been successfully raised from eggs laid by these South American condors. The techniques learned from this captive breeding program were then used with captive California condors held at the San Diego Wild Animal Park and the San Francisco Zoo with similar success.

In 1981 four of the captive-reared Andean condors were released in the mountains of South America, demonstrating that they could be successfully reconditioned for life in the wild. By 1995 thirty-nine of these captive-reared birds had been released—ten in Venezuela and twenty-nine in Colombia, where there were only about twenty condors left in the wild. The program was helping to insure the survival of condors in both North and South America.

*Man has planted his footsteps in the underwater realm
that for centuries caused all but a venturesome few to
tremble. . . . He may exploit and ravage this new world
as he has the land, or he may by careful conservation
make of it a self-renewing source of countless benefits.
The choice is his.*

James Dugan
World Beneath the Sea

10

THE WORLD'S OCEANS

The many ways in which the terrestrial areas of planet Earth
have been mistreated—overcutting the forests, overcultivating
the land, strip-mining, polluting, destroying natural habitat, and
making wastelands of vast areas—have become increasingly familiar in recent years. Not so well known is the fact that the world's
oceans and all the marine plants and animals that live in them are
also being severely threatened by human arrogance and greed.

Many people still think of the oceans as so vast that nothing
we do can harm the deep waters. But the reverse is true. The oceans
cover about 71 percent of the earth's surface; yet, like a piece of
cellophane over a big rubber ball, that liquid covering is very thin.
The average depth of the oceans is a little over a mile. Many seas
and bays are much shallower. The North Sea, for example, averages
about 200 feet in depth.

What's more, about 90 percent of all marine animals live in
the shallow waters above the continental shelves. And these waters—only about 4 percent of the oceans' total volume—surround

and wash the main land bodies and are, therefore, the most vulnerable to human depredations and pollution. They are also the places where human beings do the bulk of their sea hunting, fishing, and other harvesting of the seas' riches.

The Developing Science of Oceanography

Humans have sailed the seven seas for thousands of years—fishermen and whalers to harvest its animal bounty, explorers and adventurers to search for unknown lands beyond the horizon. Over the centuries they gradually learned much about the *surface* of the oceans and the continents and countless islands that rose from their depths. But they still knew very little about the world *beneath* the sea—except for the tantalizing glimpses free divers got as they held their breath and swam down several fathoms into the depths to gather shellfish or sponges.

The first advance was the diving bell. More than two thousand years ago the Greek philosopher Aristotle noted that "they can give respiration to divers by letting down a bucket [upended], for this does not fill with water but retains its air." The free swimmer was able to swim up into the barrel-like bucket and gulp air, enabling him to remain below the surface for a longer time. In 1691 the English astronomer Edmund Halley made a large diving bell in which he and four companions spent an uncomfortable hour and a half at a depth of 60 feet. Luckily, they did not suffer the agonies of the bends, which results when nitrogen in air breathed under pressure causes the victim's blood to start frothing when a diver returns to the surface too quickly. The nineteenth century saw the development of the heavy, watertight diving helmet and suit, in which a man, supplied with air through a hose from the surface, could walk about slowly on the bottom.

The first systematic exploration of the depths of the sea was undertaken in 1872 when the British corvette *Challenger*, a small war ship, set out on a three-and-a-half year voyage to take soundings, gather samples from the ocean bottom, chart ocean currents and temperatures, and collect marine plants and animals for study and research.

The science of oceanography finally came of age in the twentieth century. In the 1920s and 1930s the Aqua-Lung and other scuba gear were invented, allowing a freeswimmer to breathe underwater. In 1934 a spherical, deep-diving chamber, the bathysphere, was lowered by cable from a ship, allowing scientist William Beebe and designer Otis Barton to view marine life 3,000 feet below the surface. In 1960 the bathyscaph *Trieste*, a free-diving, self-contained research vessel, descended to a depth of more than 35,000 feet—nearly 7 miles—in the Mariana Trench north of New Guinea.

Since then, many kinds of diving saucers and miniature submarines have been developed—vessels which allow scientists not only to explore and chart the depths of the oceans in detail but also to expand their knowledge of marine life at every depth. What humans have been slow to learn, however, is how to protect the seas' bounty and harvest it on a sustained-yield basis. Instead of that, we have recklessly overexploited the oceans' abundance of shellfish, fish, and marine mammals and polluted the saltwater habitat.

Over the centuries, marine mammals have perhaps been hardest hit by human overexploitation. Steller's sea cow is extinct, and so, almost certainly, is the Caribbean monk seal. Many whales and dolphins are presently threatened with the same fate. So are the surviving sea cows and several species of seals. If the mammals of the sea are to be saved, *Homo sapiens* must strictly regulate their hunting and protect the feeding, breeding, and resting areas these animals need in order to survive.

Instead of preserving these vital areas, we have used our rivers and coastal waters as convenient dumping grounds for sewage and waste disposal. In addition to human sewage and garbage, we also dump industrial wastes and harmful chemicals of many kinds into the waters: heavy metals such as lead and mercury; long-lived pesticides such as DDT and its relatives; synthetic compounds such as plastics and PCBs; radioactive and nuclear wastes. These materials are rapidly making the coastal waters in many places in the world unfit for most marine life. The poisonous effect is being passed on to fish and marine mammals, and to human beings when they consume food from the polluted seas. All over the globe beds of coastal shellfish are also being killed off or rendered unfit for consumption.

At the same time the increasing demand for energy has hastened the drive to build more giant tankers to transport oil and to drill more offshore oil wells. As a result, not only coastal waters but the high seas are becoming polluted at an ever-increasing rate with oil spills from tankers and undersea blowouts of offshore wells.

Finally, not only the marine mammals but many species of food fishes and other ocean animals are now being endangered by overharvesting. As a result of increasing numbers of fishermen and improved techniques, the world's fish catch increased tenfold in the hundred years between 1850 and 1950. The total doubled in the decade that followed; then it doubled again in the next ten years.

Beginning in 1970, the world's fish catch started to dwindle as overharvesting caused the populations of many of the most important food fishes to plummet.

Laws Affecting the Seas

In bygone times the only laws of the sea that were generally recognized were those regulating navigation. Each nation claimed control and jurisdiction within a 3-mile limit around its coasts (3 miles is the distance that a cannonball could be shot by the cannons of eighteenth-century wooden ships of the line). The remainder of the oceans was considered "high seas" where every nation was free to do practically anything it wished. Eventually the 3-mile limit was increased to 6, then to 12 miles.

The laws of the sea began to undergo a fundamental change after World War II, however, when President Truman asserted that the United States had jurisdiction over the continental shelf bordering her coasts. In 1958, an international conference at Geneva affirmed that stand and gave all coastal nations the right to exploit seabed resources, either animal or mineral, to a depth of 200 meters (656 feet) off their shores.

Since 1974, when the first of many lengthy sessions of an International Law of the Sea conference was convened by the United

Nations, all countries have been grappling with the many complicated problems of negotiating an international treaty on the use and
care of the oceans. The hope was that this conference would be
able to define each nation's fishing rights, regulate the transit of
international shipping through straits and other narrow bodies of
water, control pollution of the seas, license and oversee oceanic
research, and legislate overall rules for the mining of the seabed
and the offshore drilling for oil.

In 1982 the Convention on the Law of the Sea was signed by
119 nations, but the United States was not one of them. Alone of
all the nations there, the United States refused to sign the treaty
because of a dispute over who had the rights for the mining of the
ocean floor. The impasse continues today.

The seas, the source of all life, are the common heritage of all
nations. The health of their waters and the creatures that live in
them is of vital importance to the future of life on earth.

WHALES
Order Cetacea

Like all other marine mammals, whales are descended from early
land mammals that at some point in their evolution returned to the
sea. Seals, sea lions, walruses, and sea otters all trace their origins
back to ancient meat-eaters, but whales, dolphins, and sea cows
come from plant-eating hoofed mammals that began their adapta-
tion for life in the seas some sixty million or more years ago. Evolving and changing over a great period of time, the whales gradually
became the most atypical of all modern mammals and among the
most specialized.

In practically every outward way, whales are completely
adapted for life in the water. Their shape is fishlike and streamlined. Their forelimbs have evolved into flat, efficient flippers useful for balance and steering, and the tail has become a huge, flat
paddle that propels the vast body through the water with powerful
up-and-down strokes. Except for a few bristles around the lips, the
whale's body has no hair. The skin is underlaid with a heavy coat
of blubber that protects internal organs and helps to preserve body
heat; the stored fat can be burned up in times of food scarcity.

According to how they gather their food, the cetaceans are

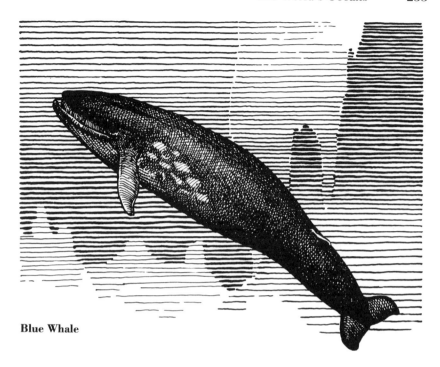

Blue Whale

divided into two suborders: the toothed whales (Odontoceti) and the baleen, or whalebone, whales (Mysticeti).

The toothed whales number more than sixty species, the vast majority of them small cetaceans known as dolphins and porpoises. The sperm whale, which may measure sixty feet or more, is by far the largest of the group and the only one considered a great whale. For the most part the toothed whales eat fish and such marine invertebrates as squid and octopus.

The baleen whales, on the other hand, depend primarily upon plankton—tiny crustaceans and other small marine organisms—for their principal food. Instead of having teeth for gathering and eating this food, the whalebone whales are equipped with rows of horny comblike plates, called "baleen," which hang from either side of the upper jaw. Fringed on their inner side, these whalebone plates act as strainers to separate the plankton, or krill, from seawater.

There are only nine species of baleen whales. The largest is the blue or sulphur-bottomed whale, which may measure as much as ninety or 100 feet long and weigh 130 tons. Dwarfing any dino-saur, the blue whale is the largest animal that has ever lived on earth.

For many centuries, humankind's only interest in whales was in hunting and killing them for oil, baleen, meat, and other prod-ucts. For thousands of years Eskimos of the Far North have pursued the bowhead whale in kayaks, skillfully guiding their frail little boats through ice floes to the side of a blowing giant and then thrusting their spears into its back. Indians of America's west coast pursued migrating gray whales in canoes, and, in similar manner, various peoples of the South Pacific have long hunted the whales that traveled close to the shores of their island homes.

The Vikings began to kill whales from their long ships many centuries ago, combing the arctic seas for their quarry. The first considerable whale fishery of record, however, was that developed during the tenth and eleventh centuries by the Basques—seafaring people who lived along the Atlantic coasts of France and Spain. Their principal quarry in the coastal waters of the Bay of Biscay was the right whale, so-called because it was the right whale to hunt. Slow and unaggressive, it was easy to pursue and kill. Sup-ported by its thick coat of blubber, it floated instead of sinking when dead. As inshore stocks of whales became depleted, the Basques ventured farther and farther offshore in pursuit of the right whale.

In America, the New England colonists also practiced coastal whaling at first, and their quarry was usually the right whale. In 1712, however, a new kind of whaling was introduced when a storm drove Captain Christopher Hussey of Nantucket and his crew far out to sea in a small sloop. Encountering a school of sperm whales, Hussey harpooned one of them and brought it home. Few sperm whales had been taken before this time, for they seldom came close to shore and had to be pursued in the open seas.

By now right whales were becoming as rare in New England waters as they were in northern seas, so the hardy New England whalers began to pursue the sperm whale instead. Nantucket boasted twenty-five whaling vessels by 1739, and, by 1775, neigh-boring New Bedford had sixty active whalers.

The expanding whaling industry survived the American Revolution intact, and about one hundred whaling ships operated from Massachusetts ports in 1788. So far, they had restricted their activities to the Atlantic Ocean. In 1791, however, five Yankee whalers sailed around Cape Horn, at the tip of South America, to try their fortunes in the Pacific.

For the next sixty years or more, countless American whaling ships scoured the Pacific Ocean in search of whales. The rugged American square-riggers carried hundreds of huge casks in which the whale oil was stored and were equipped for voyages that sometimes lasted three or four years. The search for whales led the Americans into the little-known waters of the southwest Pacific, to Australia and New Zealand, and to the discovery of many hitherto unknown islands.

The sperm whale was still the most sought-after whale, for its oil was unsurpassed for illumination and as a lubricant. Spermaceti—the pure, waxy oil obtained from the great domed head—was especially valued. An occasional sperm whale also yielded ambergis, a foul-smelling stomach secretion which was highly prized as a fixative for perfumes.

New England whalers so dominated the industry during the mid-nineteenth century that of some nine hundred whaling vessels of all nations operating worldwide in 1846, more than seven hundred were American.

After that time, a slow but steady decline began. In 1848, when gold was discovered in California, many whalers tied up at West Coast ports, and their crews took off to search for gold in the foothills of the Sierra Nevada. In 1859 another event occurred that had an important effect on whaling—the discovery of petroleum at Titusville, Pennsylvania. This find opened up a whole new industry of extracting inexpensive fossil fuels from the ground, which began to compete with old-time whaling.

But while American whaling dwindled, other nations developed innovations and improved techniques. The first was the invention in the 1860s, by enterprising Norwegian whaleman Svend Foyn, of a harpoon gun with an explosive charge in its tip. Foyn also helped to develop an improved type of whaling ship—a smaller, speedier whale catcher that was powered by steam instead of the traditional sail.

The opening decades of the twentieth century also saw the development of huge factory ships. These floating bases acted as mother ships for fleets of smaller whale-chasing vessels. The speedy whale chasers did the hunting and brought their kills back to the big mother ship. There teams of specialists cut up the victims, hauled them aboard, and efficiently rendered them for their oil and other products.

Seven factory ships were operating in the Arctic by 1905, and another had already sailed to the Antarctic, which had been little exploited previously. A land-whaling station had been established on the island of South Georgia in 1904, and the island quickly proved a convenient gateway to the riches of the antarctic seas. By 1910 there were six land-whaling stations on South Georgia and at least fourteen factory ships were operating in the polar seas to the south.

In the 1930–31 season over 42,000 whales were killed in the Antarctic, nearly 30,000 of them blue whales. By 1938 the world catch had risen to nearly 55,000. About 30,000 were fin whales. World War II gave the whales a temporary respite. But once the conflict was over, full-scale whaling began once again with renewed enthusiasm and efficiency. Sonar and other underwater detection equipment had been perfected during the war, and with these devices the giants could be hunted with virtually no chance of their escape.

During the ten-year period from 1958 to 1968 more than 60,000 whales were killed annually worldwide. Smaller specimens of the biggest whale species were taken each year as their stocks began to be exhausted. By this time the small whale species were being pursued more vigorously as well. A peak of 66,090 whales were killed in 1962, and 63,000 the year after. The same number were slaughtered in 1964, but only 372 of them were blue whales (compared to 30,000 blue whales taken in 1931). Obviously, unless some protection was afforded them, the blue whales would soon be extinct. Others would follow, if such slaughter continued. Worldwide, more than 1.6 million whales had been killed between 1925 and 1964.

The first serious attempt to slow down the killing of whales in the Antarctic came in 1935 when the principal whaling nations agreed to prohibit the hunting of right and bowhead whales, which were almost extinct by this time, and to stop the taking of female whales accompanied by calves. No quotas were set for any of the other whale species, however.

Realizing the inadequacy of existing regulations, the United States called for another whaling convention in Washington, D.C., in 1946. This time an International Whaling Commission (IWC) was organized, with representatives from the major whaling nations as its members. This new international regulatory body promptly made the gray whale a protected species, along with the bowhead and right. But the yearly overkill of all other species was allowed to continue unabated.

In 1964 both Britain and the Netherlands finally dropped out of the whaling business. Stocks were too scarce and costs too high to make whaling a profitable venture for them. At the 1964 meeting the IWC's scientific advisers issued another sharp warning about the dangers of overkill, and once again the member nations refused to pay attention. Instead, they set their own higher quotas for both 1964 and 1965—quotas that they were unable to fulfill.

In 1970 the United States secretary of the interior placed eight of the great whales on the endangered list, omitting only the Bryde's and the minke. The United States took further action at the 1971 IWC meeting in London by calling for a ten-year moratorium on the killing of all whales. That same year the United Nations Environmental Conference in Stockholm also called for a ten-year whaling moratorium.

For three successive years the members of the IWC turned down the proposals for a moratorium, mainly because of the refusal of Japan and the USSR to agree to it. Faced with the possibility of the disappearance of all the great whales, Australia and the United States proposed an alternative quota system based on the concept of "optimum sustainable yield" for each species. In effect, the catch would be limited to only as many whales of each species as the total population could sustain and still flourish under prevailing conditions. This new management system was accepted. At last there seemed to be a faint glimmer of hope for the future of the great whales. But the killing continued on a lesser scale, and whale populations continued their decline.

In 1982, over the strong objections of Japan, the Soviet Union, and Norway, the IWC voted a five-year moratorium on all commercial whaling, to start in 1986. The Soviet whaling fleet was old and badly maintained, and in 1987 the Russians discontinued most of their whale hunting. Japan, Norway, and Iceland continued to kill a limited number of whales for what they termed "scientific research."

In 1991 the IWC moratorium on all commercial whaling was reaffirmed as established policy. In protest, Iceland resigned from the IWC the next year. In 1994 the commission continued its strong stand against whale hunting by voting to create an 11-million-square-mile whale sanctuary in the southern oceans around Antarctica.

Norway and Japan have continued to kill a limited number of small minke whales each year. Most of Japan's whaling operations are financed by selling the meat, considered a great delicacy in Japan, Taiwan, and South Korea. Both Japan and Norway insist that the world population of minke whales is large enough to allow a limited hunt without threatening the species, and the Revised Management Scheme (RMS) of the IWC's scientific committee supports that view. But the IWC as a whole rejected the plan at its 1993 meeting. If accepted, it could have been the first step in reestablishing commercial hunting of other whale species.

"There are enough minkes—some million worldwide—to allow for a limited harvest," whale specialist Richard Ellis concedes in the March-April 1996 issue of *Audubon* magazine. "The question is whether whales should be killed at all." Norway evidently thinks they should. In May 1996, it opened its annual minke whale hunt, nearly doubling its quota to 425 whales from 232 in 1995, despite protests from conservation organizations and other governments.

Perhaps the main reason minke whales are so plentiful today

is that they were seldom pursued by commercial whalers until the populations of big whales such as the blue and fin were so depleted that it was not profitable to pursue them any more. It was only then that whalers began to turn their attention to the minke and other small whales.

The sperm whale is another species with a healthy and flourishing present-day population. Pursued relentlessly during the nineteenth century, its numbers sharply depleted, the hardy and enduring sperm whale survived. What's more, it rebuilt its populations during the twentieth century when the main whale hunt shifted to antarctic seas. Today the sperm whale's worldwide population totals nearly two million.

The other big whales have not been so fortunate. Several are perilously close to extinction. Perhaps ten to twelve thousand blue whales survive, and the same number of humpbacks. About seventy-five hundred bowheads range through arctic waters from the Beaufort Sea to the Sea of Okhotsk, but only three hundred to five hundred remain in the North Atlantic. The right whale is the rarest of them all. According to 1993 estimates less than three thousand southern right whales survive in southern seas and a bare three hundred northern right whales live in the North Atlantic.

Common Dolphin

DOLPHINS AND PORPOISES
Suborder Odontoceti

The ancient Greeks revered dolphins, believing that they were messengers of the gods, the bringers of good fortune. They used the

240 LAST OF THE WILD

figure of a dolphin on coins and frescoes and featured the animals in many of their myths and stories. Aristotle studied them and compared them to humans. He noted that they breathed air, nursed their young, and could utter sounds. Plutarch, in an essay on animal intelligence written nearly two thousand years ago, observed that the dolphin "has no need of man, yet is the friend of all men, and has often given them great aid."

True then, and still true today. For almost thirty years, until its death in 1912, a friendly Risso's dolphin escorted ships across Cook's Strait, New Zealand, between the towns of Wellington and Nelson. So faithful was the engaging animal in this self-appointed task that it became known far and wide, and ships' passengers felt betrayed if they did not see "Pelorus Jack," as it was called.

"Opo" was the name of another New Zealand dolphin that began following boats near the seashore town of Oponino in 1955. Opo swam with the bathers along the seashore, played ball with children in the shallow water, and seemed to enjoy thoroughly the company of human beings.

These are isolated incidents, but many others could be told to illustrate the seeming good humor, friendliness, and intelligence of dolphins. During World War II a cooperative dolphin pushed six American aviators, adrift in a rubber raft in the South Pacific after their plane had been shot down, from the open sea to the beach of a nearby island. A woman who fell overboard from a ship in the Bahamas in 1960 was nudged and escorted to shore by a dolphin.

Whether these true-life stories show a genuine helpful spirit of cooperation on the dolphin's part or just a lively curiosity about something in the water could be debated. But modern scientific experiments show without question that the engaging mammals are highly intelligent and cooperative.

What is the correct name—dolphin or porpoise? Some experts say that dolphins have a beak, a sickle-shaped dorsal fin, and pointed teeth, while porpoises have a blunt nose, a triangular dorsal fin, and spade-shaped teeth (the little harbor porpoise, *Phocoena phocoena*, for example). By this definition, which is followed here, the trained stars of many aquatic shows should be called bottle-nosed dolphins instead of porpoises. Both dolphins and porpoises are members of the suborder Odontoceti, or toothed whales. This big group numbers more than seventy species.

Like the great whales, dolphins and porpoises emit a variety of whistles, chirps, and other sounds by which they communicate with one another. They also give out series of staccato, high-pitched squeaks that serve to locate objects underwater through echolocation. This sonar system is very highly developed.

Most people enjoy watching dolphins and porpoises play about their boats and would not think of killing them. But this attitude is not present everywhere. Members of some primitive societies—and some advanced societies too—kill dolphins and porpoises for food and other products. Dolphins that live in the rivers of China, southern Asia, and the Amazon Basin have long been hunted by native peoples for food. A number of ocean species are regularly killed for their meat in the North Pacific Ocean. Japanese hunters take thousands of them yearly. Such kills, however, are dwarfed by activities of the tuna-fishing fleets of other advanced nations that for many years killed dolphins by the hundreds of thousands annually, incidentally drowning them as they harvested yellowfin tuna by a technique known as "purse seining."

The yellowfin tuna, which travels in large schools, is the most important commercial member of the tuna family in the Pacific Ocean. It often travels with dolphins or porpoises, most frequently with those known as spotted and spinner dolphins. These common dolphins of the eastern Pacific also travel in large schools—sometimes several hundred or a thousand strong. They swim at or near the surface, while the school of yellowfin tuna swim many feet beneath them.

Until the 1950s yellowfin tuna were usually caught on individual hooks and lines cast from the boat by the crew, or by an alternate method of bait fishing in which many baited hooks were attached to a very long line. Then the American tuna fleet perfected a new method of surrounding and catching tuna by means of purse seine nets. These nets are vast, half a mile to three-quarters of a mile long and about 200 feet deep.

Once the net is in place around the tuna—and incidentally the dolphins and sometimes seals, sharks, sea turtles, and other marine animals—a power winch purses up its bottom, much as a woman's purse is closed by drawstrings. A portion of the net is then hauled in, crowding the imprisoned dolphins into a much smaller area.

The fishermen do not want the dolphins, only the tuna. At this point, therefore, the captain executes a complicated maneuver called "backing down," which is an attempt to jerk the net out from under the dolphins without freeing the deeper-swimming tuna. Many clipper captains are quite skillful in this technique, but in spite of every care, many dolphins remain caught in the nets and die. According to some estimates, nearly eight million dolphins have been killed in this manner during the past thirty years.

The Marine Mammal Protection Act of 1972 made it illegal for United States citizens, except peoples such as Eskimos, to kill any marine mammals, except under special license and permit. And although the powerful tuna lobby on Capitol Hill had tried for many months to exempt the killing of marine mammals (especially dolphins) "incidental to commercial fishing operations," they were unsuccessful. The dolphin kill had risen to about 360,000 that year, but the tuna industry assured Congress that improved techniques would soon make the dolphin losses insignificant. With this assurance, the government gave the industry a twenty-four-month grace period to perfect their methods and equipment, with the stipulation that the dolphin kill during that time must be reduced to "insignificant levels approaching zero."

In the meantime the National Marine Fisheries Service set up a quota system under which the U.S. tuna fleet was allowed to kill only a certain number of dolphins, and "countries that want to export tuna products to the United States are required to conform to the same kill per ton regulations imposed on the U.S. fleet."

By 1990, operating under this quota system, and with improved equipment and techniques, the U.S. tuna fleet's kill of dolphins had declined more than 90 percent.

Even better, as the 1993 annual report of the Marine Mammal Protection Act of 1972 reported, "mortality for the United States fleet was 439 dolphins in 1992 and 115 in 1993, down from 20,692 dolphins in 1986 . . . a reduction in dolphin mortality of over ninety-nine percent."

Foreign fleets, unfortunately, were still killing many dolphins in their pursuit of tuna, and in 1990 the United States put an embargo on tuna imports from nations whose dolphin kill was more than that of the U.S. fleet. Bowing to this market pressure, many of these nations are now striving to improve their records.

As reported by the Environmental Defense Fund in early 1996, "Twelve nations meeting in Panama recently agreed to strengthen dolphin protection and improve the 'dolphin safe' label for tuna caught in the Eastern Tropical Pacific Ocean." Among other provisions, the Panama Declaration would cut allowable dolphin deaths by nearly 50 percent, and also increase protection for sea turtles, seals and sea lions, and other marine species such as sharks and sailfish that also become entangled in tuna nets.

The Clinton administration and a number of respected environmental organizations hailed the Panama Declaration and urged support for proposed legislation that would lift the tuna embargo to reward fishermen who have reduced their dolphin kill. Other equally respected environmental groups opposed the legislation, however, claiming it would be a sell out—a "dolphin death bill."

In July 1996, as reported by the Associated Press, the U.S. House of Representatives "voted to change the 'dolphin safe' tuna label requirement to allow the designation to be used even when fishermen harass, chase or injure dolphins in pursuit of tuna, as long as no dolphins die in the nets." Several months later, however, legislation to lift the embargo died in the Senate. The debate over dolphin safety continues.

STELLER'S SEA COW
Hydrodamalis gigas

On November 5, 1741, the Russian ship *Saint Peter*, under the command of Vitus Bering, a Dane, made its way into the harbor of a small uninhabited island in the uncharted seas east of Kamchatka, Siberia. Disabled by storms, its captain and many of its crew sick with scurvy, the *Saint Peter* had been beating its way back toward the Asian mainland after an epic voyage of discovery, during which

Steller's Sea Cow

the crew had glimpsed the mountainous mainland of Alaska and briefly explored several of its offshore islands. The battered ship barely made its way into the harbor, and everyone aboard knew that it could not hold together much longer. They would have to survive the winter as best they could on the barren, rocky shores of the unknown island. The prospect was not an inviting one.

Bering Island, named for the unfortunate commander of the expedition, is one of the remote Komandorskiye (Commander) Islands, lying between the Aleutian Islands and the Asian mainland. The ailing commander and his crew suffered great hardships there during that winter of 1741–42 as they struggled to survive on its cold and desolate shores. The men dug out shelters for themselves in the earth and carried ashore such supplies as they could rescue from the ship, which was slowly breaking up. The island abounded with blue foxes which were so bold they invaded the camp night and day and snatched whatever they could find to eat. There were many sea otters on the island too. The crew killed them for food as well as for their lustrous pelts, which would be of great value if the men were ever able to make their way back to Kamchatka. They also hunted sea lions and fur seals for their flesh. But the animals that provided the best and most abundant meat were the giant sea cows they discovered in the waters around Bering Island.

Georg Wilhelm Steller, the German naturalist with the ill-fated expedition, made detailed studies of these great beasts, which have never been known to exist anywhere except along the shores of Bering Island, neighboring Copper Island, and in the surrounding seas.

"These animals, like cattle, live in herds at sea, males and females going together and driving the young before them about the shore," Steller noted in his journal. "They are occupied with nothing but their food. . . . They tear the sea weed from rocks with the feet and chew it without cessation. . . . When the tide falls they go away from the land to the sea but with the rising tide go back again to the shore, often so near that we could strike and reach them with poles from shore."

Measuring twenty-eight to thirty-five feet in length, Steller's sea cow had wrinkled, brownish-black skin and a horizontal, crescent-shaped tail. One of the giant beasts would easily provide food for many days for the whole crew of the *Saint Peter*. Steller noted that the meat tasted like fine veal, and "the boiled fat surpassed in sweetness and taste the best beef fat."

Nourished on sea cow meat and similar food, the crew survived the winter. In the spring of 1742 they built a small boat out of the wreckage of the *Saint Peter* and that August sailed back to the port of Petropavlovsk on the Kamchatka Peninsula. All that Steller was able to take with him as proof of the sea cow's existence, however, were his notes and a couple of horny mouth plates that served as teeth for the huge animals.

Back in Kamchatka, the survivors of the *Saint Peter* told stories about the sea cows, as well as tales of the abundance of sea otters on the islands they had found. Soon the stampede was on to harvest the fur riches of the new lands to the east. More and more ships stopped at Bering Island and its neighbors every year, not only to hunt sea otters but also to stock up on fresh sea cow meat. By 1768, a scant twenty-seven years after its discovery, the Steller's sea cow was gone. No sightings of the species have ever been verified since that date.

The only tangible remains that we have today of Steller's sea cow—and there were probably no more than fifteen hundred or two thousand of them in all when Steller first saw and described them— are a few incomplete skeletons dug from the rocky soil of Bering and Copper islands.

DUGONG
Dugong dugon

The closest living relative of Steller's sea cow is the dugong, thought to be the source of the mermaid stories of ancient writers. It has a forked or whalelike tail, like that of its giant northern relative. The relatively smooth skin ranges from reddish brown to olive gray, with lighter underparts, and is very sparsely covered with hair. Adults usually range from seven to nine feet in length; the largest one on record measured slightly more than thirteen feet and was said to have weighed a ton. Unlike any of the other sea cows, male dugongs have protruding upper incisor teeth. These short tusks are normally not exposed.

Exclusively marine mammals, dugongs are found only in shallow coastal waters in warm climates where plenty of food—seaweeds and sea grasses of various kinds—is available. They usually come close inshore to feed as tides are rising, advancing head-down and "walking" on their flippers as they graze. In the past they often banded together in herds of several hundred animals.

The dugong was a familiar sight to early navigators and explorers of the Old World, for they frequently encountered it on voyages to India and the Far East. Perhaps the way the female nursed her young one, or the way she sometimes swam with the baby riding on her back, seemed human. In any event, the resemblance was sufficient for the dugong and its close relatives, the manatees, to be given the group name Sirenia, after the fabled Sirens of Greek mythology—nymphs whose singing lured sailors near dangerous rocks, causing the ships to break up and the crews to drown.

Both dugongs and manatees are completely aquatic; they have no hind limbs, and the forelimbs have evolved into flippers. The flat, horizontally broadened tail is stroked up and down in the same way that whales use their great tails to propel themselves through the water. They are the largest aquatic herbivores, feeding on seaweeds which they draw into their mouths with their bewhiskered upper lips. The flexible lips move from side to side to draw and manipulate food into the mouth. Inside are the grinding teeth, or molars, that grow continually out and forward, like those of elephants, until they wear out in succession toward the front of the mouth. Their thick hide is almost hairless, and a layer of oily blubber lies beneath it.

For hundreds of years the dugong has been hunted and killed for its meat, oil, and hide, which can be fashioned into a fine quality, durable leather. In the late nineteenth century a regular commercial dugong fishery flourished, mainly along the coast of northern Australia. The animals were usually taken by harpooning them from boats or by snaring them in nets.

Dugong meat was prized, for it was tasty and nourishing. In order to keep it fresh, the inhabitants of Hoen Island, in the Torres Strait just north of Australia, kept living captives by tethering them in shallow water with ropes tied around the narrow part of the tail. The oil was also prized, for it was clear and pure, free from any disagreeable odors, and was believed to have the same health-supporting qualities as cod-liver oil. Even the dugong's so-called tears, which consist of a viscous substance that is secreted from the animal's eyes when it is taken out of the water, were valued. The Malays believed that this fluid had powerful influences as an aphrodisiac.

Historically, the dugong ranged through coastal waters from the Red Sea and East Africa westward through the Indian Ocean to Australia, New Guinea, and various islands of the far western Pacific. Today it is still found over much of this area, but in greatly reduced numbers and with many gaps where it has been completely exterminated. The largest present populations live in the waters of northern Australia and New Guinea, between India and the island of Sri Lanka, and along the East African coast and the Arabian Gulf.

The species is listed by the IUCN as vulnerable, with its populations dwindling nearly everywhere. It is given legal protection in many countries, however, and if commercial hunting and exploitation are effectively curbed, the dugong's chances of survival, and even an increase in its population in many areas, are favorable.

MANATEES
Trichechus species

Although the dugong had long been a familiar sight to Old World travelers, the first Westerner who seems to have noted manatees in the New World was Christopher Columbus. He sighted one of the beasts on January 9, 1493, off the coast of Hispaniola, or Haiti. "They are not so beautiful as they are painted," he noted in his journal, "though to some extent they have the form of a human face." Later Spanish explorers and colonists called the species ei-

West Indian, or Caribbean Manatee

ther *manati* or *vaca marina*: "sea cow." The Portuguese called it *peixe boi*, or "cowfish."

Although very much like the dugong in outward appearance, the manatees have been placed in a separate family and are usually divided into three distinct species according to the three different regions in which they live. The West Indian, or Caribbean, manatee (*Trichechus manatus*) once ranged throughout the West Indies and along the coasts of the Carolinas and Florida southward along the Gulf Coast of Mexico to Guyana and Surinam in South America. Today, however, it has disappeared from many of its old haunts. The Amazon manatee (*Trichechus inunguis*) inhabits the slow-moving, black waters of the Amazon and possibly the Orinoco River systems, and coastal waters of Brazil. The West African manatee (*Trichechus senegalensis*) lives in coastal rivers of West Africa, from Senegal to Angola.

Whereas the dugongs are exclusively marine animals, manatees inhabit brackish bays and fresh water as well. Manatees have no tusks, and instead of the dugong's forked tail, they have a distinctly rounded or fan-shaped paddle.

Just as is true of the dugong, the manatees have been hunted for centuries for their delectable meat, high-grade oil, and durable hides. The Caribbean and West African species are listed as vulnerable, while the Amazon manatee is seriously endangered. Ruthless hunting for its meat has brought it nearer to extinction than perhaps any other mammal in the Amazon region.

The Florida form of the West Indian manatee (*Trichechus m. latirostris*) is presently afforded complete protection, and its population may be fairly stable at about 2,600 animals. The chief threats to the Florida manatee today are injuries inflicted by motorboat propellers, the locks of canal systems, and waters that sometimes become too cold during winter. Manatees seem unable to withstand water temperatures much below 65 degrees Fahrenheit and may readily succumb to pneumonia or other ailments during cold spells. In Florida winters manatees tend to congregate in the mild waters of Everglades National Park, as well as in natural warm-water springs and around other warm-water outlets. During the winter and spring of 1996 more than two hundred manatees were found dead in Florida's coastal waters, making that year the worst on record for this endangered form. Extensive laboratory research revealed that the cause of most of the deaths was an infection brought about by red tide—a bloom of poisonous, one-celled, plantlike animals in the waters of Florida's southwest coast.

STELLER'S SEA LION
Eumetopias jubatus

Largest of all the eared seals, Steller's sea lion ranges from northern Japan and Kamchatka through the Aleutians to islands of the Bering Sea and coastal Alaska, south to California's Channel Islands. Adult males may measure nearly thirteen feet in length and weigh more than a ton.

From a world population of 250,000 or more in the 1960s, the numbers of Steller's sea lion have dropped to less than 100,000. During that time, the species has suffered a more than 90 percent die-off in some of its core habitat in Alaska.

No one knows for sure what has caused this precipitous decline, but there are a number of theories: disease; pollution of the marine habitat by oil spills, PCBs, mercury, and other poisons taken in with the fish they eat; and malnutritional stress caused by a drastic depletion of the sea lion's principal food supply because of human overfishing.

The human exploitation of Steller's sea lion's primary food fish, the pollock, may be an important part of the answer. In 1991 5 million metric tons of pollock (nearly 5 billion fish) were taken by commercial fishermen, and populations of the species plummeted. Sad to say, some 5 million pounds of the fish are wasted every year. They are netted, but thrown back because they are too small, or are not the primary catch of the day.

Because of its steep decline in numbers, Steller's sea lion was listed as threatened under the Endangered Species Act in 1990. Three years later a government study predicted that the species would be extinct within the next sixty to one hundred years at the current rate of decline.

ELEPHANT SEALS
Mirounga angustirostris and *Mirounga leonina*

By far the largest of all seal species, the elephant seals get their common name not because of their size but because the adult male has a trunklike proboscis that hangs over his muzzle. Inflated, the proboscis acts as a resonating chamber when the bull bellows. Both the northern elephant seal (*Mirounga angustirostris*) and the southern elephant seal (*Mirounga leonina*) were slaughtered ruthlessly for their oil during the nineteenth century.

Adult males of the northern elephant seal may measure fifteen to sixteen feet in length and weigh 5,000 pounds or more. The smaller cows run to eleven feet and 2,000 pounds. The species

Northern Elephant Seal

originally ranged through the coastal waters of California and Baja California, where it bred on coastal islands and beaches. By the 1890s it had almost disappeared because of excessive hunting. In 1892 scientists found nine elephant seals on Guadalupe Island, the species' last outpost some 180 miles west of central Baja California, and promptly killed seven as museum specimens.

A few survived, however, and in the early years of the twentieth century the Mexican government put the species under complete protection. Slowly the population began to recover. Today the northern elephant seal has a population of 130,000 or more, and has reoccupied all of its old breeding grounds, including California's Farallon and Channel islands, and Coronado Island.

The southern elephant seal breeds on islands to the south of South America, Africa, and Australia, all around Antarctica. Adult males may measure sixteen feet in length and weigh as much as 7,000 pounds. Like their northern relatives, southern elephant seals were taken relentlessly during the eighteenth and nineteenth centuries for their oil.

For many years the killing of adult males on South Georgia Island, about a thousand miles east of South America's southern tip, was a British government-licensed industry, with a yearly quota of six thousand taken, calculated on a sustained-yield basis that would keep the population stable. "However, when the whaling industry collapsed in 1964, because of gross overexploitation," as authority Nigel Bonner notes in his book *Seals and Sea Lions of the World*, "the sealing industry which was intricately tied to it, also ceased. The elephant seal now lives in peace."

Under management and protection, the numbers of southern elephant seals have recovered very satisfactorily. In 1990 the world population was estimated at 664,000. About half of them haul up on South Georgia Island, and a flourishing colony of about 42,000 breeds on Peninsula Valdes, Argentina. It is the northernmost breeding colony, and the only one located on the South American continent rather than on an island.

WALRUS
Odobenus rosmarus

In colonial times the Atlantic walrus (*O.r. rosmarus*) occasionally appeared as far south as the coasts of Maine and Massachusetts. Under constant exploitation for tusks and oil, its numbers dwindled sharply by the end of the eighteenth century, and it had retreated far to the north. In the early days of the twentieth century there were still enough Atlantic walrus, however, for the Hudson's Bay Company to export about 175,000 of their hides between 1925 and 1931. Soon thereafter the Canadian government restricted the hunt to Inuits and other permanent residents of the Far North.

Today the population of the Atlantic walrus is estimated at about thirty thousand in two main groups: north of Russia to eastern Greenland, and from western Greenland to Canada's arctic islands.

Inuits in eastern Canada and Greenland are permitted to take about 6 percent of the population yearly in legal and regulated hunts.

The Pacific walrus has longer and less diverging tusks than the Atlantic walrus and is considered a distinct subspecies (*O.r. divergens*). Today it ranges through the Bering Sea and along the coasts of western and northern Alaska to the shores of arctic Siberia. Traditionally hunted by Eskimos as well as by commercial sealers and whale hunters, the population declined steadily during the nineteenth and early twentieth centuries. By the 1950s no more than an estimated forty to fifty thousand remained.

Protected from large-scale commercial hunting for most of the time since then, the Pacific walrus population has rebounded very encouragingly. Today there are about 250,000 of them—probably close to their original numbers. The aboriginal peoples in both Russia and Alaska take several thousand of them yearly in regulated subsistence hunts.

BLUEFIN TUNA
Thunnus thynnus **and** *Thunnus maccoyyi*

More than forty species of tuna and their close relatives—albacore, skipjack, bonitos, yellowfin, and many others—roam the world's oceans. They are among the most sought-after food fish. In western countries their meat is a popular choice for sandwiches, salads, and casseroles, while in Japan and other eastern nations tuna is considered a great delicacy.

Most prized and sought-after of all the tuna is the giant bluefin, called the "titan of tunas." In Japan, red tuna meat, *maguro*, is an indispensible part of a good meal, and giant bluefin *maguro* is considered, as bluefin specialist Douglas Whynott notes in his book *Giant Bluefin*, "quintessential *maguro*, the food of perfection." By 1990, he goes on to say, "Japanese were consuming 800,000 tons of tuna a year—30 percent of world landings. The Japanese tuna fleet, fishing worldwide, was able to supply 690,000 tons per year between 1985 and 1990, a lot of fish but only 74 percent of demand. Consequently, imports swelled to $1 billion worth of tuna, bought from fisheries in sixty-one countries." In 1992, as reported by Michael Parfit in *National Geographic*, one 715-pound bluefin was sold in Tokyo for $67,500.

Forty years ago Japanese longline trawlers began tuna fishing in the Atlantic. By 1965 their fleet of several hundred trawlers was setting 100 million hooks. Every year the take of tuna increased.

The giant bluefins can grow to twelve feet or more in length and weigh 1,800 pounds. Streamlined and built for speed, they have been known to swim at speeds of 50 miles per hour in brief spurts. There are three forms of giant bluefins: the Pacific bluefin (*Thunnus t. orientalis*); the southern bluefin (*Thunnus maccoyyi*); and the Atlantic bluefin (*Thunnus t. thynnus*). The Atlantic bluefin has two distinct stocks, or populations. The western Atlantic stock spawns in the warm waters of the Gulf of Mexico and the Caribbean and migrates northward to summer feeding areas in the western North Atlantic. The eastern Atlantic stock spawns in Mediterranean and Spanish waters and migrates to feeding areas in the Bay of Biscay and the waters around Norway.

In 1975 the western Atlantic stock had an estimated population of 250 thousand but, due to overexploitation, the population had fallen to twenty-two thousand by 1992—a more than 90 percent decrease. As a result, the U.S. National Marine Fisheries Service urged that the legal catch be cut in half. Since 1960 the tuna catch had been regulated by yearly quotas set by the International Commission for the Conservation of Atlantic Tuna (ICCAT). "Since 1960," the Service states in its 1991 publication, *Our Living Oceans*, "the top species in the U.S. harvest has shifted from bluefin tuna to swordfish to yellowfin tuna as each species became increasingly over-utilized." It also noted that international regulations were being developed for swordfish fishing, as that specimen was fast becoming overexploited as well. As a result, as noted by the ICCAT's scientific advisory group in 1994, "the 20 countries that catch bluefin tuna have agreed to halve their catch in the Atlantic by 1995." In 1996, however, bowing to political pressure, the ICCAT voted to *increase* western Atlantic quotas.

Overexploitation of other tuna species is taking its toll as well. In 1990, one of Australia's most important commercial fish, the yellowfin tuna (*Thunnus albacares*), was reported "close to extinction" because of overfishing by Pacific nations.

Caribbean Reef Shark

SHARKS
Order Selechii

An ancient and enduring group, sharks first appeared in the seas some 300 million years ago. Today, more than three hundred species are recognized worldwide. In size they vary from small species no more than two to three feet in length to the whale shark and basking shark, giants that may measure forty-five feet or more.

These slow and inoffensive behemoths are plankton feeders, and pose no threat to humans.

Sharks as a group have a bad reputation with humans, however, and many people fear and hate them, often depicting them as savage killers and man-eaters. A few species, such as the tiger, mako, hammerhead, and great white shark, are dangerous indeed, but the vast majority of sharks pose little threat to people. "Most attacks on humans by sharks are a matter of mistaken identity," declares Grant Gilmore, of the Harbor Branch Oceanographic Institute in Fort Pierce, Florida. "What people have to realize is the ecological role they play. You remove the top predator from the food chain and you change the whole ecosystem. The entire balance is threatened."

For many years commercial fishermen considered sharks of little value and took them only for their livers, a source of vitamin A, and for their thick skin, which makes good leather. Many sharks were caught in long line fishing for tuna and swordfish, but most were discarded. In 1989 an estimated 2,800 tons of juvenile sharks were caught by the U.S. shrimp fishery in southeastern waters alone. Practically all of these were discarded.

In the 1980s shark flesh—inexpensive in comparison to tuna or swordfish—increased in popularity as food. Countless thousands of sharks are also taken for their fins alone. The fins are cut off, and the helpless victims are then usually thrown overboard to die. In the decade from 1980 to 1990 the annual volume of world shark fin exports doubled, with 95 percent going to Asian markets where the fins are prized for making health remedies and soup stock.

Along with the growing commercial shark fishery, the taking of sharks by recreational fishermen has increased rapidly too. According to environmental writer Roger DiSilvestro, "Sport fishermen alone caught nearly one billion pounds per year of sharks worldwide in the late 1980s. . . . This take, which affected about two-thirds of all shark species, was a threat to shark survival, because most sharks breed slowly, and their populations tend to drop precipitously under heavy hunting." In U.S. waters alone, sport fishermen were taking 22 million pounds of sharks each year.

Alarmed by figures such as these, the National Marine Fisheries Service took action, and an Atlantic Coast Shark Fisheries Management Plan, limiting and regulating the allowable catch of sharks, was passed in April 1993.

In all seas and oceans, the populations of dozens of shark species are plummeting because of the growing demand for shark products. Samuel Gruber, chairman of the World Conservation Union's Shark Specialist Group, declared in 1993 that "as many as 100 million sharks and related species are killed each year." Unless this extensive slaughter is stopped and the yearly harvest regulated worldwide, many members of this ancient group will disappear.

Other Threatened Marine Life

As already noted at the beginning of this chapter, humans have treated the oceans with wreckless arrogance over the years, using them as convenient dumping grounds for sewage, industrial wastes, oil, garbage, and nuclear wastes. The oceans are so vast, we have reasoned, that we cannot harm them and that they will cleanse themselves. Such treatment and such attitudes are increasingly threatening the health of the seas and all the life that lives in them.

The second serious threat to sea life is our overexploitation of its riches, our overfishing the waters so that species after species of our most important food fish are rapidly disappearing.

"Technology has helped quadruple the world's catch of seafood since 1950," writes Michael Parfit in the November 1995 issue of *National Geographic* magazine. "There are too many fishermen and not enough fish." More than a million fishing vessels now roam the oceans of the world, harvesting seafood, and Parfit goes on to note that the annual fish catch in the sea is about 86 million short tons (172 *billion* pounds)! Sad to say, much of the catch is wasted—and not even counted in the fish catch total— because fishermen often dump all but the most valuable specimens. Many of those dumped are undersized fish—young ones not yet sexually mature. For depleted species whose populations have plummeted, these are the last hope for renewal. As a result, many of our most valuable commercial fish species are disappearing.

For many centuries the Grand Banks of Newfoundland have been famous for cod fishery. In recent years giant fleets of draggers, factory trawlers, and other fishing vessels have arrived at the Grand Banks from all over the world to fish twenty-four hours a day, every day of the year, and fill their holds with cod. They have been so efficient and so successful that cod populations have plummeted, with smaller and smaller catches being made each year. Canada finally closed down its own cod fishery there in 1992, putting 42,000 people out of work, because of the drastically reduced catch. Other countries, however, have continued to fish at the outer edges of the Banks, just outside Canada's 200-mile limit. If the overfishing continues, the cod may finally disappear completely.

The story is the same in Europe, where the cod catch in the North Sea dropped from 287,000 metric tons in 1981 to 86,000 metric tons ten years later. In British waters, 70 percent of all commercial fish species are disappearing. The same sort of thing is happening in many of the world's most productive fisheries in the Atlantic, Pacific, and Indian oceans, and in arctic and antarctic seas as well.

As one side effect of overfishing, the giant sea turtles are also threatened with extinction because so many of them are killed when accidentally caught in longline and other forms of fishing. Every year Spanish longlines for swordfish hook about twenty thousand loggerhead turtles, and up to half of them die as a result. In 1988 Japanese tuna long-lining alone hooked about twenty-one thousand sea turtles, killing about twelve thousand of them.

The rapidly developing science of aquaculture and fish farming will help to make up for the diminishing stocks of seafood in the oceans. Oysters and clams and other shellfish are now being grown in large quantities under controlled conditions in sheltered bays and inlets. Many kinds of fish are also being raised in freshwater ponds and in marine net-pens. Norway alone has 700 salmon farms in its fjords. More than half of the total world production of salmon (277,500 metric tons) in 1990 came from these Norwegian fish farms. But useful as fish farming is in helping to satisfy constantly increasing demands for seafood, it cannot take the place of international agreements and common sense in preserving the wild stocks and harvesting them on a sustained-yield basis.

As the world demand for fish and other seafood grows, the fish themselves continue to be scarcer and scarcer—and smaller and smaller. In response to this alarming situation, the World Wildlife Fund in 1996 launched a global Endangered Seas Campaign, with the aim of establishing a Marine Stewardship Council, promoting ecologically sound fishing practices, and reducing by 50 percent the 27 million metric tons of "by-catch" fish taken and wasted every year by bottom trawlers, longlines, and other commercial fishing operations.

*As the twentieth century draws to a close, an impres-
sively large percentage of the world's most familiar
wild animals are facing extinction. The creatures that
we introduce our children to at bedtime as a part of
their initiation into the world—lion, leopard, rhinoceros, tiger—will soon exist only in zoos and in the wilderness of the imagination.*

Richard Ives' informant
Of Tigers and Men: Entering the Age of Extinction

11

THE GIANT KILLER
Homo sapiens

The preceding chapters look at what has happened—as well as
what *is* happening—to land and wildlife around the world
because of man's destructive activities. Today, many giant wildlife
species—and thousands of smaller animals—are heading toward
extinction and will soon disappear unless the harmful effects of
human destructive forces can be reversed.

Wildlife writer and editor Les Line emphasized that message
in an article, "1,096 Mammal and 1,108 Bird Species Threatened," in the October 8, 1996 *New York Times*. In that article he
reported that the Species Commission of the World Conservation
Union—formerly known as the International Union for the Conservation of Nature (IUCN)—had just finished updating its Red List
of endangered and threatened wildlife on every continent, "and the
news is grim: 1,096 mammals, nearly one-fourth of all known species, are considered threatened, as are 1,108 birds, more than 11
percent of the world's bird species. . . . The document lists 253

reptile, 124 amphibian, and 734 fish species as being at risk of extinction, but it emphasizes that thousands of species in these taxonomic groups have not been assessed."

"Rarity is the attribute of a vast number of species of all classes in all countries," Charles Darwin observed more than a century ago in his classic book, *The Origin of Species*. "If we ask ourselves why this or that species is rare, we can answer that something is unfavorable in its condition of life: but what that something is, we can hardly ever tell." The first part of that statement is as true today as it was when Darwin wrote it, but not the last part. Today we can almost without exception tell what the unfavorable factors are, and in practically every case they are the result of human activities.

As the number of people in the world increases, the results become ever more marked. All over the world tropical rain forests fall under the ax and bulldozer. Mountain slopes are cleared for more croplands. Vital wildlife habitats everywhere, whole ecosystems and natural areas, are disappearing under the onslaught. As environmental writer David Quammen observes in his book *The Song of the Dodo*, "The problem of habitat fragmentation and the animal and plant populations left marooned within the various fragments under circumstances that are untenable for the long term, has begun showing up all over the land surface of the planet. The familiar questions recur. How large? How many? How long can they survive?"

As a result of all human activities, wildlife disappears at an ever more rapid rate, and the overall quality of human life decreases. A few industrialized nations may be living well for the moment, but only at a high cost to all other countries and to planet Earth itself. The declining fortunes of much of the earth's wildlife as a result of environmental destruction could serve as a clear indication of what lies in store for us if we do not alter our attitudes and ways. Species that can't change their ways to adapt to new and perhaps harmful conditions, whether caused by natural forces or by human activities, face extinction.

The dodo, the elephant bird, the great moa, and the passenger pigeon all disappeared because they were unable to change their ways when faced with harmful conditions brought about by human beings. Even though the wheels of natural evolution turn exceedingly slow, none of the higher animals *except* man can adapt quickly to extensive change in their environment. Human beings are unique in that they *can* change their ways quickly when the need arises. The important questions are: Will we recognize the need to change our ways? Will we change them before it is too late—for wildlife, for ourselves, and for planet Earth? "Man's attitude toward nature is today critically important simply because we have now acquired a fateful power to alter and destroy nature," Rachel Carson, the noted author of *Silent Spring*, observed. "But man is a part of nature and his war against nature is inevitably a war against himself."

A Rising Ecological Conscience

There is some evidence that we are, at last, beginning to recognize the seriousness of our situation and starting to do something about it. Most of the highly developed nations, for example, are making substantial—although usually insufficient—efforts to deal with the problems of increasing population. Even so, another seventy-five years or more will pass before most of them, even if they make an all-out effort, can achieve zero population growth. Meanwhile, the populations of developing nations continue to increase—and starve.

One horn of the dilemma is the fact that the highly industrialized nations represent only about a third of earth's human population, but that one third is using up nearly 90 percent of the planet's resources, and in the process is creating much of the basic problem. However late, these advanced nations are beginning to realize that they bear a great deal of the responsibility for the pollution and environmental destruction that occurs around the world and that they must take the lead in stopping such activities.

Many nations are enacting legislation designed to protect their lands and wildlife; many are establishing new wilderness preserves and parks within their borders. Attitudes toward killing animals merely for sport are undergoing significant changes in many nations, and the practice of wildlife management is shifting away from the aim of helping only game species to the concept of managing areas for the general benefit of all the wild species.

All such trends are cause for some optimism about the future of endangered wildlife—and for mankind's future as well. So are the recent scientific breakthroughs, and the new concepts and techniques that are being used to help an increasing number of threatened species.

New Knowledge, New Techniques

Many of the current practices—both old and new—used to help endangered wildlife have been mentioned in previous pages. Species as different as the ibex, the rhinoceros, and the wolf are being successfully transplanted from areas of concentration to regions where they formerly lived but had long since disappeared. The technique of shooting large animals such as the rhinoceros with tranquilizer darts that temporarily immobilize them makes transporting them without danger possible. Tiny radio transmitters are sometimes fastened on captured animals in order to monitor and map their movements after release. Skilled behavioral studies, such as those conducted by George Schaller and Dian Fossey on the gorilla, have shed new light on how endangered species may be helped. Survival centers have been established for some endangered species—the chimpanzee and orangutan, for example— enabling captive specimens to be reintroduced to life in the wild gradually.

The science of breeding wild animals in captivity has made great advances in recent years. Species such as Père David's deer and the European bison survive today only because they were kept and protected in captive herds for many years. Careful breeding records and stud books are kept for a number of threatened species with captive groups in zoos and protected reserves all over the world. A few groups of animals are propagated in special breeding centers established just for them. The Ornamental Pheasant Trust and the Wildfowl Trust, both in England, are two examples. A number of leading zoological parks—London, San Diego, New York, and Washington among them—have established huge natural areas covering many hundreds of acres, where endangered species can live and propagate under simulated natural conditions. Various zoos and animal study centers are also working to perfect techniques for breeding threatened species by artificial insemination. Commercial wild animal farms successfully keep and breed such diverse species as African antelopes, kangaroos, crocodiles, and green turtles. These captive-breeding programs are most worthwhile when they hold forth the eventual possibility of reintroducing specimens to the wild under favorable conditions.

Our Fossil Fuel Civilization

As beneficial as these activities are, however, they are only a Band-aid treatment for a long-festering cancer—the deteriorating health of the earth's environment. Planet Earth is ailing because of our fossil fuel civilization, and our ever-increasing industrial development and growth. Our burgeoning human population wants and needs more and more *things* every year, and poor and undeveloped nations want to reach the same level of development as the advanced industrial nations.

"We find ourselves near the end of a process that will, within the next couple of decades, result in the wholesale destruction of the natural world as it has always existed," writes naturalist and writer Richard Ives in his book *Of Tigers and Men: Entering the Age of Extinction*. Author Bill McKibben agrees. In his 1989 book *The End of Nature*, he writes that "over the last century, a human life has become a machine for burning petroleum. . . . Oil is what has allowed us finally to dominate the earth instead of having the earth dominate us." Under the onslaught, our world—the finite home for all living things—is deteriorating tragically.

Global Warming, Ozone Holes, and Acid Rain

One result of our dominating the earth in this fashion is the so-called greenhouse effect, the global warming that results from the burning of fossil fuels and the consequent build-up of carbon dioxide and other gases in the atmosphere. The opacity of these gases inhibits the earth's surface heat from radiating back into space. Predicted consequences are a 2 to 9 percent increase in global temperatures in the twenty-first century, the melting of polar ice caps, rising sea levels, drastic changes in global climate patterns, and other very unpleasant and possibly disastrous consequences for humans and all other life.

Another serious problem is the thinning of the protective ozone layers in the atmosphere, causing "ozone holes" over both the Arctic and Antarctic polar regions. This thinning of the ozone layer allows increased deadly ultra-violet radiation to get through to the earth. It is caused for the most part by our use of chlorofluorocarbons (CFCs) for refrigerants, air conditioning, and aerosol sprays. Released into the atmosphere, they break down into ozone-destroying chemicals.

A third potentially disastrous outcome of our excessive use of fossil fuels is acid rain, resulting from the emissions of sulfates and nitrates into the atmosphere. There they combine with oxygen to form acids, which are returned to earth as acid rain or acid snow, stunting or killing whole forests, and rendering countless lakes and ponds around the world unfit for fish, amphibians, and other aquatic life.

All of these potentially disastrous effects upon earth as a fit living place will inevitably increase as human populations increase, unless we change our habits and aims. We total 5.7 billion today, and our numbers increase by 95 million persons every year. At our current rate, we will number 10 billion by the year 2030, and 20 billion by 2070—standing room only. If we continue consuming earth's resources then as we do now, the result will be catastrophe.

Is Technology the Solution?

Early in his vice presidency, Al Gore was interviewed by Bill McKibben, and told him: "We are in an unusual predicament as a global civilization. The maximum that is politically feasible, even the maximum that is practically imaginable right now, still falls short of the minimum that is scientifically and ecologically necessary."

Not so, claim many scientists, who staunchly believe that human ingenuity and rapidly advancing technological skills will enable people to live comfortably no matter how many of them there are, or what they have done to the natural world.

Technology advocates wax enthusiastic over their vision of the twenty-first century, declaring that applied science and technology will transform the earth. Food will be produced in chemical nutrients on vast indoor farms. There will be underseas farms too, where seaweed and plankton and fish can be continually grown and harvested. Disease will be conquered, and scientists will be able to manipulate human genes to produce "desirable" types of humans at will.

All of these marvels are indeed possible—and that very fact profoundly disturbs a great many people. What will be the effect of such a machine-dominated civilization, not only upon our natural environment but upon our soul and spirit as well? Opinions vary widely.

"With technology and free trade," Stephen Budianski writes in the September 12, 1994 issue of *U.S. News and World Report*, "earth can defy the doomsayers—and feed twice as many people."

The opposite viewpoint is held by Pulitzer prize-winning scientist E. O. Wilson in an article, "Is Humanity Suicidal?" in the *New York Times Magazine* for May 30, 1993:

> With people everywhere seeking a better quality of life, the search for resources is expanding even faster than the population. The demand is being met by an increase in scientific knowledge, which doubles every ten or fifteen years. It is accelerated further by a parallel rise in environment-devouring technology. Because Earth is finite in many resources that determine the quality of life—including arable soil, nutrients, fresh water, and space for natural ecosystems—doubling of consumption at constant time intervals can bring disaster with shocking suddenness.

Genetic Engineering and the End of Nature

The new science of genetic engineering or biotechnology—the creating of new life forms and altering of existing ones—has made amazing strides in the past few years. Having learned the mystery of the gene, biotechnologists are now busy experimenting with the creation of new forms of life: new, high-yield food plants, free of disease and easy to grow; new kinds of domestic animals that are just efficient machines for laying eggs or for producing milk, wool, or high-grade fat-free meat. Genetic engineering could be used to produce human babies that have any traits desired, whether of sex, eye color, hair color, features, or specific abilities in music, mathematics, art, or other fields.

Under such technology, Jeremy Rifkin observes in his book *Declaration of a Heretic*, "Our children will view all nature as a computable domain. They will redefine all living things as temporal programs that can be edited, revised, and reprogrammed." In his book *The End of Nature*, noted environmentalist Bill McKibben writes:

> This ideology argues that man is at the center of creation and it is therefore right for him to do whatever pleases him. It is the method that offers the most hope for continuing our way of life, our economic growth, in the teeth of the greenhouse effect. It promises crops that need little water and can survive the heat; it promises cures for all the new ailments we are creating as well as the old ones we've yet to solve; it promises survival in almost any environment we may create. It promises total domination.

It also promises the end of nature as we know it. Sad to say, a great many people around the world go along with that premise. They will settle for an artificial world, a world in which most wild animals as we know them will no longer exist.

Sustaining Our Planet

There are many millions of people the world over, however, who hold the opposite view. They are those who want to keep the earth a fit living place for both humans and wild animals and plants. They want us to begin thinking of ourselves not as the one and only species for which the world was created, but as just one species among the countless others that live on earth along with us. More than a century ago Alfred Russel Wallace observed that "all living things were *not* made for man." How true! And since we are supposedly more intelligent than the other animals and able to reason (our species name, *Homo sapiens*, means "knowing man"), it is up to us to preserve the world as a suitable home for all living things.

"At the heart of the environmentalist world view is the conviction that human physical and spiritual health depends on sustaining the planet in a relatively unaltered state," E. O. Wilson writes in his article, "Is Humanity Suicidal?"

Concerned people everywhere hope that such an attitude will become stronger day by day and year by year. They do not want a future in which generations will look back at the last quarter of the twentieth century and say, "There were still tigers and rhinoceroses and gorillas living in the wild in those days. But the people living then allowed them to be killed off; all that remains to remind us of them are a few zoo and museum specimens."

Rather let us hope that they will be able to say, "Our earth is alive and well, and we share it with all God's creatures. Perhaps we never will see a rhinoceros or a tiger in the wild, but at least we know that they are still there."

SELECTED BIBLIOGRAPHY

Publications of the International Union for the Conservation of Nature and Natural Resources (IUCN), particularly the Red Data Books on endangered species, have been very helpful references in the preparation of this work. Reports issued by the U.S. Fish and Wildlife Service (Department of the Interior) and the National Marine Fisheries Service (Department of Commerce) have also been very useful. Among the most informative magazines and periodicals have been the following: *Wildlife Conservation* (Wildlife Conservation Society) and its predecessor *Animal Kingdom* (New York Zoological Society); *Audubon* (National Audubon Society); *Defenders* (Defenders of Wildlife); *Focus* (World Wildlife Fund); *International Wildlife* (National Wildlife Federation); *National Geographic* (National Geographic Society); *Natural History* (American Museum of Natural History); *Oryx* (Fauna Preservation Society); and *Smithsonian* (The Smithsonian Institution).

In Section I of this bibliography, I am listing for each chapter selected books and articles that should be of special interest to the reader who wishes to pursue a particular subject further. Section II lists a few selected titles on exploration and discovery throughout the world, and on the human effect on land and wildlife of all continents.

The editions given here are my own. Very many of these books are now in modern editions and readily available; due to their historic nature, many of the older ones will still be in libraries, though out of print. Some, however, may exist only in special collections.

SECTION I

1. The Human Rise to Dominance
Gore, Rick. "The Dawn of Humans: Neanderthals." *National Geographic* 189, no. 1 (January 1996).

Hermann, Paul. *Conquest by Man*. New York: Harper & Brothers, 1954.

Howell, F. Clark, and the editors of *Life*. *Early Man*. New York: Time, 1965.

McNeill, William H. *The Rise of the West*. Chicago: The University of Chicago Press, 1963.

Osborn, Fairfield. *Our Plundered Planet*. Boston: Little, Brown, 1948.

Swimme, Brian, and Thomas Berry. *The Universe Story*. New York: Harper Collins, 1994.

2. Europe: Cradle of Western Civilization

Bourlière, François, and the editors of *Life*. *The Land and Wildlife of Eurasia*. New York: Time, 1964.

Curry-Lindahl, Kai. *Europe: A Natural History*. New York: Random House, 1964.

Jennison, George. *Animals for Show and Pleasure in Ancient Rome*. Manchester, England: Manchester University Press, 1937.

Ley, Willy. *Exotic Zoology*. New York: Viking, 1962. (Account of the woolly mammoth and other wildlife species)

Murray, Marion. *Circus! From Rome to Ringling*. New York: Appleton-Century-Crofts, 1956.

3. Asia: the Immense Land

Durant, Will. *The Story of Civilization; Vol. I, Our Oriental Heritage*. New York: Simon & Schuster, 1954.

Fox, Helen M., ed. and trans. *Abbé David's Diary, Being an Account of the French Naturalist's Journeys and Observations in China in the Years 1866 to 1869*. Cambridge, Mass.: Harvard University Press, 1949.

Hendrix, Steve. "Quest for the Kouprey." *International Wildlife* 25, no. 5 (September–October 1995).

Jackson, Peter. "Status of the Tigers of the World." *CBSG* (Captive Breeding Specialist Group) *News* 4, no. 4 (1993).

Linden, Eugene. "Tigers on the Brink." *Time*, March 28, 1994.

McClung, Robert. "Can We Save the Tiger?" *Princeton Alumni Weekly*, September 13, 1995.

Pfeffer, Pierre. *Asia: A Natural History*. New York: Random House, 1968.

Polo, Marco. *The Book of Marco Polo*. New York: Grosset & Dunlap Universal Library, n.d.

Ripley, S. Dillon, and the editors of *Life*. *The Land and Wildlife of Tropical Asia*. New York: Time, 1964.

Saberwal, Vasant K., James P. Gibbs, Ray Chellam, and A. J. T. Johnsingh. "Lion-Human Conflict in the Gir Forest, India." *Conservation Biology* 8, no. 2 (June 1994).

Schaller, George B. *The Last Panda*. Chicago: University of Chicago Press, 1993.

Ward, Geoffrey C., with Diane Raines Ward. *Tiger Wallahs. Encounters with the*

Men Who Tried to Save the Greatest of the Great Cats. New York: HarperCollins, 1993.

Wise, Jeff. "If a Sao La Is Seen in the Forest, But Not by Scientists, Does It Exist?" *New York Times Magazine*, June 19, 1994.

4. Africa: Land of the Last Great Herds

Bonner, Raymond. "Crying Wolf Over Elephants." *New York Times Magazine*, February 7, 1993.

Bridges, William. "An Okapi Comes to the Zoological Park." *Animal Kingdom* 40, no. 5 (September–October 1937).

Brown, Leslie. *Africa: A Natural History*. New York: Random House, 1965. (Includes material on Madagascar)

Butler, Victoria. "The Call of South Africa: Wildlife Prospers in a Country Where Nature Is a National Asset." *Wildlife Conservation* 99, no. 1 (January–February 1996).

Carr, Archie, and the editors of *Life*. *The Land and Wildlife of Africa*. New York: Time, 1964. (Includes material on Madagascar)

Chadwick, Douglas H. "Elephants, Out of Time, Out of Space." *National Geographic* 179, no. 5 (May 1991).

———. "A Place for Parks in the New South Africa." *National Geographic* 190, no. 1 (July 1996).

Du Chaillu, Paul B. *Explorations and Adventures in Central Africa*. New York: Harper & Brothers, 1861.

Fauna Preservation Society. "The Nile Crocodile in Zimbabwe—A Case of Sustainable Use." *Oryx* 28, no. 3 (July 1994).

Fossey, Dian. *Gorillas in the Mist*. Boston: Houghton Mifflin, 1983.

Karesh, William. "Rhino Relations." *Wildlife Conservation* 99, no. 2 (March–April 1996).

Keller, Bill. "Africa Thinks about Making Wildlife Pay for Its Survival." *New York Times*, December 27, 1992.

Lang, Herbert. "In Quest of the Rare Okapi." *Animal Kingdom* 21, no. 3 (May 1918).

Linden, Eugene. "Bonobos, Chimpanzees with a Difference." *National Geographic* 181, no. 3 (March 1992).

Matthiessen, Peter. *The Tree Where Man Was Born*; Eliot Porter. *The African Experience*. New York: Dutton, 1972. (Two volumes in one)

Miller, Peter. "Jane Goodall, Crusading for Apes and Humans." *National Geographic* 188, no. 6 (December 1995).

Moorhead, Alan. *No Room in the Ark*. New York: Harper & Row, 1959.

———. *The White Nile*. Rev. ed. New York: Harper & Row, 1971.

Morland, Hilary Simons. "Looking for Grauer's Gorilla." *Wildlife Conservation* 98, no. 5 (September–October 1995).

Ricciuti, Edward R. "Rhinos at Risk." *Wildlife Conservation* 96, no. 5 (September–October 1993).

Schaller, George B. "Gentle Gorillas, Turbulent Times." *National Geographic* 188, no. 4 (October 1995).

———. *The Year of the Gorilla*. Chicago: University of Chicago Press, 1964.

Sunquist, Fiona. "Cheetahs, Closer than Kissing Cousins." *Wildlife Conservation* 95, no. 3 (May–June 1992).

5. Madagascar and Islands of the Indian Ocean

Bangs, Richard. "Lemurs in the Midst." *Wildlife Conservation* 95, no. 3 (May–June 1992).

Jolly, Alison. "Madagascar's Lemurs, on the Edge of Survival." *National Geographic* 174, no. 2 (August 1988).

Ley, Willy. *The Lungfish and the Unicorn: An Excursion into Romantic Zoology.* New York: Modern Age Books, 1941. (Account of the dodo and other wildlife species)

McNulty, Faith. "Madagascar's Endangered Wildlife." *Defenders of Wildlife* 50, no. 2 (April 1975). (A special issue on Madagascar)

Silverberg, Robert. *The Auk, the Dodo, and the Oryx.* New York: Thomas Y. Crowell, 1967.

Wetmore, Alexander. "Re-creating Madagascar's Giant Extinct Bird." *National Geographic* 132, no. 4 (October 1967).

Wright, Patricia Chapple. "Lemurs' Last Stand." *Animal Kingdom* 91, no. 1 (January–February 1988).

6. The Malay Archipelago

Browne, Malcolm W. "They're Back! Komodos Avoid Extinction." *New York Times*, March 1, 1994.

Galdikas, Biruté M. F. *Reflections of Eden. My Years with the Orangutans of Borneo.* Boston: Little, Brown, 1995.

Hutton, Angus F. "Butterfly Farming in Papua New Guinea." *Oryx* 19, no. 3 (July 1985).

MacKinnon, John. *In Search of the Red Ape.* New York: Holt, Rinehart & Winston, 1974.

Morris, Jaqui. "New Hope for Queen Alexandra's Birdwing." *Oryx* 28, no. 3 (July 1994).

Rabinowitz, Alan R. "On the Horns of a Dilemma." *Wildlife Conservation* 97, no. 5 (September–October 1994). (Sumatran rhinoceros)

Speart, Jessica. "Orang Odyssey." *Wildlife Conservation* 95, no. 6 (November–December 1992).

Starowicz, Mark. "Leakey's Last Angel." *New York Times Magazine*, August 16, 1992.

Stevens, Jane. "Facing the Dragons." *International Wildlife* 23, no. 3 (May–June 1993). (Komodo monitor)

Wallace, Alfred Russel. *The Malay Archipelago: The Land of the Orangutan and the Bird of Paradise.* London: Macmillan, 1922. (First printed in 1869)

7. Australia and New Zealand: Strange Lands Down Under

Bergamini, David, and the editors of *Life. The Land and Wildlife of Australia.* New York: Time, 1964. (Includes material on New Guinea and New Zealand)

Carlquist, Sherman. *Island Life: A Natural History of the Islands of the World.* Garden City, N.Y.: Natural History Press, 1965.

Dawson, Terry. "Red Kangaroos, the Kings of Cool." *Natural History* 104, no. 4 (April 1995).

Keast, Allen. *Australia and the Pacific Islands.* New York: Random House, 1966.

Sidney, John. "New Zealand's Rare Birds: Threatened Species Breed at a Mountain Reserve." *Animal Kingdom* 72, no. 6 (December 1969).

Stivens, Dal. "The Thylacine Mystery." *Animal Kingdom* 76, no. 3 (June 1973).

Troughton, Ellis. *Furred Animals of Australia.* New York: Scribner's, 1947.

8. North America: The Conquest of a New World

Allen, Thomas B., ed. *Wild Animals of North America.* Washington, D.C.: National Geographic Society, 1979.

Chadwick, Douglas H. "Dead or Alive: The Endangered Species Act." *National Geographic* 187, no. 3 (March 1995).

DeVoto, Bernard, ed. *The Journals of Lewis and Clark.* Boston: Houghton Mifflin, 1953.

Díaz del Castillo, Bernal. *The Discovery and Conquest of Mexico, 1517–1521.* New York: Grove, 1956. An abbreviated edition of this title is available: *Cortez and the Conquest of Mexico by the Spaniards in 1521*, B. G. Herzog, ed. North Haven, Conn.: Linnet Books, 1988.

DiSilvestro, Roger L. *The Endangered Kingdom: The Struggle to Save America's Wildlife.* New York: Wiley, 1989.

Dunlap, Thomas R. *Saving America's Wildlife.* Princeton, N.J.: Princeton University Press, 1988.

Ehrlich, Paul R., David S. Dobkin, and Darryl Wheye. *Birds in Jeopardy.* Stanford, Calif.: Stanford University Press, 1992.

Farb, Peter, and the editors of *Life. The Land and Wildlife of North America.* New York: Time, 1964.

Fishbein, Seymour L., ed. *Our Continent: A Natural History of North America.* Washington, D.C.: National Geographic Society, 1976.

Garretson, Martin S. *The American Bison.* New York: New York Zoological Society, 1938.

Manning, Richard. "The Buffalo Is Coming Back." *Defenders* 71, no. 1 (Winter 1995–96).

Matthiessen, Peter. *Wildlife in America*; updated and expanded edition. New York: Viking, 1987.

McClung, Robert M. *America's Endangered Birds: Programs and People Working to Save Them.* New York: Morrow, 1979.

———. *Lost Wild America. The Story of Our Extinct and Vanishing Wildlife,* revised, expanded, and updated edition. North Haven, Conn.: Linnet Books, 1993.

Rattner, Robert. "Make Way for Manatees." *Wildlife Conservation* 98, no. 5 (September–October 1995).

Shoemaker, H. W. *A Pennsylvania Bison Hunt.* Middleburg, Pa: Middleburg Post Press, 1915.

Storer, Tracy I., and Lloyd P. Tevis, Jr. *The California Grizzly.* Berkeley, Calif.: University of California Press, 1955.

Trefethen, James B. *Crusade for Wildlife.* Harrisburg, Pa.: Stackpole, 1961.

Turbak, Gary. "Where the Buffalo Roam." *Wildlife Conservation* 98, no. 6 (November–December 1995).

U.S. Department of the Interior, Fish and Wildlife Service. *Fish and Wildlife 91, A Report to the Nation.* Washington, D.C.: U.S. Government Printing Office, 1990.

———. *Report to Congress: Endangered and Threatened Species Recovery Program.* Washington, D.C.: U.S. Government Printing Office, 1990.

9. South America: Land of Contrasts

Bates, Henry Walter. *The Naturalist on the Amazons.* 5th ed. London: John Murray, 1884.

Bates, Marston, and the editors of *Life. The Land and Wildlife of South America.* New York: Time, 1955.

Benirschke, Kurt, and Warner P. Heuschele. "Proyecto Tagúa: The Giant Chaco Peccary Catagonus Wagneri." *International Zoo Yearbook* 32. London: The Zoological Society of London, 1992.

Cutright, Paul Russell. *The Great Naturalists Explore South America.* New York: Macmillan, 1940.

Darwin, Charles. *The Origin of Species.* New York: Collier, 1909. The Harvard Classics Edition. (First printed in London, 1859)

Dorst, Jean. *South America and Central America: A Natural History.* New York: Random House, 1967.

Laidler, Keith, and Liz Laidler. "Giant Among Otters." *Wildlife Conservation* 98, no. 3 (May–June 1995).

Lemonick, Michael D. "Can the Galápagos Survive?" *Time.* October 30, 1995.

Margolis, Mac. "Single Lonely Parrot Seeks Companionship." *International Wildlife* 26, no. 1 (January–February 1996).

McClung, Robert M. *Vanishing Wildlife of Latin America.* New York: Morrow, 1979.

Wallace, Alfred Russel. *A Narrative of Travel on the Amazon and Rio Negro.* London: Macmillan, 1870. (First printed in 1853)

Wilcove, David. "Is There a Cure for the Blues?" *Wildlife Conservation* 99, no. 2 (March–April 1996). (Macaws)

10. The World's Oceans

Bonner, Nigel. *Seals and Sea Lions of the World.* New York: Facts on File, 1994.

Carey, John. "Embattled Behemoths." *International Wildlife* 25, no. 3 (May–June 1995).

Dugan, James, Robert C. Cowan, Bill Barada, Louis Marden, and Richard M. Crum. *World Beneath the Sea.* Washington, D.C.: National Geographic Society, 1967.

Graves, William. "The Imperiled Giants." *National Geographic* 150, no. 6 (December 1976). (Whales)

Harrison, Richard J., and Judith E. King. *Marine Mammals.* London: Hutchinson, 1968.

Holthouse, David. "The Mystery of the Disappearing Species." *National Wildlife* 33, no. 1 (December–January 1995). (Steller's sea lion)

King, Judith E. *Seals of the World.* London: Trustees of the British Museum (Natural History), 1964.

McClung, Robert M. *Hunted Mammals of the Sea.* New York: Morrow, 1978.

Parfit, Michael. "Diminishing Returns: Exploiting the Ocean's Bounty." *National Geographic* 188, no. 5 (November 1995).

Scheffer, Victor B. *A Natural History of Marine Mammals.* New York: Scribner's, 1976.

Scopes, Jack. "A Big Fish Story." *Wildlife Conservation* 97, no. 4 (July–August 1994). (Sharks)

U.S. Department of Commerce/National Marine Fisheries Service. *Endangered Whales: Status Update,* June 1991. Silver Spring, Md.: Office of Protected Resources.

———. *Marine Mammal Protection Act of 1972.* Annual Report January 1, 1992 to December 31, 1993. Silver Spring, Md.: Office of Protected Resources.

———. *Our Living Oceans. Report on the Status of U.S. Living Marine Resources, 1991.* Silver Spring, Md.: Office of Protected Resources.

Votier, Mark, photographer. "Whale Kill." *Audubon* 96, no. 2 (March–April 1994).

Whynott, Douglas. *Giant Bluefin.* New York: Farrar Straus Giroux, 1995.

Wuethrich, Bernice C. "Into Dangerous Waters." *International Wildlife* 26, no. 2 (March–April 1996). (Sea turtles)

11. The Giant Killer: *Homo sapiens*

Carson, Rachel. *Silent Spring.* Boston: Houghton Mifflin, 1962.

Dasman, Raymond F. *The Last Horizon.* New York: Collier, 1971.

DiSilvestro, Roger. *Audubon: Natural Priorities.* Atlanta: Turner, 1994.

Ehrlich, Paul R. *The Population Bomb.* New York: Ballantine, 1968.

Gore, Al. *Earth in the Balance. Ecology and the Human Spirit.* Boston: Houghton Mifflin, 1992.

Ives, Richard. *Of Tigers and Men: Entering the Age of Extinction.* New York: Doubleday, 1996.

Line, Les. "1,096 Mammal and 1,108 Bird Species Threatened." *New York Times,* October 8, 1996.

Mann, Charles C., and Mark L. Plummer. *Noah's Choice: The Future of Endangered Species.* New York: Knopf, 1995.

McKibben, Bill. *The End of Nature.* New York: Random House, 1989.

————. *Hope, Human and Wild. True Stories of Living Lightly on the Earth.* Boston: Little, Brown, 1995.

————. "Not So Fast." *New York Times Magazine.* July 23, 1995.

National Geographic Society. *National Geographic* 174, no. 6 (December 1988). (A special issue on man and the endangered earth)

Quammen, David. *The Song of the Dodo: Island Biogeography in an Age of Extinction.* New York: Scribner, 1996.

Rifkin, Jeremy, and Carol Grunewald Rifkin. *Voting Green.* New York: Doubleday, 1992.

Scheffer, Victor B. *The Shaping of Environmentalism in America.* Seattle: University of Washington Press, 1991.

————. *A Voice for Wildlife.* New York: Scribner's, 1974.

Smithsonian Associates. *Smithsonian* 21, no. 1 (April 1990). (A special issue on the environment)

Udall, Stewart L. *The Quiet Crisis and the Next Generation.* Salt Lake City:Peregrine Smith Books, 1988.

U.S. Department of the Interior. Conservation Yearbooks no. 1, *Quest for Quality* (1965); no. 2, *The Population Challenge* (1966); no. 3, *The Third Wave* (1967); no. 4, *Man . . . an Endangered Species?* (1968). Washington, D.C.: U.S. Government Printing Office.

Wicker, Tom. "What Can the Next President Do?" *Audubon* 94, no. 5 (September–October 1992).

Wilson, Edward O. *The Diversity of Life.* Cambridge, Mass.: Harvard University Press, 1992.

————. "Is Humanity Suicidal?" *New York Times Magazine* , May 30, 1993.

SECTION II

Exploration and Discovery throughout the World

Armstrong, Richard. *The Discoverers.* New York: Praeger, 1968.

Cary, M., and E. H. Warmington. *The Ancient Explorers.* London: Methuen, 1929.

Darwin, Charles. *The Voyage of the Beagle.* New York: Collier, 1909. The Harvard Classics edition. (First printed in London, 1839)

Gillespie, James Edward. *A History of Geographical Discovery, 1400–1800.* New York: Henry Holt, 1933.

Golder, F. A., ed. *Steller's Journal of the Sea Voyage from Kamchatka to America and Return on the Second Expedition, 1741–42* (Volume 2 of *Bering's Voyages*). New York: American Geographical Society, 1925.

Hyde, Walter Woodburn. *Ancient Greek Mariners.* New York: Oxford University Press, 1947.

Morehead, Alan. *The Fatal Impact: An Account of the Invasion of the South Pacific, 1767–1840.* New York: Harper and Row, 1966.

Morrison, Samuel Elliot. *The European Discovery of America: The Northern Voyages, A.D. 500–1600.* New York: Oxford University Press, 1971.

———. *The European Discovery of America: The Southern Voyages, 1492–1616.* New York: Oxford University Press, 1974.

Stefansson, Vilhjalmur. *Great Adventures and Explorations.* New York: Dial, 1947.

Sykes, Percy. *A History of Exploration from the Earliest Times to the Present Day.* London: George Routledge & Sons, 1934.

Wright, Louis B. *Gold, Glory, and the Gospel.* New York: Atheneum, 1970.

Man's Effect on Land and Wildlife of All Continents

Burton, John A. *The Collin's Guide to the Rare Mammals of the World.* Lexington, Mass.: Stephen Greene, 1987.

Chadwick, Douglas H. "Elephants—Out of Time, Out of Space." *National Geographic* 179, no. 5 (May 1991).

Collar, N. J., and P. Andrew. *Birds to Watch; The ICBP World Checklist of Threatened Birds.* ICBP Tech. Pub. no. 8. Washington, D.C.: Smithsonian Institution Press, 1988.

Collar, N. J., L. P. Gonzago, N. Krabbe, A. Madrono Nieto, L. G. Varanjo, T. A. Parker III, and D.C. Wege. *Threatened Birds of the Americas.* The ICBP/IUCN Red Data Book, 3d ed., Part 2. Washington, D.C.: Smithsonian Institution Press, 1992.

Crowe, Philip Kingsland. *World Wildlife: The Last Stand.* New York: Scribner's, 1971.

Curry-Lindahl, Kai. *Let Them Live: A Worldwide Survey of Animals Threatened with Extinction.* New York: Morrow, 1972.

Edinburgh, the Duke of, and James Fisher. *Wildlife Crisis.* New York: Cowles, 1970.

Fisher, James, Noel Simon, and Jack Vincent. *Wildlife in Danger.* New York: Viking, 1969.

Greenway, James C. *Extinct and Vanishing Birds of the World.* New York: American Committee for International Wildlife Protection, 1958.

Harper, Francis. *Extinct and Vanishing Mammals of the Old World.* New York: American Committee for International Wildlife Protection, 1945.

Hornaday, William Temple. *Our Vanishing Wildlife: Its Extermination and Preservation*. New York: Scribner's, 1913.

International Zoo Yearbook 32 and 33. London: The Zoological Society of London, 1992 and 1993.

IUCN Red Data Books: Vol. 1, *Mammalia*, 1972, with additional sheets through 1974; Vol. 2, *Aves*, 1966, with additional sheets through 1971; Vol. 3, *Amphibia and Reptilia* , 1968, with additional sheets through 1970; *Mammal Red Data*, Part 1, 1982; *Threatened Mammalian Taxa of the Americas and the Australian Zoogeographic Region* (excluding Cetacea), 1982; *Threatened Primates of Africa*, 1988; *Amphibia-Reptilia* Part 1, 1982; *Invertebrates*, 1983. Gland, Switzerland: IUCN.

Kaufman, Les, and Kenneth Mallory, eds. *The Last Extinction*. Cambridge, Mass.: MIT Press, 1986.

King, Warren, in cooperation with ICBP. *Endangered Birds of the World. The ICBP Bird Red Data Book*. Washington, D.C.: Smithsonian Institution Press, 1981.

Linden, Eugene. "A Curious Kinship. Apes and Humans." *National Geographic* 181, no. 3 (March 1992).

McClung, Robert M. *Lost Wild Worlds: The Story of Extinct and Vanishing Wildlife of the Eastern Hemisphere*. New York: Morrow, 1976.

Regenstein, Lewis. *The Politics of Extinction: The Shocking Story of the World's Endangered Wildlife*. New York: Macmillan, 1975.

Simon, Noel M., and Paul Geroudet. *Last Survivors: Natural History of 48 Animals in Danger of Extinction*. New York and Cleveland: World, 1970.

Sleeper, Barbara. *Wild Cats of the World*. New York: Crown, 1995.

Wildlife Conservation Society. *Wildlife Conservation* 99, no. 3 (May–June 1996). (A special issue on the world's cats)

INDEX

(Asterisks after page numbers indicate illustrations)

Acid rain, 265, 266
Adams, John (Grizzly), 205; quoted, 183
Aepyornis. *See* Elephant bird
Africa, 4–5, 11, 67–109, 172; early exploration of, 67–68, 70–71; early man in, 4–5; East, 72, 83; future of wildlife of, 106–09; land and people of, 72–73; map of, 69; modern exploration of, 71–72; parks and reserves in, 74, 77, 81, 82, 84, 93, 94, 97, 99, 103, 107–08; South. *See* South Africa
Akeley, Carl, 90
Alaska, 174, 184, 185, 188, 189, 191, 194, 244
Alaskan Native Claims Settlement Act, 185
Albert National Park (Zaire), 90
Aldabra Atoll, 112, 119, 120–21
Aldabran giant tortoise, 119–22, 120*
Alexander the Great, 32, 35–36
Alligator, American, 194–95; Chinese, 66
Amaghino, Florentino, 214
Amazon Basin, 198, 199, 207; rain forests of, 198
Amazon River, 198, 208, 217, 219, 220, 249
American Association of Zoological Parks and Aquariums, 139

American bison, 23, 175*, 175–81
American Bison Society, 179
American elk (Wapiti), 65, 162, 191
American Museum of Natural History, 90, 102
Andes, 199, 225, 226
Angola, 98, 99
Anoa, 144
Anteaters, 210; giant (*Myrmecophaga tridactyla*), 210*, 210–11; prehensile-tailed, 198; spiny. *See* Echidna
Antelopes, 65, 95, 265; blackbuck, 65; blesbok, 95; Bontebok, 95; giant sable (*Hippotragus niger variani*), 98*, 98–100; hartebeest, 95; pronghorn, 192; saiga (*saiga tatarica*), 45–47, 46*; springbok, 95; wildebeest, 95
Aquaculture, 259
Aqua-lung, 230
Argali, 65
Aristotle, 14, 36, 240; quoted, 229
Armadillos, 170, 210; giant (*Priodontes maximus*), 211–13, 212*; nine-banded, 212
Asia, 28–66, 167; early civilizations in, 29–32; and Europe, ancient trade routes between, 32–34; map of, 30-31; parks and reserves in, 39, 40–41, 44, 51, 53–54, 58, 62–63, 65, 132; size of, 28; Southeast, 145

286   Index